POVERTY

Opposing Viewpoints®

Other Books of Related Interest in the Opposing Viewpoints Series:

American Government
Economics in America
Social Justice

Additional Books in the Opposing Viewpoints Series:

Abortion
AIDS
American Foreign Policy
The American Military
American Values
America's Elections
America's Prisons
The Arms Race
Biomedical Ethics
Censorship
Central America
Chemical Dependency
Civil Liberties
Constructing a Life Philosophy
Crime & Criminals
Criminal Justice
Death & Dying
The Death Penalty
Drug Abuse
The Environmental Crisis
Latin America and U.S. Foreign Policy
Male/Female Roles
The Mass Media
The Middle East
Nuclear War
The Political Spectrum
Problems of Africa
Science and Religion
Sexual Values
The Soviet Union
Teenage Sexuality
Terrorism
The Vietnam War
War and Human Nature

POVERTY
Opposing Viewpoints®

David L. Bender & Bruno Leone, *Series Editors*

William Dudley, *Book Editor*

OPPOSING VIEWPOINTS SERIES ®

Greenhaven Press   577 Shoreview Park Road   St. Paul, Minnesota 55126

Library of Congress Cataloging-in-Publication Data

Poverty: opposing viewpoints / William Dudley, book editor.
    P.   cm. — (Opposing viewpoints series)
   Includes bibliographies and index.
   Summary: Presents opposing viewpoints on various aspects of poverty, including its causes, ways to end it, the welfare system, the homeless, and the relationship between poverty and discrimination.
   ISBN 0-89908-432-X (lib. bdg.) : $13.95.
   ISBN 0-89908-407-9 (pbk.) : $6.95.
   1. Poor—United States. 2. Economic assistance, Domestic—United States. 3. Public welfare—United States. [1. Poverty. 2. Poor.]
I. Dudley, William, 1964—   . II. Series.
HC110.P6P63 1988
362.5'0973—dc19
                                           87-36794
                                               CIP
                                               AC

"Congress shall make no law... abridging the freedom of speech, or of the press."

First Amendment to the US Constitution

The basic foundation of our democracy is the first amendment guarantee of freedom of expression. The Opposing Viewpoints books are dedicated to the concept of this basic freedom and the idea that it is more important to practice it than to enshrine it.

Contents

Chapter 3: How Should Society Deal with the Homeless?

Chapter 4: Why Does Poverty Disproportionately Affect Minorities?

Chapter 5: Can Government Programs Alleviate Poverty?

Why Consider Opposing Viewpoints?

"It is better to debate a question without settling it than to settle a question without debating it."

Joseph Joubert (1754-1824)

The Importance of Examining Opposing Viewpoints

The purpose of the Opposing Viewpoints books, and this book in particular, is to present balanced, and often difficult to find, opposing points of view on complex and sensitive issues.

Probably the best way to become informed is to analyze the positions of those who are regarded as experts and well studied on issues. It is important to consider every variety of opinion in an attempt to determine the truth. Opinions from the mainstream of society should be examined. But also important are opinions that are considered radical, reactionary, or minority as well as those stigmatized by some other uncomplimentary label. An important lesson of history is the eventual acceptance of many unpopular and even despised opinions. The ideas of Socrates, Jesus, and Galileo are good examples of this.

Readers will approach this book with their own opinions on the issues debated within it. However, to have a good grasp of one's own viewpoint, it is necessary to understand the arguments of those with whom one disagrees. It can be said that those who do not completely understand their adversary's point of view do not fully understand their own.

A persuasive case for considering opposing viewpoints has been presented by John Stuart Mill in his work *On Liberty*. When examining controversial issues it may be helpful to reflect on this suggestion:

> The only way in which a human being can make some approach to knowing the whole of a subject, is by hearing what can be said about it by persons of every variety of opinion, and studying all modes in which it can be looked at by every character of mind. No wise man ever acquired his wisdom in any mode but this.

Analyzing Sources of Information

The Opposing Viewpoints books include diverse materials taken from magazines, journals, books, and newspapers, as well as statements and position papers from a wide range of individuals, organizations and governments. This broad spectrum of sources helps to develop patterns of thinking which are open to the consideration of a variety of opinions.

Pitfalls To Avoid

A pitfall to avoid in considering opposing points of view is that of regarding one's own opinion as being common sense and the most rational stance and the point of view of others as being only opinion and naturally wrong. It may be that another's opinion is correct and one's own is in error.

Another pitfall to avoid is that of closing one's mind to the opinions of those with whom one disagrees. The best way to approach a dialogue is to make one's primary purpose that of understanding the mind and arguments of the other person and not that of enlightening him or her with one's own solutions. More can be learned by listening than speaking.

It is my hope that after reading this book the reader will have a deeper understanding of the issues debated and will appreciate the complexity of even seemingly simple issues on which good and honest people disagree. This awareness is particularly important in a democratic society such as ours where people enter into public debate to determine the common good. Those with whom one disagrees should not necessarily be regarded as enemies, but perhaps simply as people who suggest different paths to a common goal.

Developing Basic Reading and Thinking Skills

In this book carefully edited opposing viewpoints are purposely placed back to back to create a running debate; each viewpoint is preceded by a short quotation that best expresses the author's main argument. This format instantly plunges the reader into the midst of a controversial issue and greatly aids that reader in mastering the basic skill of recognizing an author's point of view.

A number of basic skills for critical thinking are practiced in the activities that appear throughout the books in the series. Some of the skills are:

Evaluating Sources of Information The ability to choose from among alternative sources the most reliable and accurate source in relation to a given subject.

Separating Fact from Opinion The ability to make the basic distinction between factual statements (those that can be demonstrated or verified empirically) and statements of opinion (those that are beliefs or attitudes that cannot be proved).

Identifying Stereotypes The ability to identify oversimplified, exaggerated descriptions (favorable or unfavorable) about people and insulting statements about racial, religious or national groups, based upon misinformation or lack of information.

Recognizing Ethnocentrism The ability to recognize attitudes or opinions that express the view that one's own race, culture, or group is inherently superior, or those attitudes that judge another culture or group in terms of one's own.

It is important to consider opposing viewpoints and equally important to be able to critically analyze those viewpoints. The activities in this book are designed to help the reader master these thinking skills. Statements are taken from the book's viewpoints and the reader is asked to analyze them. This technique aids the reader in developing skills that not only can be applied to the viewpoints in this book, but also to situations where opinionated spokespersons comment on controversial issues. Although the activities are helpful to the solitary reader, they are most useful when the reader can benefit from the interaction of group discussion.

Using this book and others in the series should help readers develop basic reading and thinking skills. These skills should improve the readers' ability to understand what they read. Readers should be better able to separate fact from opinion, substance from rhetoric and become better consumers of information in our media-centered culture.

This volume of the Opposing Viewpoints books does not advocate a particular point of view. Quite the contrary! The very nature of the book leaves it to the reader to formulate the opinions he or she finds most suitable. My purpose as publisher is to see that this is made possible by offering a wide range of viewpoints which are fairly presented.

David L. Bender
Publisher

Introduction

"We in America are nearer to the final triumph over poverty than ever before."

US President Herbert Hoover, 1929.

Poverty in the United States seems paradoxical. America is a country remarkably rich in resources and technological development, and is also a country that prides itself on its generosity and idealism. Yet in spite of these qualities, poverty remains a disturbing and consistent problem. Robert Reich writes:

> No nation talks more about the importance of charity towards the less fortunate. No people organize more concerts, bake sales, telethons, walkathons, and national hand-holdings to raise money for the hungry and homeless. None takes as seriously the problem of poverty or the ideal of equal opportunity. But few Western industrialized nations fail as miserably to bridge the gap between their richest and poorest citizens.

There is little argument today over the injustice of poverty or that, theoretically, America has enough material wealth to eliminate it. But there is much disagreement over poverty's causes and cures. The central question of the poverty debate is: Does poverty result from the failings of poor people, or the failings of society?

During colonial times the common belief was that poverty was a moral condition; the poor were poor because of laziness, drunkenness, ignorance, or some other individual failing. People who were old or disabled were deserving of charity, but the able-bodied poor were often whipped, imprisoned, or auctioned off as servants.

These attitudes persisted through the nineteenth century even as the industrial revolution gave poverty new meaning. Men, women, and children moved to the cities to work in factories up to fourteen hours a day, six days a week, for less than a living wage. Millions of immigrants arrived in America to work these jobs and live in crowded urban slums.

During this time some people began to question traditional views on poverty. They examined social and economic factors like unemployment, low wages, and child labor. The poor began to be thought of not as moral failures, but as victims of social structures and forces over which they had no control. This new view gained widespread acceptance during the Great Depression of the

1930s. With 25 percent unemployment and millions of Americans made suddenly destitute by losing their homes and life savings, the view that poverty was a result of individual rather than social failure became less credible.

The Great Depression also revolutionized the role of the federal government. Previously, most government officials, including Herbert Hoover, believed that governments, especially the federal government, should not be extensively involved in "relief." During the 1920s, Hoover and many others believed that, left to itself, the nation's economy would eventually eliminate poverty. After Franklin Roosevelt defeated Herbert Hoover in 1932, his New Deal programs proceeded to enlist the federal government in unprecedented ways to help the poor. He used the government to employ millions of people, to provide assistance to the needy, and to initiate programs like Social Security. Some New Deal programs remain active today.

Full economic recovery for the US did not arrive until after World War II. In the general prosperity that followed, poverty was not an important public issue. Yet it remained, if in less visible forms than during the Depression. In 1964, President Lyndon Johnson declared a "War on Poverty." Johnson's programs differed from Roosevelt's New Deal in several respects. First, they were launched in a time of economic growth. Second, the goals of the programs were different, aiming at eliminating poverty altogether. Finally, they targeted certain groups—the elderly, the poor in Appalachia, blacks—groups who traditionally had been poor regardless of the condition of the economy. Through the establishment of new programs such as Medicare and Medicaid, and the expansion of programs like food stamps and AFDC (Aid to Families with Dependent Children), the amount of government money spent to fight poverty greatly increased. As a result, the official poverty rate was halved between 1960 and 1973. Since then the rate has remained at an average of about thirteen percent.

In the 1980s America is experiencing a renewed backlash against welfare. Some critics have argued that government programs to help poor people have increased their number. They say that instead of giving poor people the opportunity to work themselves out of poverty, government programs absolve them of individual responsibility. Welfare thus forms a "poverty trap" of dependency. These critics believe the real roots of poverty are individual problems such as a lack of the work ethic, thriftlessness, crime, chemical abuse, divorce, and illegitimacy. This emphasis on morality and responsibility is in some respects reminiscent of nineteenth-century views on poverty.

Yet others have held that government programs, if adequately funded, can help alleviate poverty. They maintain that poverty is a social problem and that serious attempts to end poverty have to involve more extensive social reform than was attempted in the past. Some proposals have included guaranteeing every American citizen a job or a minimal income.

As America enters the 1990s, the question of what should be done about poverty remains an unresolved issue. The topics debated in this book include: Is Poverty in America a Serious Problem? What Causes Poverty in America? How Should Society Deal with the Homeless? Why Does Poverty Disproportionately Affect Minorities? Can Government Programs Alleviate Poverty? As in all Opposing Viewpoints books, the purpose is not to give final answers, but to enable the reader to form his or her own conclusions.

Is Poverty in America a Serious Problem?

Chapter Preface

America does not have the widespread poverty found in many nations such as Mexico or India. Since the end of World War II, in fact, this country has experienced unprecedented and widespread prosperity. Many people who live below the official poverty line still own homes, cars, television sets, and other items considered luxuries in many other countries. This has led some people to conclude that while poverty in America has not been completely eliminated, full-scale government attacks on poverty are unwarranted and inappropriate.

Others argue that beneath the veneer of prosperity many Americans still lack food, homes, health care, and hope for the future. Poverty has merely become easier to hide and ignore as those who are not poor move to the suburbs and other neighborhoods where the poor can't be seen. Those who believe that poverty is a serious problem conclude that it can and should be cured.

The viewpoints in the following chapter demonstrate the widely differing opinions on the extent and meaning of poverty in the US.

"Over 30 million Americans live below the government's official poverty level. . . . It's still America's national disgrace."

Poverty in America Is a Serious Problem

Allan Sheahen

Allan Sheahen is a businessman and writer who has studied the welfare systems of many countries. In the following viewpoint, he uses a question-and-answer format to describe the poverty problem in the United States. Structural changes in the economy, according to Sheahen, have made it more difficult for many Americans to work themselves out of poverty.

As you read, consider the following questions:

1. What reasons does the author list to explain why poverty has not declined despite government programs?
2. Does Sheahen believe education can alleviate poverty?
3. How has automation affected poverty, according to the author?

Allan Sheahen, *Guaranteed Income: The Right to Economic Security.* Van Nuys, CA: Gain Publications, 1983. Reprinted with permission.

Does poverty still exist in the United States?

Yes.

Over 30 million Americans live below the government's official poverty level. About 14% of the population. One American in every seven.

It's still America's national disgrace.

The 1981 official poverty level was $9287 for an urban family of four. It was $4620 for a single person and $5917 for a couple. Today it's higher. Inflation pushes the levels up each year.

Anyone with an annual cash income below these levels is living in poverty, the government says.

• 31.8 million Americans have incomes below these levels.

• Two-thirds are white. One-third are non-white.

• 3.9 million Americans over age 65 live in poverty. That's one in every six.

• 12.3 million children live in poverty. That's one in every five.

• 11% of whites, 34% of blacks, and 26% of Hispanics live in poverty. . . .

Poverty Is Growing

But isn't the number of poor declining each year?

No.

The number of people living in poverty dropped from 39 million in 1960 to 25 million in 1969, stayed at that level during the seventies, then rose to 29.3 million in 1980 and 31.8 million in 1981.

In 1965, the War on Poverty was declared. Today, that war is still bogged down in the trenches, little closer to victory than when it began.

Despite all the innovative programs, despite the hundreds of billions of dollars spent, the number of people classed as poor is higher than a decade ago.

Reasons for Poverty

Why isn't the number of poor declining?

Four reasons:

1) Old age. More people are reaching retirement age than ever before. Once out of the job market, their incomes often slip below the poverty line.

2) Inflation. It's driven people into poverty as prices rose faster than income. 17% of poor family heads worked full time, but couldn't earn enough to rise above the poverty line. Those on fixed incomes are really hit hard.

3) The poverty cycle itself. Once in, it's hard to get out. Poverty means poorly fed pregnant women. That means poorly fed fetuses in their wombs. That means fetuses that fail to synthesize proteins and brain cells at normal rates. That means a high rate of mortality of these infants. It means appallingly high rates of prematurity and mental retardation in the survivors. It means fur-

18

ther lack of brain growth because of poor feeding in the crucial years of early childhood. It means millions of Americans today have permanently stunted brains.

4) Automation. Unskilled and semi-skilled workers simply can't get jobs anymore. The nation's unemployment rate varied between 3% and 4% in the 1960s. Now it's 8% to 10%. The government used to define "full employment" as just that: everyone works. Then it said 3% is full employment. Now the goal is 5% and heading up. Each recession is a little worse. We've always relied on the job market to provide jobs and income for the American people. But it doesn't work anymore. . . .

A Vicious Circle

Why can't we all pull ourselves up by our own bootstraps?

It's too hard. Poverty's a vicious circle. You get knocked down a few times. Each time it's tougher to get up. One day you don't. You say to hell with it.

Down deep, we know how tough it is. Everytime someone from "the ghetto" rises up to be somebody, we're so shocked we make a big deal out of it. We make an example of him and say, "See, if he can do it, so can you."

A Social and Moral Scandal

Harsh poverty plagues our country despite its great wealth. More than 33 million Americans are poor; by any reasonable standard another 20 to 30 million are needy. Poverty is increasing in the United States, not decreasing. For a people who believe in "progress," this should be cause for alarm. These burdens fall most heavily on blacks, Hispanics, and Native Americans. Even more disturbing is the large increase in the number of women and children living in poverty. Today children are the largest single group among the poor. This tragic fact seriously threatens the nation's future. That so many people are poor in a nation as rich as ours is a social and moral scandal that we cannot ignore.

National Conference of Catholic Bishops, 1986.

It takes money to break out of the poverty cycle. There's no easy way out. In a rural area, where do you go to find work if none exists? You can go to the city, but only if you can raise the money to move. If, somehow, you manage to get to the city, you're limited by the spread of the city itself. Often, you become trapped in one little area. Distances are too vast to walk. Public transportation, what there is of it, costs.

If you somehow manage to find your way to a potential job, what are your chances of getting it? Are you well-groomed? Neatly dressed? That costs. Are you alert? Ready to work? Not if you haven't had a decent bed to sleep in. Are you confident, positive, sure of yourself? Hardly.

There are two problems with leaving poverty—the money to get out, and once out, getting a job, food, bed and help. Today, in America, none of these are available to a lot of people who are really trying to fit in.

Isn't sports a good way out of poverty?

No. There's more chance of becoming a surgeon or architect than an all-star outfielder.

For every Reggie Jackson, Magic Johnson or Bruce Jenner, hundreds of thousands of young American athletes try and fail.

The Problems with Education

Isn't education the best way to reverse the poverty cycle?

No.

American folklore says a child born in poverty can reasonably hope to rise by his or her ability, to become a doctor, lawyer or industrial chief.

It's a myth.

While there's *some* upward mobility, Americans generally reach the same relative level of education and financial success as their parents.

In otherwords, the higher your status at birth, the more education you're likely to get. So those born to money tend to make money. Those born to poverty tend to stay there.

The odds are long against certain children making it in America. And those odds haven't changed much throughout American history.

You've heard—and maybe you believe—that each individual is the master of his or her fate. Well, that's not so. It's a false belief which leads to the misconception that poverty is the individual's own fault. When, in fact, it's the fault of the structure of our society.

A 7-year study by the Carnegie Corporation attempted to learn "why American social policy, apparently aimed at providing equal opportunity for all, has not made much progress in that direction."

It found: "The hereditary aristocracy that some of the Founding Fathers hoped to stop is today a reality."

The study said the public schools perpetuate inequality by steering poor, working class and minority students into vocational and remedial programs. But they allow upper-income students to enter college prep programs. This guidance system, along with the "low expectations and prejudices of many public school teachers," means the poorest children get the *worst* education.

Why can't everyone get a job?

The aged, sick and disabled can't. Children and many mothers can't. Even able-bodied men can't. There aren't enough jobs to go around.

Over 17% of blacks are unemployed.

Over 40% of black youth are unemployed.

And, according to the Daniel Yankelovich Co. public opinion poll, nearly 25 million Americans are looking for work.

"The government unemployment rate," says the survey, "badly underestimates the problem of the American labor force."

Mary Smith

Mary Smith is twenty years old. She was laid off from a secretarial job in Minneapolis eighteen months ago. Unable to find work, she lost her apartment and had to sell her furniture. She lived on yogurt and water for a month. One night she went to a hospital waiting room and, without anyone seeing her, slipped into an empty bed. When a nurse found her, she sent Mary to a shelter, where the homeless are given a bed and their meals. "It's very scary to be like this," Mary said.

Milton Meltzer, *Poverty in America*, 1986.

But what about all the jobs advertised everyday in the paper?

You hear it all the time. There's plenty of work out there, but a lot of people just don't want to work. They'd rather live off welfare. They're lazy. Just look at all the want ads in the paper. Jobs are going begging. Anyone who wants to work can find it.

Sure.

Okay, let's look at all those want ads.

One morning, there were 1059 help wanted ads in the *Washington Post*.

Reporter Martha Hamilton checked them out.

At first glance, she thought, the ads looked deceptively promising. 1059 notices of dreams and opportunity.

But on that same day, according to the unemployment figures, 77,600 people were out of work in the Washington area. More than 70 times the 1059 jobs listed.

"For the unskilled," wrote Hamilton, "wading through the want-ads is like unwrapping a large, elaborately wrapped present, only to discover another smaller box inside, a still smaller box inside that, and nothing in the end." . . .

A Closer Look

Looking closely at the ads eliminated most of them as full-time jobs for the hard-core unemployed. There were 64 jobs that were part-time or temporary. Next were 29 that required you to move and live on the job site—jobs like apartment manager.

Fourteen of the 1059 ads weren't even real jobs but come-ons for real estate courses and the like. Another 16 jobs were out of town, from Baltimore to Israel.

At least 30 more jobs weren't salaried, but for commission only, or required an investment.

In other words, there were 85 times as many people out of work as there were jobs left after these subtractions.

Of the 906 jobs left, 157 ads were for managers or professionals . . . architects, engineers. Still another 223 jobs were for skilled craftspeople, such as carpenters, mechanics and electricians.

Another 25 jobs required some type of license, such as a beautician's license. And 245 were for clerical jobs. That left 256 jobs for the really unskilled and undereducated job hunter.

Too Many Applicants

According to those offering these jobs, the ads produced a large number of applicants, many of them anxious to work.

"When I advertise for a driver," said one, "I often get as many as 100 calls. They say things like 'I'm out of work,' and 'the kids need food.'"

An ad for a hostess for a Howard Johnson's Restaurant drew about 50 responses.

"It seems as if an awful lot of people in D.C. are out of work," said the woman who took the calls. "I think a lot of people are getting fairly desperate." . . .

"There is a big structural unemployment problem in this area," said John Gallahan, a labor economist for the District of Columbia. "The people that are unemployed don't match up with the jobs that are available."

Within 3 weeks, 79% of the jobs had been filled. Of the unfilled jobs, over half were clerical.

A year later, on September 15, 1980, over 12,000 men and women, mostly black and young, stretched around 3 Baltimore city blocks in response to a job call for 75 openings by the Social Security Agency.

Four years earlier, when Marriott's Great America amusement park was about to open in Santa Clara, Calif., it advertised for 2200 unskilled workers at the minimum wage. The office had 14,000 application blanks on hand, but an estimated 30,000 job seekers showed up, clogging traffic for miles. Most of them were under 25.

On February 9, 1982, in Pittsburgh, the Post Office said it would hire 60 workers. 15,000 showed up for the 60 jobs.

On February 23, 1982, 2400 lined up to compete for 300 apprenticeships at the Long Beach, Calif. Naval Shipyard.

The Changing Job Market

Why aren't there enough jobs to go around?
The job market has changed.

First, more women are in the work force than ever before. In an effort to beat inflation, both wives and husbands are working full-time jobs.

Second, automation and technology are displacing thousands of workers a year.

Technological change is making it impossible to provide jobs for all who want them.

The evidence shows that those with inadequate education and training won't find jobs in the future. Their talents simply won't be economically competitive with the machine.

Robotics is a new word in the dictionary. For years, robots have performed such unpleasant and hazardous jobs as spray-painting cars, handling hot forgings and lifting heavy castings. Now they're performing quality control inspections, parts loading and assembly operations.

They're perfect. Unlike human operators, they never make a mistake. And they never get bored. . . .

Examples of Automation

• Radio stations which needed a dozen people to operate, can now be run by three with automated recording equipment.

• In one insurance company, there were 539 persons employed in the commercial department prior to the installation of automatic methods. 133 persons were replaced. . . .

• A wholesaler displaced 150 tally clerks with a computer and 10 workers. . . .

• Robots will undoubtedly raise productivity at lower labor costs. For instance, a $40,000 robot working two shifts at an auto plant over an 8-year period costs about $4.80 per hour, compared with current labor costs of about $15 per hour for a comparable human worker. And after its working life is over, the robot won't collect retirement pay. . . .

The Concentration of Wealth

Why does poverty exist if the United States is so rich?

Because the wealth of America is concentrated in the hands of a few.

The income gap between rich and poor families in the United States has widened since World War II.

The income gap between the richest 5% of families and poorest 20% widened from $10,565 in 1947 to $19,150 in 1970 and to $32,590 in 1977. The top 5% have consistently earned 5 times the income of the lowest 20%.

The top 20% of the U.S. population receives 43% of all national income. The bottom 20%—more than 40 million men, women and children, including the unemployed, the aged and the disabled— receive only 4.8% of all national income.

The wealth gap is even greater than the income gap. The richest 20% of all people own 75% of all assets. The poorest 20% own no assets at all. . . .

23

The gap isn't narrowing. In 1958, the top 1% owned 26.9% of the wealth. In 1962, it was 27.4%. In 1969, 25.6%. And in 1972, 25.9%.

Control of Investments

Economist Ferdinand Lundberg calculated that one-half of one percent of our population—each worth over half-a-million dollars—owns 32% of the nation's investment assets, from which real financial control is derived. Through an interlocking chain of corporate and bank directorships, this one-half of one percent virtually controls most of the financial and political power of the country.

Experts concede that a 5% ownership stake in a large corporation is enough in most cases to give corporate control. Lundberg calculates that 13 families own 8% of the stock in the 200 largest corporations. . . .

"These 200 corporations, in turn," said Lundberg in 1970, "own 67% of the manufacturing assets of the country, up from 48% in 1948. The duPont family, alone, controls 17% of General Motors. 0.2% of the shareholders of General Electric control 33% of the stock. 0.2% of the shareholders control 45% of Sears. One bank, J.P. Morgan Co. of New York, controls more than twice the total budget of any state government, and more than the combined Gross National Products of Greece, Israel, Jordan, Syria, Algeria, North Vietnam, South Vietnam, Laos and Cambodia."

The top 49 banks hold over $1 trillion in trust funds. They own at least 5% of the stock in 147 of the 500 largest corporations, and control 768 interlocking directorships in 286 of the top 500 corporations. . . .

That's why a few people are wealthy and why most of us are struggling to make ends meet.

"For nearly a billion human beings elsewhere, poverty, American style, would seem like unleashed luxury."

Poverty in America Is Not a Serious Problem

Bud Shuster

Bud Shuster is a Republican congressman from Pennsylvania. In the following viewpoint, he argues that poverty in America should not be assessed by a comparison with Utopia, but rather with conditions elsewhere in the world. Viewed in this light, Shuster concludes, America's poor not only have a higher material standard of living than the poor in other places or times, but also have the American advantage of the opportunity to better their condition.

As you read, consider the following questions:

1. How does the typical poor American family live, according to the author?
2. How does Shuster's view of technology and employment differ from that of the opposing viewpoint?
3. How does the author sum up the difference between poverty in America and poverty elsewhere?

Excerpts from *Believing in America* by Bud Shuster. Copyright © 1983 by Bud Shuster. By permission of William Morrow & Company.

Overall, Americans enjoy a better standard of living than any other people on Earth. Starting with the basics, Americans have available the most nutritious, balanced, tasteful, and diverse diet at the lowest relative cost. That some do not avail themselves of proper nutrition is another story. Based on a shopping basket of thirty-nine basic food items including bread, milk, meat, fish, vegetables, and fruit, the United States continues to lead the world in purchasing power and affluence. Even high-priced foods in America are bargains compared to their cost in other countries. For example, 2.2 pounds of medium-quality steak cost $7 in America, as compared to $24 in Western Europe and $41 in Japan. As a percentage of the average American family's cost of living, food has dropped from 23 percent in 1950 to 18 percent in 1981.

Contrary to a widely held view that starvation in under-developed countries is caused mainly by an unbalanced diet, it is in fact caused by an inadequate number of calories in the daily diet. On the average, people in India consume only 90 percent of the calories essential to the maintenance of their bodies, meaning that about half the population—325 million people—are under-nourished. For 14 million people in Ethiopia, the picture is even worse, since they consume only 74 percent of the minimum daily calories required. Americans, embarrassingly, consume 135 percent of their daily caloric requirements.

Housing Luxuries

Breaking an early-morning crust of ice in a water bucket, shivering while starting a fire, bundling up for a dash to the privy, chilling milk in a cellar cistern, feeling the warmth of an oil lamp on the palm of the hand cupped to blow out its flame remain everyday experiences for millions around the world; but they are only dim memories, or strange stories of distant days, for that most privileged of all people—the Americans. Virtually every American home now enjoys indoor plumbing, central heating, and electricity, although at the turn of the century, fewer than 10 percent could claim such luxuries. The typical American family lives in a home with 5.1 rooms, and almost 20 percent of those homes consist of seven or more rooms. About a million new homes are built annually, averaging 1,600 square feet, with two bathrooms, three bedrooms, a fireplace, and a garage. In 1966, 25 percent of new U.S. housing construction included central air conditioning; by 1979, that figure had increased to 60 percent. . . .

Typical of millions in underdeveloped countries, almost half the homes in India have only one room, and almost all are without indoor plumbing. Even in prosperous Japan, the average housing unit is only 3.8 rooms, with no central heating, and general-purpose rooms convert into bedrooms at night, with mats rolled out for sleeping on the floor. Kuwait, with the world's highest per-person GNP, has 3.5 rooms per housing unit, but 82 percent of the homes are without running water.

American homes are filled with appliances unavailable in many parts of the world, and at costs lower than those in other areas in which they are available. Combined, an electric or gas oven, refrigerator, washing machine, color TV set, vacuum cleaner, and electric iron cost about $2,500 in America, while averaging $3,200 in Western Europe and $5,200 in the Middle East.

Cars and Telephones

Americans enjoy a level of personal mobility unmatched anywhere. Americans can go where they choose, conveniently and economically. Over 114 million automobiles are registered in the United States: one car for every two people, or 1.8 vehicles for every household. Compared to Japan, America has three times as many cars per person, twice as many as Britain, and twenty times as many as the Soviet Union. . . .

There are 742 telephones for every thousand Americans. That's nearly twice as many as in Japan, Britain, or France, nearly three times as many as in Italy, and over nine times as many as in the Soviet Union.

No Poverty in America

When compared with living conditions throughout the world there may be no poverty at all in the U.S. Most Americans have never seen the true face of poverty, which is visible in many other countries. It reveals hunger, disease and early death. In the U.S. even the least productive members of society live in relative abundance and comfort when compared with their counterparts abroad. Among his foreign peers the American pauper is an object of envy and the U.S. the target of pauper immigration.

Hans F. Sennholz, *The Freeman*, January 1985.

The various elements of personal prosperity combine to provide Americans with the overall highest standard of living the world has ever known. Certainly, when compared to the pre-Depression "good old days" of the high-flying 1920s, the average American is better off economically in virtually every respect. Compared to those earlier days, known firsthand only by senior citizens, today's average American has to work only half as many hours to pay for a new car, a child's education at a state university, a gas range, an electric washing machine, a lady's wool skirt, a dozen oranges, ten pounds of potatoes, or a half gallon of milk; he need work only one-fifth the time to purchase a vacuum cleaner, an electric sewing machine, or a ticket for public transportation.

Within two decades, the real purchasing power of the average American family has increased 40 percent, and the number classified as poor has declined 35 percent.

Despite the recurring problems, the fact remains that compared to earlier generations, Americans are vastly better off. Economic prosperity surely is not shared equally by all, nor will it ever be, so long as talents and ambitions differ. While opportunities abound, they fall imperfectly and unevenly on a heterogeneous people separated by climate, class, and culture, but joined in freedom to pursue their own enlightened ends.

The Great Utopia

Economic prosperity provides the base, the material bedrock from which noneconomic values may most securely be pursued, but it carries with it no warranty, neither written nor implied, for happiness or peace of mind.

When the car payment and mortgage are due, when the supermarket cash register slip ratchets upward every week, when children's flimsy summer sneakers cost more than the sturdy winter shoes did a few years back, the indisputable fact that one is really better off may be hard to swallow, even though it's true.

Life always loses when compared with what it ought to be. The great Utopia one subconsciously seeks but never finds debases the reality in which one must live. Measured against the ideal, America falls far short; but against the humanly attainable, here or anywhere around the globe, America soars.

Comparisons

For Americans, the average life expectancy has surpassed the biblical three score and ten, reaching 70.5 years. Life expectancy in the underdeveloped world is twenty years less, and that stark statistic does not begin to measure the suffering experienced by almost one billion of the world's population who do not have adequate food, shelter, or sanitation. For example, infant deaths in America average 13 per 1,000 born, while in most underdeveloped countries they exceed ten times that rate, topping 162 in Ethiopia. While virtually all Americans enjoy access to a safe water supply, less than one-third of the people in the underdeveloped world have such access, and only 6 percent of the Ethiopians enjoy such a basic necessity, taken for granted by Americans.

A comparison of the standard of living between the United States and the Soviet Union is particularly instructive. On November 7, 1977, the ruling Communist Party of the USSR celebrated the sixtieth anniversary of its Bolshevik takeover of Russia. Sixty years in which the "dictatorship of the proletariat" had absolute power to remake the society it ruled; sixty years in which it could have capitalized (pardon the expression) on such natural advantages over America as more land, more tillable acreage, more minerals, and more people; sixty years in which Russia's rich heritage of literature and music could have been further cultivated, rather than destroyed, debased, or driven westward. After sixty years of iron control, and despite its superiority of natural resources, the Soviet Union lags far behind the United States by virtually every measure. . . .

Absolute vs. Relative Poverty

Much of the confusion is caused by the definition of poverty. If poverty is given an ABSOLUTE definition, such as "a fixed bundle of goods," then relative to 1940, poverty has been eliminated in the U.S. Back in 1940 it was unheard of for poor people to own such luxury items as cars, telephones, designer clothes, or to travel the nation and even the world by plane. They were lucky if they could afford to vacation by bus. However, if poverty is given a RELATIVE definition, such as a certain percentage of the national median income, poverty is impossible to eliminate. We could quintuple everybody's income and, relatively speaking, the poor would still be with us.

Walter E. Williams, *Manchester Union Leader*, March 7, 1985.

The typical poverty family in today's America lives in a rental unit of 3.7 rooms—1.7 bedrooms, one bath, a complete kitchen, and modern plumbing. The unit is located in a forty-year-old structure of two to four units, and rents for about $170, part of which is subsidized. The family's personal belongings include a television set, radio, and motor vehicle. Adequate clothing is taken for granted, for even the poorest have shoes, shirts, dresses, and pants. Free health care is provided through Medicaid in modern medical facilities located within a dozen miles of most homes; food stamps and free school lunches provide for a balanced nutritional diet, if used properly. In setting up the Food Stamp Program, the federal government established a scientifically based formula for a family of two adults and two teenagers to ensure that poverty-level families could enjoy a nutritious diet. Entitled the Thrifty Food Plan, it spelled out the quantities of food to be consumed weekly in various groups including: milk, meat, vegetables and fruit, and bread and cereals. The problem was, however, that the plan's promoters never bothered to distribute the Thrifty Food Plan to food-stamp recipients, realizing that few would have adhered to it since, under the law, recipients can buy any kind of food they want. The Thrifty Food Plan established Recommended Dietary Allowances as set by the National Academy of Sciences for protein, calcium, iron, magnesium, vitamin A, thiamine, riboflavin, niacin, vitamin B_6, vitamin B_{12} and vitamin C. Dr. Robert Rizek, director of the

Consumer Nutrition Center for the U.S. Department of Agriculture, told a congressional committee that "the plan provides twenty-three pounds of red meat and seven pounds of poultry (monthly), despite the fact that chicken is a more economical source of protein than most types of red meat." He added: "Many households, whether or not they are eligible for food stamps, do not select nutritious assortments of food."

That many Americans do not avail themselves of good nutrition is one of the many choices that they are free to make. But even the poorest of the poor seldom goes to bed hungry for want of food or the wherewithal to get it.

Poverty and the American Dream

Compared with most of the world, poverty in America loses much of its sting. For nearly a billion human beings elsewhere, poverty, American style, would seem like unleashed luxury. Yet, to the extent that people in America who have the capacity and desire to participate in the production and consumption of America's wealth cannot do so, they are, indeed, disadvantaged. Their plight is a festering sore on the most productive and prosperous national body the world has ever seen, and must be healed in order for that body to be entirely healthy.

In centuries past, kings lived neither so well nor so long as the poor in America today. Yet, for those at the bottom of the U.S. economic ladder, the bottom is still the bottom—and the genius of America has been that it has held out real opportunity for people to better themselves—to bootstrap themselves out of poverty, however officially defined. Should that opportunity no longer exist, a vital part of the American soul would surely die. But the good news is that, while still imperfect, the opportunity shines as bright as ever, and the desire to achieve it burns fiercely in the hearts of millions. The substantial decline in the number of Americans defined as poor, the doubling of the average American's standard of living every twenty years, the explosion of young people enrolled in higher education, and the increasing numbers of college graduates and professionals among the minorities, are but a few of the measurements which confirm the continuing health, vigor, and viability of the American dream.

The New Technology

The opportunities for growth and upward mobility are no better exemplified than by the electronic-computer industry, in which I worked for seventeen years, from the early days of vacuum-tube computers through the explosion of the software revolution and introduction of microprocessors. During that exciting period, thousands of young men and women were introduced to new technologies, as they entered exotic worlds of bits and bytes, of microseconds and logic boards, of binary arithmetic and excess-three codes, of machine language and COBOL, of high-speed printers and random-storage devices, of display terminals and acoustic couplers. As young people just out of college learned to electronically manage data to tell factories how to run, planes where to fly, and investors what to buy, they participated in a technological revolution that rocketed America ahead. The sons and daughters of steel-mill workers and gas-truck drivers, electronically redesigning blast furnaces and calculating where to dig for oil, were doing so at salaries four times the earnings of their parents.

Aristotle had said mockingly: "When looms weave by themselves, man's slavery will end," to make the point that slaves would always be necessary, because looms would never weave alone. America proved him wrong. Today, a whole nation "weaves" by itself, building products and scheduling events automatically, at the touch of a button. But behind the button is the ingenuity and effort of people making machines to do the work for them, faster, better, and more productively than ever before.

Soviet Poverty

Soviet spokesmen tirelessly condemn the West for the existence in the democracies of poverty, unemployment, homelessness and racial prejudice. . . .

It is true that 14 percent of the U.S. population in 1985 lived beneath the official government poverty line. A family of four with an annual income below $10,989 is considered poor. Excluded from this income is the value of food stamps, Medicare, housing subsidies and other benefits.

Yet if the U.S. definition of poverty were applied today to the Soviet Union, *a majority of the Soviet population would fall beneath the official U.S. poverty line.*

Arnold Beichman, *The Washington Times*, August 17, 1987.

Hundreds of new companies have been spawned by the high technology explosion, creating thousands of new, exciting jobs, and making poor men rich. Bittersweet for some, as life most always is, and mixing failure with success, American high-technology engineers and entrepreneurs tried whole new ways of doing things and, in the process, changed the world. Not content, now they reach for worlds beyond, with *Columbia* shuttling between Earth and space, and deep probes peering into Mars and Venus. But while Americans try to touch the stars, others around the globe still scratch for food.

For much of the world, poverty is still poverty. Over eight hundred million people live in absolute poverty, meaning they go to bed malnourished and hungry, and live a quarter-century less than people in industrialized areas. Meanwhile, three out of every four can expect to die without ever having learned to read or write.

Poverty, then, has different faces for different people. For millions in Africa, Asia, and South America, it means total despair and resignation. It is existing, rather than living, while waiting to die. It is life without hope, relief only through death. It is Edwin Markham's "Man With the Hoe," only painted brown or yellow and having even less: "The emptiness of ages in his face, and on his back the burden of the world. . . . a thing that grieves not and never hopes, stolid and stunned. . . "

For Americans, it is a condition to be changed. Not stopping to note how well-off even poor Americans are compared to well-to-do citizens of underdeveloped countries, Americans dream of better days. They hope because they have been taught to hope. It is part of the great American dream, of a better tomorrow, however good today. Surrounded by prosperity, what they see so widely spread about them, they know they too can touch and have.

"Accounting for taxes, underreporting, and in-kind income appear to reduce poverty estimates by nearly 50 percent."

The Poverty Rate Is Overestimated

The President's Task Force on Food Assistance

How poverty is defined and measured can have a profound impact on determining just how many poor people there are. Many people have criticized government poverty statistics as being either too high or too low. The following viewpoint is taken from the report of the 1984 President's Task Force on Food Assistance. It concludes that government poverty statistics exaggerate poverty.

As you read, consider the following questions:
1. How is the poverty line calculated?
2. According to the authors, what is the most common criticism of poverty statistics?
3. What are the different methods of measuring in-kind benefits?

President's Task Force on Food Assistance, Staff Working Paper, January 1984.

The concept of the poverty line was developed by the Social Security Administration in 1964. The index consists of a set of cash income cutoffs that vary by the size and the number of children in a family. The original poverty index was based on USDA's 1961 Economy Food Plan (the predecessor to the Thrifty Food Plan) and reflected the different consumption requirements of families based on their size and composition. USDA's 1955 Food Consumption Survey showed that families of three or more persons spend an average of one-third of their after-tax income on food. The poverty level was therefore set at three times the cost of the Economy Food Plan.

Poverty levels are adjusted each year by the percentage change in the Consumer Price Index (CPI). Other than the annual adjustment for inflation, the poverty thresholds in 1983 are essentially the same as they were in 1963.

Poverty Thresholds

It is frequently argued that the poverty thresholds, as currently estimated, no longer meet their goal of measuring the costs of minimum adequate expenditures on food and nonfood items (however defined). For 1963, the year the index was defined, it can be argued that one-third of the poverty threshold represents a minimum adequate expenditure on food and two-thirds represents a minimum adequate expenditure on nonfood items. Over the years, however, the poverty threshold has been adjusted by the CPI which reflects the price in the *average* consumers' market basket of expenses, not a market basket of "necessities." Energy, shelter, medicine, and food weigh more heavily in the market basket of low-income consumers compared to the average consumer.

Thus, there is no basis for breaking down the current set of poverty thresholds into components reflecting food and nonfood items. Adjusting the poverty threshold by the CPI can either over- or underadjust for changes in the cost of necessities. As a result, no one understands exactly what poverty statistics measure.

It is frequently argued, however, that for technical reasons, problems in measuring consumer prices have artificially inflated poverty thresholds and thus poverty counts. For example, the Bureau of Labor Statistics has recently revised the calculation of the housing component of the CPI to represent more accurately residential living costs. If this revised housing component had been utilized beginning in 1972, the CPI (and thus poverty thresholds) would have been 12 percent lower in 1980, reducing estimates of the number of people in poverty by about 18 percent. . . .

The source of data on poverty is the March Supplement to the Bureau of the Census' Current Population Survey, the monthly survey that provides the basis of unemployment estimates and other population characteristics. Approximately 60,000 households are interviewed each month. The March supplement contains detailed data on family income for the previous calendar year.

For the purpose of measuring poverty, only cash income (including cash transfer payments) is counted. Noncash transfer payments are *not* counted as income for the purposes of measuring poverty status. The failure to account for sources of in-kind income is the most frequently cited criticism of poverty statistics.

As such, receipt of food stamps, free or reduced-price school lunches, Medicaid, Medicare, public housing, etc. have no effect on the official estimates of poverty. The exclusion of noncash benefits was not considered a major issue when poverty thresholds were developed because most government aid to the poor was provided in cash. Since then, however, the importance of in-kind transfers has grown tremendously. In terms of 1982 dollars, noncash transfer payments grew from $7 billion to $107 billion between 1966 and 1982. Noncash benefits have also come to account for the lion's share of all means-tested transfer benefits that are determined by recipient's income.

Noncash Transfer Payments
(1982 Dollars)

	Noncash Total (billion $)	Noncash Means-Tested (billion $)	Noncash As % Total Transfer	Noncash As % Means-Tested
1959	$ 1.3	$ 1.3	1.8%	10.5%
1966	6.8	6.8	6.1%	33.8%
1973	50.0	29.3	21.7%	56.0%
1982	106.9	56.4	29.5%	71.6%

Failure to account for the growth of noncash transfers thus distorts interpretation of long-term trends in poverty. There is little disagreement that in-kind transfers should be factored into calculations of economic well-being. There is disagreement, however, as to how they should be valued. Two methods of valuation have been widely cited by economists:

(1) the *market value* approach assigns a value to the transfer equal to the purchase price in the private market of the goods received by recipients, e.g., the face value of food stamps.

(2) the *cash equivalent* value is the amount of cash that would make the recipient just as well-off as the in-kind transfer. This is generally less than or equal to the market value.

A recent study by the Bureau of the Census (1982) estimates the impact of incorporating income from in-kind transfers on estimates of the size of the poverty population. The size of the reduction depends on which benefits are considered and the particular valuation method utilized.

Poverty Rates in 1979

	Market Value	Cash Equivalent
Cash Income (official measure)	11.1%	11.1%
Plus Food and Housing Only	9.4%	9.5%
Plus Medical (excluding institution care expenditures)	6.6%	8.7%
Plus Institutional Care Expenditures	6.4%	8.2%

Source: U.S. Bureau of the Census, 1982.

Thus, incorporating the value of in-kind transfers reduces the poverty count for 1979 by 26 to 42 percent. The difference between these estimates is attributable largely to problems in the valuation of medical benefits which account for the largest share of the estimated poverty reduction. Inclusion of the value of noncash benefits has a larger impact on the poverty rates of blacks and families maintained by women since these groups have higher participation rates in the noncash transfer programs.

Poverty statistics have been further criticized due to their reliance on pre-tax measures of income when economic well-being depends on after-tax income. Adjusting poverty statistics to reflect after-tax income would increase estimated poverty rates by two-tenths of a percentage point.

Underreporting Income

Yet another shortcoming in the measurement of poverty is that individuals tend to underreport sources of cash income as well as the receipt of in-kind transfers to survey interviewers. This phenomenon is observed in most surveys, not only the CPS which provides the basis of poverty statistics. The underreporting of cash income has the effect of inflating estimates of the poverty population from the "true" level.

Comparison of CPS and Administrative Estimates of Income and In-Kind Benefit Recipiency

	Administrative Data Source	CPS	CPS as a % of Independent Source
Income (billions of dollars):			
Earned Income	$1345.4	$1293.3	96.1
Unearned Income	362.9	235.9	65.0
In-Kind Benefits (millions of people):			
Food Stamps	22.8	17.5	77.0
Free and Reduced-Price School Lunch	11.6	10.3	88.1
Medicare	26.3	25.7	98.0
Medicaid	20.8	18.1	87.2

Source: U.S. Bureau of the Census, Current Population Reports Series P-60, No. 137, p. 137.

Previous attempts to adjust poverty statistics for the underreporting of income find that the size of the poverty population is reduced by about two percentage points.

Poverty Rates Estimates (1979)

	Official	Adjusted for In-Kind Income	Adjusted for Taxes, Reporting, and In-Kind Income
1979	11.6	8.7	6.1

Although methodological refinements can be debated endlessly, accounting for taxes, underreporting, and in-kind income appear to reduce poverty estimates by nearly 50 percent from unadjusted levels.

"Most of the changes which would make our poverty line more realistic would increase the number of people classified as poor."

The Poverty Rate Is Underestimated

William P. O'Hare

William P. O'Hare is the director of policy studies for the Population Reference Bureau in Washington, DC. In the following viewpoint, he argues that official poverty measurements do not reflect the full extent of American poverty. He argues that including non-cash benefits as income is not a realistic poverty measure, and that a more accurate poverty assesssment would show the number of people in poverty to be much higher than official figures.

As you read, consider the following questions:

1. What objections does the author have to including "non-cash income" in counting the poor?
2. What evidence does O'Hare give to show that the poverty line is too low?
3. Why does the author believe that his recommendations on measuring poverty will not be used?

William P. O'Hare, "Keeping Track of the Truly Needy." Reprinted from USA TODAY MAGAZINE, September 84. Copyright 1984 by the Society for the Advancement of Education.

The disparity regarding the perceived size and growth of the poverty population in America is captured in two statements: "The number of people remaining in poverty is very small and it grows smaller every day" (Martin Anderson, Stanford University economist, 1978; and ". . . there were 34,400,000 persons classified as poor in 1982, an increase of 2,600,000 over 1981" (U.S. Bureau of the Census, 1983).

The two contradictory views expressed above also indicate how important the proper measurement of poverty is in shaping public policy. If the first statement above is correct, it implies that there is little need for public programs to assist the poor and that the recent Federal cuts in social programs are of little consequence. On the other hand, if the Census Bureau is correct, there is not only a large number of people living in poverty, but their numbers are growing. If the Census figures are correct, the past two years has hardly been the time to cut back public assistance programs. . . .

The Poverty Line Controversy

Because of its importance, the measurement of poverty has been a subject of controversy since the inception of an official poverty definition in the mid-1960's. The official government definition of poverty consists of a table of separate income thresholds which vary by size of family, number of children under 18, and age of the head of household (over or under 65). The yearly income of a family or individual is compared to the appropriate income threshold from this 48-cell matrix to determine poverty status. . . .

The basis for establishing these income thresholds can be traced back to the original conception of the poverty guidelines formulated by the Social Security Administration in the early 1960's, primarily under the direction of Mollie Orshansky. The original poverty threshold was computed by taking the cost of purchasing the U.S. Department of Agriculture's (USDA) "Economy Food Plan" and multiplying this cost by three, based on findings from a 1955 USDA survey which showed that one-third of a family's budget usually goes for food. The resultant figure was then adjusted for family size and other characteristics to create a matrix of poverty income thresholds. This definition, often referred to as the Orshansky index, and the assumptions upon which it is based have had only slight modifications since their inception in the mid-1960's. . . .

Inclusion of Noncash Income

Although there have been numerous suggestions for changing the way the government measures poverty, one particular recommendation has received most of the attention in the last few years—inclusion of noncash or in-kind benefits in calculating income for the poor. (Cash transfer payments, such as Aid to

Families with Dependent Children and other public assistance, are already counted as income in the determination of income and poverty status.) Although the number of people officially below the poverty line climbed from just under 23,000,000 in 1973 to over 34,000,000 in 1982, many have argued that the official statistics on poverty actually overstate the real number of poor people because they do not include noncash government welfare benefits—such as food stamps, subsidized housing, and free health care—in calculating income. . . .

There are two sorts of concerns with the way the in-kind benefits issue has evolved: first, some considerations regarding the inclusion of noncash benefits as income that have not been fully appreciated, and second, other issues surrounding the way we define poverty which are equally important, but have not received sufficient attention.

A Modest Decline

How many poor people are there? Honest analysts can sincerely differ on the definition, but the reasons given for the alleged great decrease in the number of the poor in recent years are simply not persuasive. I would suggest that there are in the range of forty to fifty million Americans who live in poverty. That is roughly the same number I suggested more than twenty years ago, but, since the population has increased during those decades, it represents an exceedingly modest decline in the percentage of the poor.

Michael Harrington, *The New American Poverty*, 1984.

So far, most of the proponents of including noncash benefits as income have focused on government benefits for the poor and have largely ignored the noncash benefits received by the nonpoor. Employer-paid health and life insurance, tax-free interest, the enormous tax expenditures given businesses, tuition subsidies for college students, and price supports for agricultural crops (including tobacco) are all government benefits which go largely to the nonpoor.

Recent data show that there are almost 61,000,000 Americans who enjoy group health insurance either entirely paid for or subsidized by their employer, and almost 48,000,000 workers are provided with a pension plan that is partially or totally paid for by their employer. One recent study shows that the value of noncash employer benefits are equal to one-fourth of total remuneration. We also have all heard of the company cars, expense accounts, and country club memberships that top executives enjoy tax-free.

If the noncash benefits to the nonpoor were counted as

income—and taxed appropriately—the increased revenue would go a long way towards balancing the Federal budget. If inclusion of noncash benefits helps determine who is really poor (truly needy), won't the inclusion of noncash benefits help determine who is really wealthy? Some proponents of inclusion of noncash benefits in measuring poverty seem to be advocating one standard for the poor and a different one for the rich—count the in-kind benefits of the poor, but not the in-kind benefits of the nonpoor.

Other Problems

Furthermore, there is seldom any mention of the general public value of some of the noncash assistance to the poor. For example, medical assistance for the poor has the effect of improving the "public health" of the entire country. Since the health of everyone is interrelated to some degree, a healthier poverty population is better for everyone.

It should also be clear that the notion of including noncash benefits as income to an individual is illogical in some contexts. For example, if one adds the payments made under Medicaid or Medicare to one's income, it implies that the more medical expenses one has, the better-off one is—the sicker, the better! To some extent, this example also holds for housing and food stamps. The larger one's family is, the larger the housing subsidy and the more food stamps one is entitled to, but it is incorrect to argue that large families make poor people economically better off.

Finally, the valuation of these noncash benefits for the poor, as well as noncash benefits for the nonpoor, is extremely problematic. This difficulty is recognized in the recent Census Bureau report on this topic, which tried three different methods for valuing noncash benefits. The results of these three methods vary dramatically from one another.

Aside from the inclusion of noncash benefits, there are many other questions about the official definition of poverty which should be addressed. To the extent that public attention is directed exclusively toward the issue of noncash benefits, these other equally weighty issues are overlooked. In other words, whether or not to include noncash benefits is *not* the best question to ask. We should be asking how we can improve the measurement of poverty in this country. In this context, examination of noncash benefits is only one small portion of the answer, and unfortunately one which has obvious political overtones.

How To Define Poverty?

In an effort to improve the measurement of poverty, we can start by looking at how the definition of poverty was derived. The original measurement of poverty, as discussed earlier, set the poverty income threshold at three times the cost of the USDA's

Economy Food Plan, assuming that families spent approximately one-third of their income on food. However, data from the 1965 Food Consumption Survey shows the income-to-food ratio is 3.4 to one, and more recent evidence from the 1972-73 Consumer Expenditure Survey (CES) shows that poor people actually spend a much lower proportion of their funds on food; therefore, a higher multiplier should be used in deriving the poverty line. The CES shows that food expenses are about one-fifth of all consumption expenses for all families ($1,625 out of $8,253) and nearly the same proportion for families in the lowest income decile ($663 out of $3,037). This would indicate that the cost of food should be multiplied by five instead of three and that the poverty line should be about five-thirds, or 1.67 times, its current level. The poverty threshold for an average family of four in 1982 would then be $16,470, rather than $9,862.

Basic Changes Needed

Poverty guidelines in the United States, though officially updated each year, are outdated and in need of major revisions. The formula for the existing standard was based on food and income data of the mid-1950s. No basic changes have been made in the fundamental assumption underlying the guidelines for 30 years! The poverty-line thresholds should be increased by about 25% to 30% to reflect 1987 standards.

Wilbur J. Cohen, *Los Angeles Times*, April 19, 1987.

The Economy Food Plan, used as the basis for the original poverty level, was the cheapest of four alternatives, and is not designed for prolonged use, but for "emergency or temporary use when funds are low." A more realistic food plan would, of course, cost more, thereby raising the poverty income threshold. Work by Mollie Orshansky shows that use of a more realistic food plan and a multiplier based on the most recent expenditure information would raise the poverty thresholds by at least 50% and increase the number of officially poor by several million. A few years ago, Ms. Orshansky, in response to a query on improving the poverty measure, stated: "My own update, to bring the measure into line with more recent nutritional standards and consumption practices, is one example. That update would change the number of the poor for 1975 from 26,000,000 to 36,000,000'—an increase of 38% in the poverty population. Using 1977 data, the increase was slightly larger, from 24,700,000 to 37,600,000 under the updated Orshansky index. If the same ratio held in 1982, the number of poor using the revised Orshansky index would have been 47,500,000, compared to the official figure of 34,400,000. This measure, commonly known as the "revised Orshansky" or the "updated Orshansky" in Federal statistical circles, has been available for several years. Yet, despite the fact that it uses technically superior and more timely information, it has not been adopted by the government and is completely ignored by many of those arguing that poverty is understated due to the inclusion of noncash benefits in the calculation of income.

A Minimum Standard of Living

Another criticism of the current measure of poverty is the fact that it makes no attempt to actually examine the costs of items generally thought to reflect a minimum standard of living. Instead, it simply updates a set of income thresholds derived nearly 20 years ago. On the other hand, the Bureau of Labor Statistics (BLS) regularly calculates the costs of a Family Budget for a Lower Standard of Living which is based on updated actual costs for a series of budget categories required for maintaining a household. The BLS Lower Family Budget was about 65% higher than the poverty standard in 1981. The BLS Lower Family Budget was $15,323, compared to the poverty line of $9,287 for an average family of four in 1981, the last year the family budgets were calculated by BLS. The Reagan Administration has decided not to fund this project any longer. Use of the BLS Lower Family Budget as the poverty line would indicate that over 50,000,000 people should be classified as poor.

The decision to stop calculating the BLS family budgets is particularly interesting since the BLS Family Budget for a Lower Standard of Living is considerably closer to the income level most public opinion polls show to be a reasonable poverty level. A long series of opinion polls show the public feels that the poverty line should be much higher than it is. In the January, 1983, Gallup Poll, the average response to the question, "What is the smallest amount of money a family of four . . . needs to get along in this community?" was $15,400. For most of us, the prospect of supporting a nonworking spouse and two children on less than $9,800 a year (before taxes) is awesome. . . .

The Census Undercount

One final factor effecting the official poverty statistics which is often overlooked is the Census undercount. In 1970, the Census Bureau estimated that it missed approximately 5,000,000 people; figures for 1980 are better, but it still appears that about five per cent of blacks were missed. Given the characteristics of the people generally missed by the Census Bureau—such as minority status and transient lifestyles—it would not be surprising if at least one-fifth and perhaps as much as one-half the missed persons were below the poverty line. In addition, if the Census and Current Population Survey (CPS) could accurately survey the undocumented alien population of the country, they would surely reflect a further increase in the population below poverty level.

Comparison of data from the Decennial Census and the Current Population Survey, which provides the poverty figures for non-census years, suggests that the CPS figures underestimate the number of poor. For example, the 1980 Decennial Census taken on April 1, 1980, reported 27,383,000 people in poverty, while the March, 1980, CPS, which purportedly measures income in the same calendar year (1979), shows about 26,072,000 poor people, or 1,300,000 fewer people in poverty. My preliminary analysis of this difference suggests that the outreach program of the Decennial Census results in the Census reaching many of the people missed in the CPS (i.e., the transient, homeless, and unemployed) —a great portion of whom are likely to be poor. Consequently, the CPS figures, which are used in nine out of 10 years, probably underestimate the true number of poor consistently.

Poverty Measures That Increase Poverty

The introduction of any of these changes in the measure of poverty would, of course, result in a slightly or substantially different measure of poverty than we have had in the past. The exact extent of the difference would depend on the change or combination of changes made. While some claim that the current poverty index overstates the number of poor because noncash benefits are not counted as income, most of the changes discussed here suggest that a more realistic poverty measure would result in a higher number of officially poor, rather than a lower number. . . .

It is not hard to understand why many of the changes to the poverty measure discussed here are not likely to be implemented. Most of the changes which would make our poverty line more realistic would increase the number of people classified as poor, and no president would like to see the number of poor increase during his administration. On the other hand, inclusion of noncash benefits as income for the poor would reduce the number of officially poor. What president wouldn't welcome that? It is easy to see that many of the improvements of the way we measure poverty are not likely to be implemented in the near future at least, not because they are not worthy adjustments, but because they are not politically expedient.

=====

"Hunger is a problem of epidemic proportions across the nation."

=====

Hunger Is Epidemic

The Physician Task Force on Hunger in America

The PTFHA is comprised of physicians, public health officials, and academic and religious leaders, and is sponsored by the Harvard School of Public Health. The following viewpoint is excerpted from its nationwide study of hunger published in 1985. The study concluded that the problem of hunger in America had grown significantly in the 1980s, and estimated that there are twenty million Americans who suffer from hunger. The report urged changes in government policies.

As you read, consider the following questions:

1. What historical background does the viewpoint provide? Why is this important?
2. According to the Task Force, what causes hunger in America?
3. Is hunger a solvable problem, according to the Task Force?

Hunger in America is a national health epidemic.

It is our judgment that the problem of hunger in the United States is now more widespread and serious than at any time in the last ten to fifteen years.

We do not reach this conclusion lightly. Some of us have spent a significant portion of our professional careers trying to eliminate hunger and malnutrition in this nation. In 1967, we accompanied a team of United States Senators to look into hunger in regions of the nation. We stood by Senator George Murphy (R-California) as he expressed his despair at what he had seen in this nation: "I didn't know that we were going to be dealing with the situation of starving people and starving youngsters."

1967: Crisis

During that year we went into health centers and homes across this nation and examined children and the elderly. We saw children whose nutritional and medical condition was shocking even to a group of doctors whose work involved them daily with disease and suffering. In child after child we saw evidence of vitamin and mineral deficiencies, severe anemia, eye, ear and bone diseases associated with poor food intake. We found children who were listless, suffering from fatigue and exhaustion, children who got no milk to drink and who never ate fruits and vegetables. They lived on grits and bread.

Some of our medical colleagues reported our findings to the U.S. Senate: "We do not want to quibble over words, but 'malnutrition' is not quite what we found. . . They are suffering from hunger and disease and directly or indirectly they are dying from them— which is exactly what 'starvation' means."

1977: Improvement

Ten years later some of us were among the teams of doctors sent into these same regions of the nation to determine whether hunger was still a serious problem. During that decade our people, through their federal government, Republicans and Democrats, responded to the problem of hunger. The food stamp program was expanded so that poor families could purchase food. School lunch and breakfast programs were increased so children could have adequate nutrition while they learned. Elderly feeding programs were established to reach lonely older Americans isolated in their homes. And the supplemental food program for poor pregnant women and their babies was established to reach recipients when nutrition makes such a critical difference.

In 1977, we went back to Appalachia where we had seen severe malnutrition a decade before. We returned to the Mississippi Delta where we had found malnourished infants and listless elderly citizens living on the brink of starvation. We again visited Indian reservations and returned to the ghettos of some of our nation's major cities. What we found gave us great professional and civic pride.

America's nutrition programs had succeeded. While we still saw immense poverty, we no longer saw widespread hunger and malnutrition. Poor people reported that they had food to eat. Teachers no longer reported children coming to school hungry. And doctors and nurses found that malnutrition was not a severe problem among the poor. To be certain, things were not perfect, but they were greatly improved.

1985: Relapse

It is now 1985, and hunger has returned as a serious problem across this nation. To be sure, hunger is not yet as bad as two decades ago, but the situation has greatly deteriorated.

We believe that today hunger and malnutrition are serious problems in every region of the nation. We have, in fact, returned from no city and no state where we did not find extensive hunger.

Jim Morin. Copyright © 1986 *The Miami Herald.* Reprinted with permission.

Nine-year-old Lee, who resides in the rural "Boot-heel" region of Missouri, has the stature of a six-year-old because he doesn't get enough to eat. He and the other malnourished children we found there are little different from the children who dig for food in the dumpsters outside apartment buildings in St. Louis.

Little Regina, a listless five-year-old who sat before her empty plate at a North Carolina day care center, is experiencing growth failure because she gets little to eat outside the program. But she may be faring better than the numerous younger children we examined that day who had no milk to drink and whose refrigerators were bare.

A young father in Pasadena, Texas, broke into tears as he told us that he sometimes cannot feed his wife and three sons. But he is little different from the fathers in Montgomery, Alabama, Peoria, Illinois, and other cities who cried as they told us the same thing.

Ninety-two-year-old Laura McAfee, who subsists on white beans and potatoes in her Nashville home, is thin and anemic. But her health status is little different from that of Mr. Alvarez, seventeen years her junior, who collects cans in his home near Brownsville, Texas, so his wife can eat and his little granddaughter can have milk to drink. And neither of these elderly Americans differs greatly from the thousands whom local churches and agencies report remain in their homes, alone, hungry, often malnourished. . . .

Major Findings and Conclusions

Hunger is a problem of epidemic proportions across the nation.

Hunger in America is a serious and widespread problem. It is in fact so widespread and obvious that its existence has been documented by fifteen national studies, and even more state-level studies, during the past few years.

While no one knows the precise number of hungry Americans, available evidence indicates that up to 20,000,000 citizens may be hungry at least some period of time each month. In the 1960s, before the expansion of federal nutrition programs, hunger was a daily problem for millions of citizens. Today, evidence indicates that weaknesses in these same programs leave millions of citizens hungry several days each month, and often more.

Hunger in America is getting worse, not better.

Evidence from the states and regions of the nation indicates that hunger continues to grow. Reported improvements in the economy appear to be having little, if any, impact on the problem of hunger.

Almost without exception, emergency food programs across the nation report significant increases in the number of hungry people. Accordingly, the pounds of food provided to alleviate this growing problem are, themselves, increasing at a steady rate. It appears that most Americans who are "recovering" economically were never hungry, and those who are hungry are not recovering.

Malnutrition and ill-health are associated with hunger.

Hunger and poverty are frequently associated with malnutrition and other forms of ill-health. Today, compelling evidence indicates that members of vulnerable population groups, particularly children and the elderly, are at increased risk of adverse health outcomes due to hunger.

Malnutrition is a problem which impacts somewhere in the vicinity of a half million American children. Growth failure, low birth-weights, and other outcomes associated with inadequate nutrition are serious among low-income pediatric populations, and health problems and chronic diseases associated with undernutrition are serious among the elderly poor.

Hunger is the result of federal government policies.

Hunger in America is the result of a series of governmental policies, some within the past few years and others of longer duration.

The Trouble with Hunger

The trouble with hunger is that it wears many disguises and often goes unrecognized. Some hungry Americans may be overweight; eating cheap food can cause this. Others may appear to be lazy or lethargic. Hungry Americans get sick more often than the adequately fed, but the basic cause of their illnesses may not be diagnosed as hunger. Pregnant mothers who do not get enough to eat may give birth to infants who have mental or physical defects or who are underdeveloped. Before the problem of hunger can be eliminated it must first be recognized, but this is harder to do than one might think.

Gerald Leinwand, *Hunger and Malnutrition in America*, 1985.

Hunger does not just happen in a nation with more than enough food to feed itself and a good part of the world. Hunger occurs because policies either produce it or fail to prevent it. Today our leaders have permitted poverty in this nation to reach record levels and then cut back on programs which help our citizens endure economic hardship. As a result, America has become a "soup kitchen society," a spectre unmatched since the bread lines of the Great Depression.

Present policies are not alleviating hunger in America.

Hunger is getting worse, and no evidence indicates that it will lessen as a problem.

Poverty in the country is at the highest rate in twenty years, and purchasing power for the poorest forty percent of the population is lower than it was in 1980. It is unlikely that economic changes helping the better-off will assist those who are hungry.

The bottom line is that policies which supposedly were to help the poor have not done so.

We believe that our political leaders must end their laissez-faire attitude toward hunger. Millions of Americans are hungry now, and political leadership—Republican and Democratic—is required to address their plight. Even if things do improve in the future, our job is to make sure that all of our citizens have the opportunity to reap the rewards of democracy today.

"There is absolutely no credible evidence that hunger in America is either widespread or on the rise."

Hunger Is Not Epidemic

S. Anna Kondratas

S. Anna Kondratas is the head of the Food and Nutrition Service for the US Department of Agriculture. In the following viewpoint, she says that the problem of hunger in America has been greatly exaggerated and that there is no evidence that hunger is increasing. She criticizes the methods of studies on hunger, including the report of the Physician Task Force, excerpted in the opposing viewpoint. Kondratas calls for the federal government to conduct annual health surveys to provide a more accurate picture of hunger in America.

As you read, consider the following questions:

1. What reasons does the author give to doubt claims of widespread hunger?
2. What distinction does the author make between hunger and malnutrition? How does this distinction affect studies on hunger?
3. What problems does the author see with the Physician Task Force report?

S. Anna Kondratas, "Holding Hands Against Hunger: How Americans Are Being Conned," *The Heritage Foundation Backgrounder*, May 21, 1986. Reprinted with permission.

It has been suggested that there may be as many as 20 million "hungry" Americans. The organizers of Hands Across America have even claimed on network television that "there is widespread hunger and famine in America."

There are no facts to substantiate this assertion. To the contrary, in the late 1970s scientific studies reported that hunger and malnutrition because of lack of income were not a problem in the U.S.; only isolated cases of it remained. Since then, federal spending on food programs has gone up, not down. A greater proportion of the poverty population is receiving food stamps today than ever before. Indeed, one in ten Americans is a food stamp recipient. Supplementary private-sector food assistance also is expanding rapidly. And food costs comprise a smaller proportion of personal income than five years ago, while per capita caloric consumption is up.

So what would explain rising hunger? Nothing. The truth is that there is no reason to believe the problem is any worse now than it was in the late 1970s, and the likelihood is that it has improved. Moreover, the degree of hunger in the U.S. is comparatively tiny, and persistent hunger is related more to dietary ignorance than to lack of federal assistance. The perception of widespread hunger is rooted in subjective, anecdotal impression, based on isolated and unrepresentative cases.

Field Work and Refrigerators

The methodologies of the much publicized studies that purported to "find" 20 million hungry Americans and to identify 150 "Hunger Counties" have been soundly discredited. Other studies, also given significant publicity, are based on equally questionable assumptions and shaky methodologies. One claim that the plight of the rural poor is worsening, for example, was based on 1976-1980 nutritional data. Political reports, such as that of the Conference of Mayors, frequently draw conclusions that the ambiguous and incomplete data presented cannot justify. "Field work" frequently consists of going to people's homes and looking in their refrigerators. When refrigerators are empty or near empty, individuals are deemed hungry even when they themselves deny it and there is no physical evidence of malnutrition. And even though it is clear that many of the poor really do have too little food, studies also show that many food stamp recipients do not spend all their incremental income solely on food. There is absolutely no credible evidence that hunger in America is either widespread or on the rise. . . .

Hunger or Malnutrition?

Malnutrition is a clinical state easily measured by physicians. Hunger, on the other hand, is a subjective impression, which can be "measured" only by the person actually experiencing it. While this may seem patently obvious, the distinction is important, because different people understand different things by the word "hunger." This complicates policy making on the issue. It is obviously not the feeling of hunger itself that is the proper focus of policy, because that feeling is experienced voluntarily by millions of dieting Americans every day. It is the association of hunger and poverty or the involuntary experience of prolonged hunger leading to malnutrition that should be of concern.

Malnutrition Not a Major Problem

There is little systematic evidence of widespread or increasing undernutrition in the U.S.

Data from the Centers for Disease Control indicate that there are not major public health problems among low-income children with regards to growth or anemia.

The Department of Health and Human Services indicates that nutrient deficiencies are not a major problem for the U.S. population.

Report of the President's Task Force on Food Assistance, January 1984.

This means that the strictly relevant policy questions are: What is the extent of malnutrition and health-threatening involuntary hunger in the U.S.? To what degree is such insufficient nutrition a function of income? What is the government doing to alleviate such hunger and what more could it be doing? And what are the limits of government intervention in terms of improving the nutrition of the poor? . . .

The Myth of Increasing Hunger

Despite the data, hunger—together with homelessness—has been attracting attention, mainly because of the efforts of such groups as the self-appointed Physician Task Force on *Hunger in America*. Despite annual federal expenditures of $18.6 billion on food programs alone, this group claims that hunger is directly "the result of federal government policies." Such statements, however, do not rest on serious studies adhering to scientific standards, but on analyses with flawed methodology and conclusions not supported by the data.

Typical is the Physician Task Force's *Hunger in America*, published in 1985 by the Harvard University School of Public Health, which concluded that there are at least 20 million hungry Americans—individuals who do not have sufficient income to buy an adequate diet. Understandably, this shocking statistic was reported by the press around the world. The trouble is that the statistic bears no relation to fact. The study simply ignored the dietary surveys available to any analyst, which find that the majority of the poor have perfectly adequate diets, and that many nonpoor have inadequate ones.

The clear implication in the study was that the hunger "findings" were based on the field work of the physicians on the task force, many of whom had participated in a similar field study in the late 1970s.

But field work had nothing to do with the method used to derive the number of supposedly hungry Americans. Dr. Larry Brown, the report's principal author, simply subtracted food stamp recipients from the total poverty population in 1983 and added to that an arbitrary number of food stamp recipients deemed to have an insufficient diet. This was done on the dubious and unproved assumption that anyone below the official poverty line, but not on food stamps, must go hungry and that the food stamp allotment itself is inadequate for many.

Shoddy Scholarship

That is shoddy scholarship, and it is dishonest. Using exactly the same methodology in 1979, for example, would result in the "finding" that 18 million were hungry that year. Yet the report contrasts the early 1980s with the late 1970s, noting that the 1977 field team "had reason to believe that the hunger problem had virtually been eliminated; they took professional pleasure in our nation's having eradicated this dreadful problem." It would seem that the physicians might have noticed 18 million "hungry" people then, if 20 million are so evident now.

In short, *Hunger in America* is a tract that rails against inhumane bureaucracies, analyzes trends in unemployment and poverty, draws analogies between today's economic conditions and the Great Depression, and makes frequent references to the "mean-spirited" political climate created by the Reagan Administration. But it fails to establish any cause-and-effect relationships between present economic policies and trends and the Task Force's supposed subject of study—hunger and malnutrition. . . .

There are dozens of such studies. And since officials, lawmakers, and the press rarely have either the background or the time to distinguish between serious work and flawed advocacy projects, the myth of worsening hunger flourishes. These studies, tragically, may discredit sincere and honest advocates of the poor, making the real problems of the poor more difficult to solve. . . .

Recommendations

Despite the mythology and exaggerations surrounding the hunger issue, policy makers should not be complacent about the plight of the poor, the hungry, the homeless, or any less fortunate American. To ensure sound policy, the federal government should fund annual health and nutrition surveys to produce reliable and current estimates of the nutritional status of all Americans as well as of the poor. This would help identify the scope of the problem and at-risk groups, as well as changes over time. There is currently no methodology to estimate the degree of hunger and malnutrition in the U.S. Both health and welfare policy makers would benefit from such information. . . .

More Confusion than Evidence

Perhaps the greatest source of confusion in the definition of hunger and malnutrition is the assumption made by economists, social scientists, and the public at large that having less than a certain disposable income means that a family will automatically not be able to purchase a nutritionally adequate diet, will go hungry on a regular basis, and will become malnourished. The "thrifty food plan," worked out by dieticians at the U.S. Department of Agriculture and used as the basis of the current definitions of poverty, includes very significant amounts of expensive items such as meat and dairy products which could be, and often are, replaced during difficult times by less expensive sources of nutrients. On a worldwide basis the four most important sources of dietary protein for man are wheat, rice, maize, and the white potato, all repeatedly maligned as "just starch.". . .

Despite vehement claims to the contrary, the most careful and objective analysis reveals what common observation would assert: that there is little evidence of major or even significant hunger and malnutrition in this country, unless some whimsical definitions . . . are used for these two terms.

George G. Graham, *The Public Interest*, Winter 1985.

The problem of hunger in America has been vastly exaggerated in recent years. While there is no credible methodology for determining its exact extent, the evidence suggests strongly that there is no mass hunger in America and that there has been no major change in the nutritional status of Americans in recent years.

Defining Poverty

   Much of the debate in this chapter over how serious poverty is in America revolves around how poverty is defined. There are two general methods of defining poverty. One is to use a *relative* definition—measuring the wealth and income of a certain population, and finding out who has the least *relative* to the others. This process does have limitations. For instance, most people would argue that the men in the foreground of the cartoon are still poor, even if there are people worse off than they are. Conversely, in a country populated by millionaires, a person with only a half-million dollars would be considered poor.

"There's Always Someone Worse Off Than Yourself."

ROTHCO
ORIGINAL

© Wiles/Rothco

Another method of defining and measuring poverty is to use an *absolute* definition. This method sets a minimum standard of income and/or wealth, regardless of how many people are above or below the standard. One example of an absolute definition is the official US poverty line, which defines as poor any couple who earned less than $7132 a year in 1986. A major drawback to absolute definitions is that they don't consider other factors, like differences in cost of living. The couple making $7132 a year will live more comfortably in rural Iowa than in New York City.

In this exercise you will create your own definition of poverty. Consider again the men in the cartoon. Most people would consider a person who does not live in some sort of home or shelter as poor. By this definition the men in the cartoon are poor. But most people would not consider poor a person who couldn't afford a cabin cruiser. Most people view cabin cruisers as luxuries, not one of life's essentials.

What does it mean to be poor?

Step 1

Working in small groups, discuss the items listed below. Mark *E* for essential items—things you believe people must have. Mark *N* for nonessential items—items that are luxuries a person could live without.

three meals a day
shelter
housing with at least one private room
enough money for occasional snacks, trips to movies, cigarettes
indoor running water
private hot shower
one "good" outfit of clothing
more than five changes of clothing
heating
air-conditioning
health care or insurance
annual dental and eye checkups
a washer and dryer
a job
a car
a television set
a VCR
electricity
a warm coat
a refrigerator
meal at fast-food restaurant once a week
high school education
post-high school education (college or vocational school)

a stereo
a radio
a telephone
a personal computer

If necessary, add other items you believe are essential.

Step 2

Discuss the following questions with your class or group.

1) Examine your list of *essential* items. Which ones are actually essential to survival and which are essential to a "humane" existence—a level above bare survival?

2) Write an item-based definition of poverty: "A person suffers from poverty if he/she lacks these items:_____, _____, _____ . . ."

3) How absolute is your group's definition? If a person lacked only *one* of your essentials, is he/she still poor? If a person has several non-essentials but lacks some essentials, is he/she still poor?

4) Do you think your definition of poverty is better or worse than the two described in the introduction of this activity? Why? What drawbacks does your definition have?

Periodical Bibliography

The following articles have been selected to supplement the diverse views presented in this chapter.

Gary Burtless — "Inequality in America: Where Do We Stand?" *The Brookings Review*, Summer 1987.

Stephen Budiansky — "A Measure of Failure," *The Atlantic Monthly*, January 1986.

Consumer Reports — "Life at the Edge," June, July, August 1987.

Dollars & Sense — "Defining Away the Poor," January/February 1987.

Fred Jordan — "America's Working Poor," *American Legion Magazine*, February 1987.

Nick Kotz — "The Politics of Hunger," *The New Republic*, April 30, 1984.

Abigail McCarthy — "Orphaned and Lost: A Country Built and Peopled by the Poor," *Commonweal*, July 17, 1987.

Myron Magnet — "America's Underclass: What To Do?" *Fortune*, May 11, 1987.

Charles Murray — "In Search of the Working Poor," *The Public Interest*, Fall 1987.

Sylvia Nasar — "America's Poor: How Big a Problem?" *Fortune*, May 26, 1986.

Richard P. Nathan — "Will the Underclass Always Be with Us?" *Society*, March/April 1987.

Ronald D. Pasquariello — "The Skewing of America: Disparities in Wealth and Income," *The Christian Century*, February 18, 1987.

Robert J. Samuelson — "Progress and Poverty," *Newsweek*, August 24, 1987.

Scholastic Update — "New Efforts To Help America's Poor," March 23, 1987.

Walter Shapiro — "The Ghetto: From Bad to Worse," *Time*, August 24, 1987.

John C. Weicher — "Mismeasuring Poverty and Progress," *The Cato Journal*, Winter 1987.

2 CHAPTER

What Causes Poverty in America?

Chapter Preface

What causes poverty? The question is important, for if the causes of poverty can be accurately identified and eliminated, then it may be possible for poverty to be prevented and ultimately stopped.

This approach—identifying and combatting a cause—is not a novel one. During the 1960s War on Poverty, for example, some authorities noted that many impoverished people were poorly educated and concluded that this was one of poverty's causes. Consequently, the Office of Economic Opportunity (OEO), formed at this time, devoted much effort to educating and training poor people. Its mixed results and ultimate abolishment were viewed by some as the result of incorrect assumptions about the cause of poverty. Michael Harrington, whose 1962 book *The Other America* focused much attention on poverty, is among those who agree that the OEO took the wrong approach. He believes the shortage of well-paid jobs is a more significant cause of poverty. Although various programs have also addressed this cause— programs creating jobs, establishing minimum wages, and so forth—poverty remains.

The question of cause is especially important when dealing with the poverty that persists from generation to generation. In recent years the term "underclass" has been used to describe this set of people who seem permanently fated to be poor. Today the word is nearly synonymous with the large minority populations of inner city ghettos. Isolated from the rest of society, these people are beset with unemployment, a high teenage birthrate, gang warfare, and crime. Two authors in this chapter debate the causes of this particularly troubling aspect of American poverty.

"Widespread, desperate, degrading poverty has always been the hallmark of industrial capitalism, in this country and everywhere else."

The Capitalist System Causes Poverty

New Unionist

The *New Unionist* is the newsletter of the New Union Party, a socialist organization which advocates the control of the United States government and economy by the workers. In this viewpoint, the editors assert that while capitalism can produce wealth, it causes poverty by distributing wealth and property unequally. The authors conclude that the poor today are worse off than the American farmer of two hundred years ago. Poverty will never be solved as long as this social structure of property ownership remains unchanged.

As you read, consider the following questions:

1. What paradox is the hallmark of capitalism, according to the editors of the *New Unionist*?
2. What did it mean to be poor two hundred years ago, according to the authors? How and why did this definition change?
3. According to the authors, what is the only way to solve poverty?

"Property for the Few, Poverty for the Many," *New Unionist*, December 1986. Reprinted with permission.

"That so many people are poor in a nation as rich as ours is a social and moral scandal that we cannot ignore," say the Catholic bishops in their pastoral letter on the U.S. economy.

But this is a scandal that is 100 and more years old: widespread, desperate, degrading poverty has always been the hallmark of industrial capitalism, in this country and everywhere else. Over the last century, wealth production has multiplied many times, yet poverty has persisted in boom times as well as bust. Today, with our ability to produce reaching a dazzling level of excellence through automation and computerization, "harsh poverty plagues our country despite its great wealth."

Twenty-Five Percent Are Poor

Using government statistical guidelines that set levels of consumption considered minimally adequate to keep body and soul together, the bishops estimate that more than 33 million Americans are poor, that is, below the minimum levels. In addition, 20 to 30 million are "needy," which would be at or near the poverty line. In other words, a full 25% of the population have the wherewithal for only a bare existence and nothing more.

This figure alone is enough to debunk any claim that America is an "affluent society," or the ridiculous assertion of right-wing ideologues that "free enterprise" is the most effective poverty-eliminating system imaginable.

But when poverty is considered in a broader—and more meaningful—sense than the absence of certain consumer goods, the picture is far, far bleaker than even what the bishops discovered.

Poverty in the Past

200 years ago in America, to be poor meant not owning the land or the tools of a trade by which to be an independent, self-employed producer—a farmer or craftsman or merchant. To be poor meant having to hire yourself out, to work for someone else who did own tools of production.

The propertyless worker received a daily or weekly wage as the price of the labor power he sold to the employer for a day or a week. The wage may have been only enough for the bare essentials, or it may have been enough for a higher standard of living. But the wage worker in either case remained a dependent of his employer, and when he lost his job he lost his only source of income because he had no productive property of his own. He could at any moment, for reasons beyond his choice or control, become destitute of even the minimum essentials of life.

In the early years of the new American republic, the majority of the people had the opportunity to be self-employed, primarily as land-owning farmers. The wage-working class—the poor—was still a small minority of the population, although there was to be

Norman Goldburg, *People's Daily World*

a growing slave class of black people, who not only owned no property but didn't even possess their own bodies to sell as the wage workers did.

As industrial capitalism began to take off in the late 1800s, the many self-employed small businessmen lost out in the competitive market to big business, which was concentrating property in trusts and corporations. As more and more farmers and other small owners lost their property, they went to work for wages for the corporations that had crushed their "American dream." The working class grew as the middle class of small owners shrunk.

Dependent on Wages

Today we have reached the point where giant corporations monopolize the important industries. Now 90% of the population are without self-sustaining, income-producing property, and being dependent on wages (or salaries) for their livelihood are included in the working class.

Of course, it now would hardly do to define poverty in terms of nonownership of productive property because if you did you'd be describing the vast majority of Americans. People might begin to wonder if this system is such a great deal after all!

Because the tiny minority that is the owning class—and the ruling class—are so small in number, they must retain the allegiance of the poor majority if they are to hold onto their wealth and power. For this they depend on a highly-developed propaganda machine that continuously bombards the wage slaves with the message of how well off and free they are, being bona fide AMERICANS, with especial good fortune if they are white, native-born AMERICANS.

A Revised Definition

In the revised definition of poverty, it is not *property* but *income* that counts, and since you can draw the income poverty line just about anywhere you want, two-thirds of the people are spared the poverty label with a stroke of a pen.

When the stock market goes down, you don't see Rockefellers, Mellons and DuPonts lining up at the food-stamp office. When the "high-paid" wage worker loses his or her job, it is the welfare line where you'll find him.

That's the difference. And that's why when unemployment goes up, so does the number of officially-recognized poor: a worker without a job has nothing.

Because the competitive capitalist market causes property to concentrate in fewer and fewer hands, growing poverty under capitalism is inevitable, despite the continual growth in the production of wealth. In fact, improved efficiency in production leads to more destitution rather than less because fewer workers are needed, with less total wages paid, to achieve a greater output.

Reforming the System

Yet despite these hard, unrelenting facts of capitalist economics and despite 100 years of historical experience to draw lessons from, our liberals persist in chasing their dreamy rainbow of alleviating poverty and other social ills within the existing economic order. Unfortunately, the bishops in their pastoral letter fall into this same hopeless mire of reformism, of trying to patch up a thoroughly decayed and collapsing edifice when a new and sturdy structure is the order of the day.

They call for such immediate government action as an increase in the minimum wage, a more progressive income tax, improved day care and increased welfare payments, as well as long-term goals as a family allowance and a "negative income tax."

Even if these measures were economically and politically feasible, their enactment would do nothing to change the way the system operates and *must* operate to generate ever-higher levels of unemployment and ever-larger numbers of people who will need assistance from the government—a government already saddled with a $2 trillion debt.

64

The bishops' letter does say that property rights are not absolute and goes on to document the extreme concentration of ownership in the U.S. But the bishops fail to draw the necessary conclusion that poverty is the direct consequence of the unequal ownership, and that not much can be done about the problem as long as property is monopolized by a few.

In this failure they reveal the essentially conservative, hierarchical nature of their church organization. Their concept of society reflects the makeup of the church, in which there are sheep and there are shepherds. While it is the duty of the shepherd to see that his flock is well cared for, his authority as shepherd cannot be questioned. Transferred to the economic arena, it means the capitalists shouldn't allow the workers to starve, but neither should the workers challenge the capitalists' right to own industry and rule society.

A Final Conquest of Poverty

Regardless of what positive moral sentiments motivate the religious leaders, their fundamental philosophy disqualifies them from leading a genuine movement for the final conquest of poverty. The only way poverty can be ended is by ending the economic and social inequality that produces it, and the only way to achieve that it by bringing the wealth-producing property under the democratic ownership and control of all society.

An Inevitable Result

Far from being a machine for bringing people out of poverty, capitalism perversely condemns millions to poverty in the midst of the means sufficient for creating an abundance for all and in the midst of obscene luxury enjoyed by the capitalist minority. . . .

The specific rate of poverty may move up and down with the ups and downs of the economy. But poverty itself is the inevitable result of a system based on the exploitation of wage labor—and it will never by eliminated until that system is eliminated.

The People, September 14, 1985.

This is a movement that the workers must initiate through their own informed and intelligent action. Neither a paternalistic government nor an administration committed to preserving the "free market" jungle will give us the freedom we must achieve for ourselves.

"Capitalism was like a bootstrap by which whole nations of people could and did elevate themselves out of misery, grinding poverty, and periodic starvation."

The Capitalist System Solves Poverty

Edmund A. Opitz

The Reverend Edmund Opitz is a staff member of the Foundation for Economic Education, an organization that sponsors studies in free-market theory and limited government. He is the author of the book, *Religion and Capitalism: Allies, Not Enemies.* In the following viewpoint, Opitz argues that mass poverty and famines were the norm for humanity until capitalism was developed in the 18th century. By increasing the production of wealth, capitalism made poverty the exception rather than the rule. Opitz believes that socialist systems cannot work because they focus on the distribution of wealth, and ignore how wealth is produced.

As you read, consider the following questions:

1. What historical fact does the author seek to establish? Why does he say that poverty was not a problem in the past?
2. How does the author's view of early American history differ from the opposing viewpoint? How is it the same?
3. What fundamental shifts in thinking about poverty did capitalism cause? How does this bear on "solving" poverty today?

Edmund A. Opitz, "The War on Poverty Revisited," *The Freeman,* February 1986.

If we look back over the history of the past two or three thousands years we realize that most people who have ever lived on this planet were desperately poor, not merely poor by our standards—poor by any standards; miserably housed, shabbily clothed, and continually on the verge of starvation, only to go over the edge by the hundreds of thousands during the regularly recurring famines.

Medieval Europe is regarded by many scholars as one of the high points in world civilization. It gave us the great cathedrals, scholastic philosophy, magnificent works of art, literature like Dante's *Divine Comedy*, specimens of craftsmanship that grace our museums, and chivalry. But the Middle Ages in Europe suffered from a number of famines. Between 1201 and 1600 there were seven famines, averaging ten years of famine per century. Coming down to 1709, there was a famine in France that wiped out one million people, five percent of the population. The last great natural famine in Europe was the Potato Famine in Ireland in the late 1840s, which claimed about one and a half million lives.

But Europe has always been a favored region, more prosperous than the rest of the world, less subject to natural disasters than Asia. There have been starving times in Western civilization, but never were they of the same order of magnitude as the disasters in the Orient. India and China have been especially vulnerable to famines. A famine in China between the years 1876 and 1879 resulted in an estimated 15 million deaths. And within living memory, a famine in China's Hunan Province in 1929 resulted in two million dead. Ten major famines in India between 1860 and 1900 caused the death of close to 15 million people. During the Bengal famine of 1943-44—in and around Calcutta—one and a half million people died of starvation and the epidemics that followed.

Poverty Is a Natural State

I have recited these rather unpleasant facts, not for their own sake, but to emphasize a neglected or overlooked truism: *Poverty is the natural state of mankind.* Poverty is the rule; prosperity is the exception. In most parts of the globe, in most periods of history—including the present—most people most of the time have been or are desperately poor. Prosperity is what the ruling class enjoys. The rich are the superior warriors, the superior hunters, the favorites of the gods, and these wealthy few—it was believed—deserve what they have.

Water runs downhill, fire burns, grass is green, the masses of people are poor. This was the perceived natural order of things, accepted and rarely questioned. Such was the mentality that prevailed throughout most of the world most of the time—until a few centuries ago. Poverty for the multitudes was simply a fact of life. It was a hardship, but being poor was not perceived as deprivation.

The rich were envied, but the envy rarely translated into thoughts of redistributing their wealth. Occasionally something triggered a peasants' revolt or a slave rebellion, but when each of these fizzled out, all ranks went back to "The good old rule/ The simple plan/ That they should take who have the power/ And they should keep who can." Universal poverty was a fact. But poverty was not a problem! The distinction is simple: a fact or situation just is; a fact or situation for which there is perceived to be a solution becomes thereby a problem, and a new mentality is generated. . . .

The Capitalist Alternative

There was a breakthrough a few centuries ago, one of those great tidal movements in human affairs resulting in a new mentality and a different way of viewing the human condition. It was the discovery by the people of a few western nations of the complex set of institutions which later came to be called capitalism. The breakthrough might be symbolized by two documents, one penned by Thomas Jefferson setting forth the vision of a nation founded upon a new philosophy, that "all men are created equal," that they are "endowed by their Creator with certain unalienable rights," and that everyone is entitled to equal justice under the law. These axioms form the cornerstone of the free society.

The Socialist Solution

The socialist solution to poverty is to redistribute the wealth capitalism has created. Taking from those who have and giving to those who have less sounds charitable, but it makes the problem worse by destroying the incentive to create new wealth. Welfare state measures cause poverty! Wealth is not static; it is dynamic and in a condition of continuous creation. Capitalism—the free economy—is productive; it is the only way to bring about prosperity.

Irving E. Howard, *The Freeman*, August 1987.

At the same time, on another continent, a man named [Adam] Smith wrote a great book which explained why the economy need not be centrally planned, directed, and controlled by the government—as it was under the mercantilism of his day. Let the law be vigilant to protect the life, liberty, and property of all—as the Whigs advocated—and the buying habits of freely choosing men and women in the marketplace will provide all the directives needed for the producers to grow and manufacture the things consumers want most. This is the market economy, the backbone of a free society. Under these conditions a free people will multiply

68

their productivity and thus generate their own prosperity.

Capitalism is the name given to the set of institutions which enable free people to produce wealth up to the limit of their time, talents, capacity, and desire; and then to voluntarily exchange the fruits of their labors with others. Capitalism becomes fully operative only when there are institutional guarantees of individual liberty, with laws designed to secure the God-given rights of every person to life, liberty, and property.

Results of Capitalism

The intelligent and ethical way of arranging human action in society, the free society-market economy way of life which we are labeling capitalism, was like a bootstrap by which whole nations of people could and did elevate themselves out of misery, grinding poverty, and periodic starvation. Capitalism tackled poverty using the only means by which poverty can be alleviated, namely, by increased productivity.

Remove every obstacle that hinders the productive and creative energies of men and women and you create an abundance of goods and services, shared by everyone involved according to his contribution to the productive process, as that contribution is judged by the man's peers. This ever-increasing supply of goods and services will move the entire society up the rungs of the ladder of wealth. Some will climb to the top rungs, but even the least well-off on the bottom rungs will experience a level of well-being that would be regarded as affluence in noncapitalistic societies past or present. . . .

A New Mentality

Capitalism generated a new mentality, a new perception of the human condition. After the experience of capitalism anywhere, people everywhere came to regard prosperity as the rule; poverty as the exception. The fact that we launched a "war on poverty" demonstrates this. No one would contemplate a war on poverty in India or Africa, where need is much more desperate than here. Only in a prosperous nation like our own, where the great war against poverty had already been won—by means of the market economy—would the elimination of the last, lingering remnants of poverty emerge as a political issue. The trouble is that if we employ the wrong remedy to eradicate the remaining pockets of poverty—as we are doing—we may find that we have destroyed prosperity instead, as in the familiar story about killing the goose that laid the golden eggs. . . .

For thousands of years the planet was regarded as a static warehouse, containing a fixed amount of wealth, impossible to increase, never enough for everyone. The serf tilling his field grumbled that he had to pay various feudal dues to the lord of the manor, but he was realistic enough to know that even if he kept everything he produced, he'd still go hungry much of the time. He was cursed by low productivity, caused by a faulty understanding of the nature of wealth.

When it is believed that the earth contains only a fixed amount of wealth, the preoccupation is with the allocation of what's already here, which means, invariably, that one man's gain is another's loss.

The new perception that dawned during the 18th century was that new wealth is in a process of continuous creation, in ever-increasing amounts, with more for everyone resulting from each new cycle of production. This new abundance would be distributed—not equally, but equitably—by voluntary exchanges in the marketplace, with each person receiving from his fellows what they think his contribution is worth to them. Each of us benefits in such a voluntary exchange. . . .

Life, Liberty, and Property

Our basic political structures were largely built around the conviction that, "to the producer belongs the fruits of his toil." We were to have a private property order. The Declaration does not mention a right to property, substituting a right to "the pursuit of happiness." We cannot read Jefferson's mind as he wrote the document, but we do know what was in almost everyone else's mind at the time; it was Life, Liberty, and *Property*.

Capitalism and Moral Values

Only a free economic system supports dynamic production of wealth for the benefit of all. A free economic system, of all the economic systems tried by mankind in its history, gives the poor an opportunity to work, invest, prosper, and become rich. Not only that, but the moral values underlying a free economy also motivate the rich to bestow much of their wealth on works of charity and compassion to the needy. And those same moral values give legitimacy to the role of government in assisting those unable to obtain a decent standard of living through their own efforts.

William E. Simon, *National Review*, April 5, 1985.

The colonists had migrated out of situations in Europe where they lived on the estate of a master, working mostly for his benefit and only partly for their own. Here in the colonies the idea of freehold property was established. You owned your farm in fee simple, which means that your estate was your very own. You could will it to your descendants, sell it, dispose of it as you wished.

What you produced on your property was yours to keep, or sell, or give away. Now, you owned what your labor created, and you had an enormous incentive to devise labor-saving devices and work harder, longer, and more skillfully because everything you produced was yours. *You* got the added benefit; not some absentee landlord. Wealth creation increased by geometrical progression under these circumstances, with free men and women living under a just system of laws, holding a strict property right in the fruits of their labor. . . .

A False Axiom

The redistributionist policies of our own welfare state, as well as similar international policies which tax Americans in order to subsidize other nations, is based on the false axiom that the wealth of some is the cause of the poverty of others. Something like this *was* true during the pre-capitalistic ages, but capitalism introduced an entirely new ball game in which each one of us prospers to the degree that he contributes to the well-being of other people, as they see it. . . .

To believe that wealth is the cause of poverty makes as much sense as to assume that health is the cause of disease. And to contend that the remedy for poverty is to soak the rich and give to the poor is as idiotic as believing that the only way to heal the sick is to make the healthy ill. The sick can be made well only as they adopt the sensible regimen of the healthy, and the poor can move out of poverty only as they become more productive. The world's economic problems and other ills will only worsen unless there is a revival of that sound philosophy, which, two centuries ago, gave us the free society and the market economy which I've been labeling capitalism. Education along these lines— replacing bad ideas with better ones—is slow, frustrating, uphill work. But there is no other way.

71

"If low-income men and welfare mothers worked regularly, the underclass would be well on its way to dissolution."

A Reluctance To Work Causes Poverty

Lawrence M. Mead

One of the main tenets of the American dream is that people who are willing to work hard can pull themselves out of poverty. This belief lies behind many critiques of costly government welfare programs. The following viewpoint is excerpted from Lawrence Mead's book *Beyond Entitlement: The Social Obligations of Citizenship*. In it, Mead argues that government programs to help the poor should emphasize individual responsibility. He maintains that much of the poor's unemployment is a result of personal choice and behavior. Mead is a professor of politics at New York University and a former policy analyst for the Department of Health and Human Services.

As you read, consider the following questions:

1. Mead believes that government poverty programs make several assumptions about unemployment. What are they?
2. How have the poor's attitudes toward work changed, according to Mead?
3. Does the author believe there are enough jobs?

Reprinted with permission of the Free Press, a division of Macmillan, Inc. From *Beyond Entitlement: The Social Obligations of Citizenship* by Lawrence M. Mead. © Copyright 1986 by Lawrence M. Mead.

Much of the remaining poverty in the United States is due to high unemployment and nonwork among the poor. If low-income men and welfare mothers worked regularly, the underclass would be well on its way to dissolution. In Washington the presumption that nonwork is due to external barriers like lack of jobs has been orthodox since the New Deal, when an economic collapse threw a quarter of the labor force out of work for reasons beyond its control. Unemployment was a comfortable issue for liberal politics, since it seemed to reflect so little on the jobless themselves. The same attitude carried over to the Great Society. "The memory of the Depression and a penumbra of Marxism lingered on," wrote Daniel Moynihan, with the moral that "individuals were not to be held accountable for their fate."

The progressive interpretation of nonwork rested on two specific assumptions. One was that people would work if they could, because to do so served their own interests. What could be more self-interested than to offer one's labor in return for income? Each worker simply made his or her own best bargain with the labor market. While jobseekers wanted the pleasantest, best-paying jobs they could get, they would accept lesser positions if they had to. Some income was always better than none. That is, they were economizers—they accepted the constraints of their environment and adjusted to them as best they could. The other assumption was that the individual search for work served the social interest as well. It produced income for the jobseeker but also contributed to economic growth, which in turn meant opportunity for others and the wealth needed to finance public benefits for those who could not work. Full employment has always been a high priority in Washington simply because it expands the "pie" for everyone. . . .

Voluntary Unemployment

The signs are that unemployment has become more voluntary, in the sense that jobseekers often choose to remain jobless rather than take the jobs most accessible to them. The problem is not that jobs are *unavailable* but that they are frequently *unacceptable*, in pay or conditions, given that some income is usually available from families or benefit programs. Many unemployed, it appears, are no longer job*seeking* in the traditional sense of accepting the best job they can get, however bad it is. Rather, they are job*shopping*—seeking work but not accepting it unless it meets their conditions. As in other shopping they have the option not to "buy" at all, that is, to remain unemployed or withdraw from the labor force.

We tend to think of the unemployed as having "lost" their jobs or been "thrown out" of work, but on average that was true for only 47 percent of the jobless between 1970 and 1982. Thirteen percent quit their jobs voluntarily. Forty percent were people just entering or reentering the labor force, that is, who had not sought work in the period just prior. Even in 1982, a year of sharp recession, only 59 percent of the jobless had lost their jobs while 8 percent had left them and a third were new entrants. Intermittent employment is one reason why, although over 95 percent of nonfarm workers are covered by Unemployment Insurance, only about a third now have a steady enough work history to collect benefits when they are jobless—down from around half in the early 1960s.

Jobs and Immigrants

When we read about the alleged inadequate number of low-skill job openings, we may wonder: how do the six to eight million undocumented immigrants find jobs, and the half million, more or less, that join them every year? They have several strikes against them, besides language, little education, no skills. Most of them are ineligible for unemployment compensation, welfare, and other social benefits. They starve without a job. That's why they try hard, are not too choosy about taking on tough work at a low rate of pay. Whenever it is suggested that the United States should strictly enforce its immigration laws, employers object strenuously because they found out that Americans tend to be unwilling to take menial and stoop jobs at low pay. That suggests that the intensity of a job search and willingness to adapt to less than ideal conditions make the difference between those who land and keep a job and those who stay unemployed.

Roger A. Freeman, *Does America Neglect Its Poor?*, 1987.

A special government survey done in 1976 revealed the demands that the unemployed now feel they can make on the job market. The average worker who had lost or left a job was prepared to enter a new one only if it paid 7 percent *more* than his or her last position. While 35 percent of these jobless were willing to return to work for less than they formerly earned, 38 percent demanded more money. Even after fifty weeks out of work the average respondent persisted in expecting nearly as high a wage as in his or her old job. If jobless demanding a wage increase were defined as voluntarily unemployed and excluded from the statistics, unemployment as officially measured would drop by more than a point, more than three points for nonwhites.

Furthermore, only 30 percent of the jobless were willing to commute more than 20 miles to a new job, and only a third were willing to move to one. Especially for married women, maintaining ties to one's existing home, property, and friends often took priority over working. The jobless often had the resources to hold out for an attractive job. The commonest means of coping with the loss

74

of earnings were simply to reduce expenses and delay major pur-
chases, followed by reliance on savings, Unemployment benefits,
and the earnings of other family members. More demeaning steps
such as seeking help from friends or relatives, borrowing, or going on welfare were mentioned much less frequently.

These findings, which apply to the unemployed generally,
demonstrate that a disinclination to accept many available jobs,
if they are unattractive, extends to the population as a whole.
Among the low-income and low-skilled, however, unemployment
is compounded by nonwork in other forms. Many disadvantaged
workers have simply withdrawn from the legal low-wage labor
market. Their place has been taken largely by illegal immigrants.

Job Turnover

When the low-skilled do work, the pattern is rapid turnover in
jobs rather than steady jobholding. Among workers generally, the
duration of unemployment is shorter than one would expect if
joblessness were involuntary. In 1980, 43 percent of the
unemployed were out of work four weeks or less, 67 percent ten
weeks or less, and only 11 percent more than twenty-six weeks,
the usual duration of Unemployment benefits. Among women,
teenagers, and nonwhites especially, cycling in and out of work
is frequent. These groups seem to be able to find jobs about as
easily as those with lower unemployment, such as adult men, but
they also leave them quickly, or leave the labor force entirely.
Turnover rather than lack of jobs largely explains why they are so
often unemployed. Of course, as in musical chairs, if the turnover
stopped there might not be enough jobs for everyone. Then government job-creation efforts would become more necessary than they
seem now. But at present, for most jobseekers in most areas, jobs
of at least a rudimentary kind are generally available.

This kind of joblessness is difficult to blame on the environment.
It is not influenced much by the ups and downs of overall business
conditions. Though the low-wage labor market has a lot of temporary jobs, the usual pattern is for the same job to be filled by
a succession of low-skilled workers. No doubt discrimination plays
a role, but the evidence suggests that the workers usually leave
for their own reasons. It is most likely that they are impatient with
menial pay and working conditions and keep quitting in hopes
of finding better. This "pathological instability in holding jobs,"
rather than lack of jobs, is the main reason for the work difficulties
of the disadvantaged. . . .

Work is unquestionably one of the keys to overcoming poverty
and dependency. But given the trends toward selective employment, among the better-off as well as the poor, steadier work at
the bottom of society is unlikely unless government does
something to motivate it.

"In 1984, over 2 million people who worked full-time, year-round, were counted among the official poor."

A Reluctance To Work Does Not Cause Poverty

Dollars & Sense

Dollars & Sense is a magazine written from a socialist perspective by an editorial collective of economists and journalists. In the following viewpoint, they call the idea that poor people are lazy a myth, and point to the number of people who work full-time and still live below the poverty line. The authors conclude that changes in the economy, the number of low-wage jobs, and federal government cutbacks are the fundamental problems facing the poor in America.

As you read, consider the following questions:

1. How do the authors define "working poor"?
2. What is the reason behind the rising proportion of men who earn low wages, according to the authors?
3. What do the authors contend about the minimum wage?

"Working, But Still Poor," *Dollars & Sense*, December 1986. Reprinted with permission. *Dollars & Sense*, a progressive popular economics magazine, is located at One Summer Street, Somerville, MA 02143.

In these Reagan years, once-moribund myths about poverty have been resurrected. The poor, seen in the 1960s as victims of racism, urban blight, and regional underdevelopment, are now accused of having lost their work ethic. The Reaganite solution is to restore the work ethic through punitive workfare programs which force the poor to work in exchange for public assistance.

But the reality is that many poor households already do participate in the workforce, many of them on a full-time basis. Because of changes in the U.S. family and industrial structure, paid work no longer offers a guaranteed escape route from poverty. In 1984, over 2 million people who work full-time, year-round were counted among the official poor, as were many others who worked at least part of the year but *still* did not make enough to cross the poverty line.

In 1984, a family was defined as poor if its total cash income fell below $10,609 (for a family of four) or $8,277 (for a family of three). Of the slightly over seven million poor families that year, nearly half worked some part of the year, and one in five worked 50 weeks or more. Since 1978, there has been a 60% jump in the number of poor workers between the ages of 22 and 64, and the number of persons who work full-time, year-round and are still poor has grown by two-thirds.

The New Working Class

Although there is no official definition of the working poor, most researchers consider a household to be among the working poor if at least one member of the household earns a wage but the household's annual income still falls below the official poverty level. Whether or not a worker is part of the working poor depends both on his or her earnings and on the size of the household. For instance, a single mother with a job that pays $10,000 a year would be classified as working poor if she had three children but not if she had only one child.

Not surprisingly, people of color, recent immigrants, and white women who head households are disproportionately represented among the working poor. All these groups face lower wages and higher unemployment rates than do white men.

Jobs with Low Pay

A study by Sheldon Danziger and Peter Gottschalk at the University of Wisconsin's Institute for Research on Poverty found that the nation is providing more and more jobs at wages that are too low to lift a household out of poverty. The study investigated the working poor by looking at households of all sizes whose heads had weekly earnings below $204 a week (in 1984 dollars). They chose that cutoff because a four-member household with one worker earning that amount would live in poverty even if that worker put in 52 weeks of work each year.

77

Of the households in the Wisconsin sample, 64% escaped poverty because the household was smaller than four persons, because more than one person had a job, or because they had additional sources of income (such as welfare or alimony) that boosted them out of poverty.

Duane Powell. © 1985 News and Observer. Reprinted by permission of Los Angeles Times Syndicate.

Danziger and Gottschalk grouped households whose heads were over 65 years old, disabled, full-time students, or mothers of children under six as "households not expected to work." In their sample, 53% of those households were poor. Among those households that were expected to work, most of them did; over 80% of the male and over half of the female heads of households worked at some point during the year. But the incidence of low weekly earnings for those who are expected to work is rising, according to the Wisconsin findings. . . .

The most important factor behind the rising proportion of men who earn low wages is the structural transformation of the U.S. economy. As high-wage, unionized manufacturing jobs are replaced by non-union, part-time service work, men's capacity to earn high wages erodes. A study by the Department of Labor showed that workers displaced from the primary metals industry (mainly steelworkers) between 1979 and 1983 took an average pay cut of 40% in their new jobs—if they were lucky enough to land new jobs at all.

These days, eligibility requirements for most government welfare programs are so strict that many of the working poor cannot qualify. Although many do receive Food Stamps, most do not have the option of complementing their meager earnings with cash public assistance as they once could. According to the Wisconsin study, more than 60% of men and roughly 40% of the women heads of households who are expected to work receive no government cash transfers at all. (More women than men have access to transfer income because they usually retain custody of their children. In 25 states, current law says that two-parent families cannot collect AFDC benefits.)

Aside from low wages, lack of health insurance comprises a serious problem for the working poor. Census data from 1982 show that only 38% of retail trade workers, 22% of personal service workers, and 49% of business service workers had group health coverage, compared to 82% of manufacturing workers. Because the working poor are ineligible for welfare, they also cannot qualify for Medicaid, the government program that is supposed to provide free health care for the poor.

The Minimum Wage

The minimum wage is another part of the safety net that is no longer doing much to help the poor. Contrary to the Reagan administration's claims, 70% of those who earn the minimum wage are adults. Since January 1981, the last time the minimum wage was adjusted for inflation, consumer prices have risen by about 25%. In effect, the real minimum wage has fallen every year since 1981. As a result, full-time, year-round work at the minimum wage lifts only a single person out of poverty. At that wage, a family of two—one parent and one child—was $1300 above the poverty line in 1978, but $306 *below* it in 1984. Even a family of four with one earner working full-time at the minimum wage and one earner working half-time will not escape poverty. The declining real minimum wage is a particular problem for women, who comprise over 60% of minimum wage earners. . . .

The recent changes in the tax code will help to alleviate the burden on the working poor, and are probably the best one could hope for from this administration and Congress. Nevertheless, the tax reforms merely restore working poor households to their pre-Reagan tax burdens and do not address the fundamental problems: the growth of low-wage jobs, continued occupational segregation, inadequate health insurance, and declining unionization.

VIEWPOINT

"There has been an identifiable black underclass for all of this century."

A Culture of Poverty Created the Black Underclass

Nicholas Lemann

Nicholas Lemann is a national correspondent for *The Atlantic*. He has written several articles on urban poverty. In the following viewpoint, he maintains that during the 1960s many blacks were able to escape from the ghettos to integrated middle-class neighborhoods. Those blacks left behind were the chronically unemployed; they became an isolated culture of poverty. Lemann concludes that efforts to help the underclass must take this culture into account.

As you read, consider the following questions:

1. According to the author, how have the ghettos changed in the past thirty years?
2. Why, according to the author, was the underclass a sensitive subject among blacks? Why is it still sensitive today?
3. What implications does the "culture of poverty" have for solving the problem of poverty, according to Lemann?

Nicholas Lemann, "Ghettos: What Has To Be Done," *The Washington Post*, September 8, 1986. © The Washington Post. Reprinted with permission.

There is an air almost of self-congratulation now about discussions of the underclass: see, we're finally talking about it! Crime is a problem in the ghettos. Out-of-wedlock childbearing has gotten out of control. The days of politely avoiding these uncomfortable subjects are over.

Usually this kind of honesty about a problem leads to change for the better. In the case of the underclass it hasn't so far. The reason is that as perceptions of what's going on in the ghettos now have changed, ideas about how things got so bad and what we might do now have stayed the same. The next step is to make breakthroughs in explanation and prescription of the magnitude of the breakthrough in honesty that has just taken place.

The ghettos weren't always as bad as they are now. In the '20s, '30s, '40s and '50s, places like Harlem, Roxbury and the South Side of Chicago were described as being amazingly lively despite the burdens of racism and poverty. They had churches, clubs, restaurants, families. Obviously only a catastrophe could have made them the empty, hopeless places they are today. But what was it?

Two Economic Theories

There are two standard answers, opposite ideologically but both rooted in economics. The conservative one, which prevails today, is that government programs, especially welfare and the War on Poverty, created "reverse incentives," which encouraged poor blacks to stay poor and to have children out of wedlock. The liberal answer is that the decline of the ghettos parallels a catastrophic rise in unemployment, not in the country as a whole but in the unskilled, inner-city, blue-collar jobs in which urban blacks have traditionally worked.

Both of these theories are partly true, and they're comfortable in the sense that they permit what's mainly a black problem to be discussed without reference to race. But that's also their flaw: Why haven't the reverse incentives built into government programs worked their evils across the whole spectrum of society? Why have millions of people of all races (mostly blacks, but also Koreans, Vietnamese and Palestinians) found enough economic opportunity to permit an escape from the same inner cities where millions of others seem trapped forever? It would seem that something more than pure economic rationality has been shaping the ghettos.

Two Mass Migrations

What created the ghettos in the first place was a mass migration of blacks from the rural South to the urban North—one of the great grass-roots dramas of American history. From World War I until the mid-1960s, about 6.5 million blacks left the South, moving up along the highways and rail lines to get manual-labor jobs that paid double and triple the southern scale.

For most of this time, nearly all blacks had to live in the traditional ghettos, because of the strict residential segregation that prevailed nearly everywhere in the urban North. This meant that the black middle and working classes controlled the ghettos and set the tone there. But in the late '60s, when opportunities of all kinds suddenly opened up for blacks, the ministers and postal workers and schoolteachers began leaving the ghettos and moving to formerly white working-class neighborhoods.

What followed was a second, and less well known, black migration: out of the ghettos. One reason old ghettos look bombed-out and empty is that they've been depopulated since the mid-'60s, often by more than half. The large, new black middle class does not live in the ghettos.

Beginnings of the Underclass

If the underclass is defined as a group prone to out-of-wedlock childbirth, crime and low educational achievement, there has been an identifiable black underclass for all of this century. It existed to some extent in the northern cities—W.E.B. DuBois' "The Philadelphia Negro" describes the poorest black class in terms that could be used today—but its other home was in the sharecropper cabins of the rural South.

The Enemy Within

For the first time in our history, the bottom segment of our society has become immobile. In our city centers, millions of people, mostly black, are trapped in a tragic cycle of deprivation, disorder and dependency. They are headed toward permanent status as wards of the state, without jobs or hope or any meaningful sense of membership in American society. . . .

While racial discrimination has by no means vanished from our society, it's time to shift the primary focus from racism—the traditional enemy without—to self-defeating patterns of behavior—the new enemy within.

Charles S. Robb, *New Perspectives Quarterly*, Winter 1987.

There, until just 20 years ago, a system not so very far removed from slavery prevailed. Education was forbidden and then severely truncated by whites; large out-of-wedlock families were common; and an ethic of dependency on "The Man" was intentionally fostered. There were no doubt many products of the system who were like the wonderful family "Sounder," but the unpleasant truth is that there were also many people debilitated by it (see, for a vivid description of one, Richard Wright's portrait of his father in "Black Boy").

The rest of black society knew perfectly well about the existence of the underclass, especially as its members drifted off the land and into the cities. It was a sensitive subject for middle-class blacks, who knew that the immense social problems of the black lower class would be held up by whites as the justification for keeping all blacks down. The way it was handled, in the days when almost all blacks had to live in ghettos, was by the middle class's using the church, social-improvement organizations and general physical proximity to preach to the underclass an ethic of acculturation. As a result the underclass stayed noticeable but small; for example, until the '60s the black out-of-wedlock birth rate was five to 10 times the white rate, but it was still low compared with today, between 10 percent and 20 percent.

Deserting the Ghettos

In the late '60s, when, the statistics show, the underclass quickly became a major problem, there was more than just the War on Poverty and the loss of many unskilled city jobs going on. Also, the leadership, the institutional structure and indeed most of the working and married population were leaving the underclass alone in the ghettos.

The mass construction of highways and housing projects during this time helped to complete the physical isolation of the underclass. At the same time, a kind of moral isolation was going on too, because the rest of society became empathetic to the underclass's problems to the point of explaining them away. The kind of preaching to the underclass that had gone on before was now dismissed as an example of "blaming the victim."

It was then that the out-of-wedlock birthrate, and the crime rate and the dropout rate, really soared; what sociologists call "social disorganization" had set in. Today, though certainly the people in ghettos are victims in every way imaginable, what distorts their lives most obviously isn't society as a whole, but the particular culture in the ghettos, whose rules often dictate such life-dooming activities as out-of-wedlock pregnancy for girls and petty crime for boys.

A Culture of Poverty

Here, though, the disagreements over what to do about the ghettos begin. In the rarefied circles in which policy is debated, the word "culture" is still regarded as deeply offensive—a code way of saying that poor blacks occupy an inferior position in society because they are innately, even racially, inferior. William Julius Wilson of the University of Chicago, who has done courageous and pioneering work on the split in black America and the irrelevance of civil rights legislation to the underclass, flatly told The Post's Dorothy Gilliam that there is no such thing as a poverty culture.

At the other end of the ideological spectrum, Charles Murray's "Losing Ground," which is really a book about the underclass, doesn't discuss culture either.

There are three leading sets of solutions to the problem of the underclass floating around right now. First is the venerable liberal cause of full employment, with perhaps targeted help given to industries in the northern cities. Second is cutting welfare, probably in the guise of creating a social services block grant to be controlled by the state governments. Third is "community development" programs that would, through a kind of mass self-help effort, make the ghettos bloom again.

Behaviors that Must Be Changed

There is, to put matters directly, an identifiable culture of poverty shaping the attitudes, values, aspirations and violent behaviors of the population trapped in long-term poverty.

What is clear from recent journalistic accounts, as well as from more scholarly, epigraphic and sociological literature, is that the behaviors and values of people living in these communities constitute an important cause of their long-term dependency. I'm referring to lack of parenting, participation in criminal activities, the use of prime drugs and detachment from the labor force. Ending that dependency, therefore, requires that there be some change in underlying behavior.

Glenn C. Loury, *New Perspectives Quarterly,* Winter 1987.

If culture is a significant part of the problem, none of these will completely solve it; if that seems like a big chance to take, then maybe we should consider culture in discussing what to do next.

A Cultural Solution

Discussing culture need not be an opening for racists. Certainly evil has been done in its name, but on the whole the sense that there is a national culture that is defined not by race but by an idealistic set of principles is something for the country to be proud of. The urge to bring people into the mainsteam is, again, a mostly noble one—it was the rhetorical underpinning of the civil rights movement.

A solution to the problem of the underclass that took culture into account would have to use work as its primary tool, but it wouldn't be limited to lowering the unemployment rate. The process of ending the underclass's segregation from the rest of the country would begin with Head Start-like education projects in earliest childhood and proceed through government-supplied jobs outside the ghettos that would be a transitional step into the real job market, whose health the government would have to safeguard too, of course.

You may think that all of this has been tried before, that government programs don't work, that the problems are too deeply ingrained to be solved. But it hasn't been tried as a major national effort with the clear-eyed goal of acculturation; and there was a time when major efforts to use the government to solve national problems did work; and many other groups in the past have been considered unassimilable, always wrongly. On race of all issues, where we have seen so much change for the better in a single generation and where there is still a healthy charge of moral righteousness left in us, it would be sad if we stopped now.

"Black Americans are still victims of a caste system and a class system."

Racism Created the Black Underclass

Jesse Jackson

Jesse Jackson is well known as a civil rights activist. He was an assistant to Martin Luther King Jr. in the 1960s and a Democratic presidential candidate in 1984 and 1988. The following viewpoint is taken from an interview in *New Perspectives Quarterly*. Jackson states that racism was and still is an important cause of the black underclass. Values and behavior are important, according to Jackson, but the primary obstacle for blacks in poverty is persisting social inequality and discrimination.

As you read, consider the following questions:

1. What are Jackson's views on the civil rights movement and the War on Poverty?
2. Why does Jackson believe blacks still exist in a caste system?
3. What solutions does Jackson propose? How do they differ from the opposing viewpoint?

Jesse Jackson, "Breaking the Cycle," *New Perspectives Quarterly*, Winter 1987. Reprinted with permission.

NPQ: As liberals contemplate the next social agenda, a consensus about new conditions is emerging. That consensus says the efforts of integration, the Great Society and affirmative action were successful to the extent of removing the barriers of racism, thus liberating a substantial black middle-class. But they were a failure to the extent of creating a dependent urban underclass.

What do you think?

Jackson: The Civil Rights movement, the 1954 Supreme Court decision on school segregation and the Great Society changes effectively struck down the *legal* caste system. Until 1964, blacks lived under apartheid. We could not use hotels, motels, public parks or libraries. In many southern states blacks, by law, could not earn as much teaching school as whites. In most places, blacks could not be policemen, firemen or bus drivers and couldn't go to schools of engineering, medicine and law.

Although the proportions may have been reversed, even then we had a middle-class and the very poor. We had teachers, doctors, lawyers, ministers and athletes who lived in single-family homes that they owned. There were the business people who owned barber shops, beauty shops, funeral parlors and small construction firms. . . .

But our people really began rising when the caste laws came down with school desegregation and the right to vote. When we could go to schools of the South *en masse*, there was more upward mobility because the greater the number who went to school, the greater their demands for full membership in society.

The Great Society

What the Great Society did was to begin to employ Title VI of the Civil Rights Act and enforce affirmative action. That opened some doors which had previously been closed, and was responsible for creating a whole new middle-class in the public sector. Blacks rushed into the post offices and the state and local government positions, in part because we were still locked out of the private sector. Also, the budgetary commitments of the Great Society to Head Start, Model Cities or various senior citizen programs created a generation of black administrators in this public sector middle-class.

In civil service jobs, we've done much better because the rules are clear and it is possible to define how to win and how to grow. Whenever rules are established, and blacks know what the rules are, we tend to do well. If we pass an exam to get a GS9 or 10 or 11 level, stick through a certain amount of time and get a promotion, we tend to advance. In the private sector where there are no defined rules and where everything is subjective, even though we may have greater skills, we don't do as well.

Brian Duffy. Copyright 1986, The Des Moines Register. Reprinted with permission.

So, the Great Society did not create a black middle-class by dispensing a lot of free money. It pulled down barriers and allowed us to go in doors we'd been knocking on all the while. The new ability to get an education gave us a new opportunity to compete. That's what created the black middle-class. . . .

NPQ: Busting the legal caste system and the Great Society fostered the growth of an upwardly mobile, at least public-sector, black middle-class. Both the lost War on Poverty and the outward bound middle-class have left the poor in the ghettos intact.

Isn't this split in the black community exactly what Stokely Carmichael warned of in the black power days? He opposed integration on the grounds that those who made it would leave the others behind, taking leadership and know-how out of the ghetto.

Other militants argued it would destroy the black community's "cultural integrity."

Jackson: First of all, this split is fragile. The college degrees that the middle-class got in the 1960s resulted in public-sector jobs, for the most part. With that, and with both husband and wife working, they were able to get credit and own nonbusiness items—a house on a thirty-year mortgage, a car, clothes. They could even go into debt for their children's college tuition. By and large, the black middle-class is not a property-owning or entrepreneurial class. They are only a payday away from poverty.

In the end, there is not a radical gap between that class and the very poor.

Secondly, because of the caste system, the black middle-class ain't going nowhere except to another black neighborhood. Sometimes the same neighborhood. Black doctors still basically have black patients. Black lawyers have black clients. Black ministers, black parishioners. Black politicians have black districts. . . .

Blacks Still Are Victims

NPQ: Do you agree with former Virginia Governor Chuck Robb, speaking for the Democratic Leadership Council (DLC), when he says that the barriers blocking black Americans from entering the mainstream have largely been removed. Now it is time for the social agenda to shift the primary focus from racism to the self-defeating patterns of behavior of a mostly black urban underclass?

Jackson: Black Americans are still victims of a caste system and a class system. As we've discussed, there has been some class mobility. But nothing has altered the caste system because we're designated and slotted by race.

Let's look at some facts that illustrate more than stasis, even regression in some cases. In 1976 the University of Michigan had a student body that was 7.7% black. In 1986, it has fallen to 5%. They had 2200 faculty members, but only 63 blacks. The University of Chicago has 1300 faculty members and 11 blacks. Harvard had 97 black freshmen last September, down 30% from 1976. Princeton had 645 faculty members, only 7 of whom were black. It had 1600 graduate students, 22 of them black.

Why have all these figures gone down? Because of Bakke. Because allies who were with us in the freedom movement have been against us in the justice movement and the equality movement. And the government has withdrawn the troops for civil rights enforcement. So, there is a cutback in recruitment, hiring and promotion of blacks.

A Culture of Poverty?

NPQ: . . . and about the self-defeating enemy within the black community?

Jackson: When people's backs are against the wall, some choose to fight back. Some have the dogged determination to fight for more education. Some tend to fight back by making the most of their meager income. Some tend to withdraw in despair and

89

cynicism, believing that nothing will work. They turn to liquor, drugs and the pursuit of pleasure to escape the pain.

Others find their basic fulfillment and gratification in sex without love, discipline or education. Or they make unwanted and unhealthy babies. Some turn to violence, turning *on* each other instead of *to* each other.

But there is nothing congenital about this kind of behavior. And since it is not natural, but social or environmental, there are ways of stemming it. But, when you cut back on college opportunities, cut back on job training, preschool education and Head Start, cut back on public sector employment and union apprenticeship programs and then shift $32 billion from the poor to the upper class through tax policy, the result is self-evident.

If you withdraw the water from the pool, the fish will die. They engage in all kinds of frantic behavior because they are living in an unnatural environment. Some fish cannot bounce back and will drown even with the resources.

NPQ: No one respectable is saying behavior is congenital. Are you saying that there is not a self-perpetuating dynamic to it?

Jackson: It's a pattern of behavior because of a pattern of circumstances.

The Solution Is Jobs

If there were more jobs for black men, there would be fewer black women having babies out of wedlock, welfare rolls would shrink, drug use and crime would decline, optimism and cheer would spread.

The idea is ancient: Put a man to work and you keep him out of trouble. But for most Americans it doesn't seem to be much of a priority. A new Gallup poll shows that blacks think unemployment is the nation's number one problem, but whites see other concerns as more important.

Instead, we are hearing a lot about what is wrong with welfare, about young, unmarried black women having babies, about what President Reagan referred to recently as "horrible crimes." But a solution to the crisis in the black community lies in putting black men to work, preferably in full-time, regular employment.

Barry Sussman, *The Washington Post National Weekly Edition,* March 3, 1986.

But let's just look at the realities first. Most poor people are not black or brown. By 4 to 1, they are white. They are also young and female. And who talks about their behavior? They are the ones who dominate the welfare rolls.

This is significant because as long as poverty has a black face, profound questions about the class nature of this country aren't raised. It reminds me of the Al Jolson act I would see growing up in the South. Put a black face on a white situation and you can laugh at it, you can throw balls at it and hope it falls over in the water when you hit it in the face. When Al Jolson takes the black off his face, it ain't so funny. When John Kennedy held a black baby in his arms in Harlem in 1960, he was a nice guy. Catholic. Do-gooder. When he held up a white baby in West Virginia, exposing the ribs, it started the War on Poverty.

Most poor people, with all the talk about dependence and pathology, are not on welfare. They work every day. They drive cabs and clean garbage cans. They clean other people's bathrooms. They change beds in hotels. They change the clothes of the feverish and empty bedpans in the hospitals. And when they get sick, they can't afford to lie in those beds! They die in emergency rooms because they don't have a green or yellow card to go upstairs where empty wings are waiting for the rich to get sick. The poor raise other people's kids, but can't raise their own.

Pathological? They catch the early bus in the morning. They can't be choosy about where they work, and when they get work, they're still below the poverty line. Pathological? Somehow, we do not illuminate their faces. We don't give them credit for being the hardest workers on the nastiest jobs, in the most hazardous conditions for the least amount of money.

That's who the poor really are. . . .

Breaking the Cycle

I was born to a teenaged mother, who was born to a teenaged mother. When I was 13, we moved to a public housing project. It was the first time we had a bathtub in the house. It was the first time we had central heating, a doorbell, an individual mailbox. The step up gave us an incentive.

My daddy had only finished third grade, but he was a veteran. He got ten points on the veteran's exam and got a job at the post office as a custodian. My mother was able to go back to school and become a cosmetologist. Then mamma could do hair cultures. With both of them working, we had a comfortable home in the projects. It helped stabilize the family. I was able to graduate from high school and go to college with a football scholarship.

With help, we were able to break out. There was nothing pathological about us. Cold air was coming through the walls and up out of the floor of our house. But there was nothing wrong with us. There was something wrong with the house.

NPQ: The fact that your family held together was undoubtedly an important factor in breaking out. Isn't family breakdown one of the problems of poor urban blacks today?

Jackson: Families are under real pressure. When men can't get jobs or an education, it severely impacts their ability to sustain mature relationships. When young men and young women have extreme sex stimulus without sex education and sex discipline, babies are irresponsibly made. When the mass media titillates our nerves and keeps us sexually stimulated from the age of five or six on, that is a factor.

No Culture of Poverty

Cultural values do not ultimately determine behavior or success. Rather, cultural values emerge from specific circumstances and life chances and reflect one's position in the racial-class structure. Thus, if underclass blacks have low aspirations or do not plan for the future, it is not ultimately the result of different cultural norms, but the product of restricted opportunities, a bleak future, and feelings of resignation originating from unpleasant personal experiences. Despite the claims of journalists about the ascendancy of an autonomous "culture of poverty," this fundamental principle has yet to be challenged seriously by systematic academic research.

William Julius Wilson, *The New Republic,* October 6, 1986.

NPQ: Your summary response to liberals thinking about a new social agenda?

Jackson: The black underclass need not be looked upon as an enigma wrapped in a mystery. Face it. We know how to stimulate people, open up doors. Moral leadership, mass education, balanced nutrition. We understand that.

As the trillion dollar deficit looms over any commitment to this effort, something else must be understood. The immorality of letting people languish in poverty is not cost-efficient. Jails cost more than schools. Ignorance costs more than intelligence. Dropouts cost more than graduates. A diseased body costs more than a healthy body. . . .

NPQ: The black agenda?

Jackson: The black agenda is equity and parity. If freedom was a horizontal movement from outside in, justice and equality is a vertical movement from bottom to top.

We've run into tremendous resistance seeking equity. Many who supported freedom do not support equality. They would agree to "Free Mandela" but not "Elect Mandela."

Distinguishing Between Fact and Opinion

This activity is designed to help develop the basic critical thinking skill of distinguishing between fact and opinion. Consider the following statement: "Twenty years after President Johnson declared a 'war on poverty,' poverty still exists in America." This is a fact with which few people would disagree. But consider another statement about poverty: "Poverty is an inevitable result of America's capitalist system." This statement expresses an opinion on what causes poverty, an opinion many people disagree with.

When investigating controversial issues it is important that one be able to distinguish between statements of fact and statements of opinion. It is also important to recognize that not all statements of fact are true. They may appear to be true, but some are based on inaccurate or false information. For this activity, however, we are concerned with understanding the difference between those statements which appear to be factual and those which appear to be based primarily on opinion.

Most of the following statements are taken from the viewpoints in this chapter. Consider each statement carefully. *Mark O for any statement you believe is an opinion or interpretation of facts. Mark F for any statement you believe is a fact. Mark I for any statement you believe is impossible to judge.*

If you are doing this activity as a member of a class or group, compare your answers with those of other class or group members. Be able to defend your answers. You may discover that others will come to different conclusions than you. Listening to the reasons others present for their answers may give you valuable insights in distinguishing between fact and opinion.

O = opinion
F = fact
I = impossible to judge

1. Over the last century, poverty has persisted in boom times as well as bust.

2. The only way poverty can be ended is by ending the social and economic inequality that produces it.

3. Work is unquestionably one of the keys to overcoming poverty and dependency.

4. Aside from low wages, lack of health insurance comprises a serious problem for the working poor.

5. Ten major famines in India between 1860 and 1900 caused the deaths of close to 15 million people.

6. The poor raise other people's kids, but can't raise their own.

7. Only a prosperous nation like our own could contemplate a "war on poverty."

8. The War on Poverty lasted only three to five years.

9. When the stock market goes down, you don't see Rockefellers, Mellons and DuPonts lining up at the food-stamp office.

10. Discussing culture need not be an opening for racists.

11. In 1980, 43 percent of the unemployed were out of work four weeks or less.

12. A worker without a job has nothing.

13. The ghettos weren't always as bad as they are now.

14. In the late 1960s many blacks moved from the ghettos to formerly white working-class neighborhoods.

15. Since 1978 the number of persons who work full-time, year-round and are still poor has grown by two-thirds.

16. As long as poverty has a black face, profound questions about the class nature of this country aren't raised.

17. Poverty is the natural state of mankind.

18. The immorality of letting people languish in poverty is not cost-efficient. Dropouts cost more than graduates. Jails cost more than schools.

Periodical Bibliography

The following articles have been selected to supplement the diverse views presented in this chapter.

Barry Bearak — "Poor Share Work Ethic, US Dream," *Los Angeles Times*, July 29, 1985.

Warren T. Brookes — "Dispelling the Big Lie of Low-Pay Jobs," *Conservative Chronicle*, February 18, 1987. Available from 9 2nd Street NW, Hampton, IA 50441.

Sheldon Danziger and Peter Gottschalk — "Work, Poverty, and the Working Poor: A Multifaceted Problem," *Monthly Labor Review*, September 1986.

James J. Drummey — "The Poor Always with Us," *The New American*, February 24, 1986.

John Kenneth Galbraith — "How To Get the Poor Off Our Conscience," *The Humanist*, September/October 1985.

Leonard M. Greene — "Progress: US Style," *USA Today*, May 1986.

John L. Hess — "Malthus: Then and Now," *The Nation*, April 18, 1987.

Irving E. Howard — "Poverty: Material and Spiritual," *The Freeman*, August 1987. Available from The Foundation for Economic Education, Inc. 30 S. Broadway, Irvington-on-Hudson, NY 10533.

Richard I. Kirkland Jr. — "Are Service Jobs Good Jobs?" *Fortune*, June 10, 1985.

Jerry Kloby — "The Growing Divide: Class Polarization in the 1980s," *Monthly Review*, September 1987.

Nicholas Lemann — "The Origins of the Underclass," *The Atlantic Monthly*, June, July 1986.

Charles Murray — "White Welfare, White Families, 'White Trash,'" *National Review*, March 26, 1986.

New Perspectives Quarterly — "A Tale of Dual Cities," Winter 1987.

Karl Zinsmeister — "Illegitimacy in Black and White," *The Wall Street Journal*, November 16, 1987.

How Should Society Deal with the Homeless?

Chapter Preface

The homeless have received much attention in recent years. They have been featured in newspaper articles, books, and movies. Telethons and other charitable events have been held on their behalf. For many people poverty ceases to become an abstract issue when they are confronted with pictures of men sleeping on heating grates or women living with their children on park benches.

Yet the increased attention has failed to create a national consensus on how to deal with this problem. Some people call for massive public and private aid to build shelters and low-cost housing and to provide jobs. Others say that many homeless people are mentally ill, and the answer is to place them in institutions rather than leave them on the streets. Still others say that attempts to help the homeless serve only middle-class sensibilities: Those who want to be homeless should be left alone.

The viewpoints in the following chapter explore some of the responses people have made to the question of homelessness.

"Up to 3 million people now live without a home in the United States."

The Problem of Homelessness Is Serious

Michael Fabricant and Michael Kelly

Michael Fabricant is an associate professor at Hunter College in New York. He has written on homelessness, and is on the board of the National Coalition for the Homeless. Michael Kelly is a social worker in New York. In the following viewpoint, they state that homelessness is a serious and growing problem in the United States. The authors point to several causes including unemployment, lower wages, and government cutbacks in welfare and public housing, and write that the principle of a right to shelter and an adequate living standard is under attack. They call for fundamental changes in the American economy and society.

As you read, consider the following questions:

1. How has the homeless population changed in recent years, according to the authors?
2. What criticisms do the authors have of shelters?
3. What do Fabricant and Kelly mean by "social wage"? What significance do they attach to it?

Michael Fabricant and Michael Kelly, "No Haven for Homeless in a Heartless Economy," *Radical America*, Vol. 20, #2&3 1986. Reprinted by permission.

Mitch Snyder, activist for the homeless and member of the Community for Creative Non-Violence in Washington, D.C., once spent the winter months living on the street. During the nights he slept on a heat grating. From this vantage point he observed:

the streets became the province of the vast army of the homeless. Scores of street dwellers would file past our corner every night . . . we could watch the bent and the broken—mostly elderly—people wandering, marching to and from nowhere. They trembled in the cold, surrounded by heated, lighted, guarded and empty government buildings.

Snyder's observations reflect a growing national recognition of the homelessness problem, which now affects an expanding number of citizens. . . .

The Problem of Homelessness

Up to 3 million people now live without a home in the United States, mostly in our cities. In cities like New York, it is difficult to comprehend the scope of the homeless problem, with its more than 60,000 homeless riding the subways or seeking refuge in the train and bus stations at night. The cold restroom floor in Penn Station becomes a bed for some 50 women. Others stay in phone booths or blend into the dark recesses of the stations. Many catch a few hours of sleep in the waiting room until rousted by the rap of a policeman's nightstick against their chair. Some of the more ingenious homeless New Yorkers get needed rest and pass the night safely by camouflaging themselves on city streets where large amounts of garbage have been placed for disposal: they crawl into cardboard boxes or cover themselves with plastic trashcan liners.

In 1981, a Chicago newspaper reported that 50 homeless people had been buried in the city's Potter's Field in January, after silently freezing to death. A year later, the Chicago Coalition for the Homeless estimated 25,000 homeless wandered the city. Charles Ford, the Director of Emergency Services said: "We have the feeling that the numbers are increasing. . . . We are finding more and more people who live on the street involuntarily—young people, who in ordinary times would be able to find jobs, and more women and children." By December 1982 every shelter in Chicago was filled to capacity and turning away 30-50 people per night.

Other cities of America's "heartland" have shared this experience. Detroit, with its massive unemployment, had over 27,000 homeless people in November 1984—a 300 percent increase from 1982. The U.S. Conference of Mayors reported that up to 1,000 people were living in cars, trailers, tents, or campgrounds in Tulsa while another 200-300 people lived under city bridges. In 1981-1982, 1,000 people in Milwaukee lost their homes.

In recent years, the prospering and temperate "Sunbelt" cities have been inundated with unemployed workers from the North-east. Yet in Dallas, Phoenix and Los Angeles, for example, they have found an extremely tight job market, high rents and a much lower level of entitlement than in their old homes.

The Union Rescue Mission of Los Angeles, the world's largest private mission, recently (for the first time in over 90 years) turned people away because all the 350 beds and 350 chairs were filled. Elsewhere, during the winter of 1983, Seattle turned away 4,000 families (roughly 16,000 people) who applied for shelter. And in Flagstaff, Arizona, many homeless families have been camping out in the National Forest which borders the city.

Jim Morin. Copyright © 1986 *The Miami Herald*. Reprinted with permission.

The homeless population has changed dramatically in appearance as well as quantity. Between 1945 and 1970 urban hobos, mostly older, alcoholic men, were the major skid row inhabitants. Since then, small but growing numbers of women have appeared. By the mid-1970's many younger black and Hispanic men, unemployed and lacking job skills, began using urban shelters and flophouses. Many had drug or alcohol problems. In New York City up to one third of them were veterans, mostly of the Vietnam War.

At the same time, discharged mental patients became more prominent on the streets following deinstitutionalization. Those supporting this policy claimed that recent advances in psychopharmacology and treatment had now made community living feasible for institutionalized mental patients. New "wonder drugs," especially phenothiazines, were to supplant incarceration. Community-based treatment models became the new road towards "recovery" and social reintegration. . . .

The price paid in human misery has been monumental. Vital services, community supports and follow-up treatments were not adequately developed. Many of the 400,000 people discharged from mental hospitals between 1950 and 1980 were forced to fend for themselves. Temporarily, some maintained a marginal existence in low-income housing, but by the mid-1970's this too disappeared. Other than the street, the only alternatives left were adult homes or shelters. In these newly emerging "deviant ghettos," one is likely to find neither compassion nor therapeutic treatments, but usually at best, some form of repressive tolerance on the outer fringes of society. . . .

Economic Victims

The high rates of inflation and unemployment during the recession of 1980-1982 produced yet another wave of homeless people. Massive layoffs and plant closings in 1983 produced situations in cities like Detroit, where in 1982 close to 20,000 workers per month lost their unemployment benefits. In 1983 Illinois had a 13.9 percent unemployment rate or 759,000 unemployed citizens, and also had the nation's highest rate of home foreclosures (1.6 percent). Shelters in Chicago, Detroit and elsewhere cited "the loss of a job" as a primary reason for homelessness.

The inability of younger blacks or Hispanics to enter the labor market has also contributed to the homelessness explosion. Their unemployment rate (over 50 percent) is the highest in the nation. Unable to find jobs or affordable housing, many young black and Hispanic men are crowded out of their family's apartment. In 1980, virtually no people under the age of twenty-one stayed in New York City municipal shelters. By 1985, they comprised 7 percent of the total shelter population. Recent estimates showed approximately 22,000 homeless youth in New York City, the single largest subgroup of homeless.

Finally, homeless families are the newest and, perhaps, most frightening wave of homelessness. Headed mostly by women, living on AFDC, they represent the fastest growing group of homeless.

Government Responses

To this grievous problem, the government response has sometimes been nightmarish. In Fort Lauderdale, a city councilman urged the spraying of trash with poison to cut off the "vermin's" food supply. In Phoenix, and President Reagan's home city of Santa Barbara anti-homeless ordinances prohibit sitting, sleeping, or lying down in public areas such as parks, and consider trash-bin refuse as public property. Hence, foraging for food is a criminal act. At the Federal level, a Department of Housing and Urban Development Survey concluded that there were but 200,000-300,000 homeless nationwide. Despite its numerous methodological flaws which considerably underestimate the problem, this survey has nonetheless been used to minimize government action. For example, HUD's recommendation against new, temporary shelters has seriously inhibited efforts for more significant change.

Not Just in Shelters

Homelessness in Chicago is a serious and worsening problem, though its scope and magnitude are poorly understood. . . . Only one scientific study has been made, and this produced a low estimate: 4,000 to 6,000 homeless over the course of a year; 1,600 to 3,100 on any one night. This study, however, employed an excessively restrictive definition of homelessness and a correspondingly narrow sampling methodology so that it measured only the number of people who spend the night either in shelters or in public places.

In truth, homeless people spend their nights in many other places. They spend them primarily in the homes of friends, relatives and acquaintances; in motels and flophouses; in church basements and spare rectory bedrooms; and in their cars. They also spend them hidden in culverts and under viaducts, in dangerous abandoned buildings and on rooftops; in railroad cars and truck trailers; and in a thousand other places where social scientists would not dare to visit but where homeless folk are desperate and ingenious enough to take refuge.

Edwin M. Conway, *Origins*, February 26, 1987.

Obviously, the need for safe, decent shelter greatly outstrips the number of slots available. Recent estimates show only 330 shelter beds in Detroit, for a homeless population of 27,000. Chicago has approximately 1,000 beds for 20,000-25,000. In Connecticut, the second richest state, the less than 950 shelter beds far underserve its 10,000 homeless men, women and children. One shelter in Hartford turned away more than 3,500 applicants in a recent 12-month period.

Shelters also fail to meet the differing needs of homeless people. Alcoholics, the unemployed, the elderly and former mental patients are all lumped into one space. Sanitary conditions are often poor. Bathroom and shower facilities are woefully inadequate given the crowded conditions. Some municipal shelters like the one in Washington, D.C. feature myriad abuses, including random beatings of homeless people by vicious security guards. Given these conditions, many homeless people have apparently "preferred the rats and the cold to contending with the degradation of the public shelters." . . .

Welfare and Housing Cuts

Recent reports by journalists, academics, advocates and the government underscore the dramatic reduction of entitlement benefits and services. Between 1980 and 1981 an intense drive emerged to make across-the-board cuts in all social welfare programs. Overall, cash welfare benefits declined by 17 percent. One million people were eliminated from Food Stamp coverage. Ninety percent of the working, AFDC families had their benefits reduced or eliminated. Finally, the value of general assistance payments has declined substantially. While these trends did not begin during Reagan's presidency, they have been dramatically intensified by this administration.

As cash benefits have eroded, both private and public sector housing investment decisions have also changed. The Federal government effectively withdrew from the public housing market. In 1979 over 40,000 units of conventional public housing were completed; by 1982 the number had dropped to 25,000 units. In 1979 there were 23,860 new starts for the elderly and handicapped; in 1983 only 14,112 units were funded. During fiscal year 1985 the Reagan administration arranged to fund only 12,500 new units of subsidized housing, 10,000 for the elderly and handicapped, 2,500 for Native Americans.

The central city renovations characterizing many U.S. cities have made matters worse. In New York, tax abatements gave incentives to convert low income housing to luxury apartment buildings. Between 1975 and 1981 approximately 35,000 units of low income housing were lost. New York City offers the most dramatic example of these market forces. Cities such as Cleveland, Phoenix, Newark, San Francisco, Denver and Chicago also report substantial losses in their low-income housing stock to downtown renovation or luxury housing development. These trends partly respond to the changing economic structure which has allowed some elite professionals and entrepreneurs to benefit from a polarized job market which has hurt most workers. The increased demand for urban housing from relatively affluent people has pushed many low-income individuals and families out of the formal housing market.

Consequences

The consequent increase in urban rents leaves poor people particularly vulnerable. Increasingly, general assistance and AFDC payments are simply insufficient to meet the new urban rent levels throughout the country. As has been noted: ". . . the amount of public assistance a recipient was allotted for rent—whether as a separate shelter allowance or as part of a flat grant, ranged from 20 percent to 60 percent of local fair market rent."

When basic rent allowances are insufficient to meet prevailing rents, then grants have more symbolic than real value. Entitlements that increasingly fail to meet basic survival needs (such as permanent housing) most dramatically indicate the growing inadequacy of today's "social wage.". . .

The homeless crisis reflects the unravelling of many of the advances of the last fifty years. Shelters and soup lines do not offer those presently homeless, or those who risk falling through the "safety net" to the streets, a basis for recreating their lives. At best, these services only temporarily halt the physical, emotional and intellectual deterioration of the homeless person. If the needs of the homeless, chronically unemployed or temporarily unemployed are to be met, then economic entitlement must be expanded or advanced, not diminished. This expansion or redefinition must begin with the economic right of citizens to housing and a job at a livable wage.

"A close look at what statistics there are reveals that nobody really knows how much— or even whether—the number of homeless is increasing."

The Problem of Homelessness Is Exaggerated

Martin Morse Wooster

Martin Morse Wooster is an associate editor with *The Wilson Quarterly* and former Washington editor of *Harper's*. In the following viewpoint, he argues that the widely circulated estimate of three million homeless is not based on fact, and that there are already many government programs set up to aid the homeless. Wooster further argues that government solutions of free housing will never solve the homelessness problem.

As you read, consider the following questions:

1. According to the author, why has homelessness been a major issue during the past few years?
2. What does the author think about the 1984 Housing and Urban Development (HUD) study that estimated the number of homeless?
3. Why does Wooster doubt the efficacy of government "solutions" to homelessness?

Homelessness is the issue by which the champions of the welfare state hope to regain lost ground. Bills pending in Congress will, if passed, use the homeless issue to increase federal welfare spending by up to $4 billion—the largest one-year increase since the Carter administration.

Yet advocates of massive federal spending for the homeless have failed to show the need for increases. Nor have they demonstrated whether spending more tax dollars on public housing—a favorite plea—will reduce the homeless population. If the Reagan administration had not tried to counter the sloppy estimates of the homeless lobby with equally bad estimates of its own, one wonders whether the question of homelessness would have ever become a "crisis" to be solved by bloating the welfare state.

A Tale of Two Lobbyists

Ten years ago there were homeless in America. Twenty years ago there were homeless. How is it that in the 1980s there is a *homeless crisis?* A close look at what statistics there are reveals that nobody really knows how much—or even whether—the number of homeless is increasing (more on this later). A little more looking, and it becomes clear that homelessness has become an issue in American life largely because of the efforts of two charismatic lobbyists—a Washington adman and a New York City lawyer.

In late 1978, Robert Hayes, an associate at the Wall Street firm of Sullivan and Cromwell, was walking to the subway when he noticed "bums . . . begging for handouts." He began to talk to the homeless and visit shelters. Appalled by what he found, he resolved to do something. Being a lawyer, he resolved to file a class-action lawsuit. He got Robert Callahan, a former short-order cook he'd met in the Bowery, to agree to be the plaintiff. In October 1979, Hayes sued New York Mayor Edward Koch and New York Governor Hugh Carey to compel the city and state government to provide shelter for the homeless.

In December 1979, New York's supreme court granted a preliminary injunction in *Callahan* v. *Carey* in favor of Callahan—and Hayes. New York City residents now had a "right to shelter"; the court ordered New York City to provide food, shelter, and showers to any resident. Shelters also had to be large enough so that no homeless person has to be bused from one shelter to another.

Callahan v. *Carey* has been a costly decision for New York City's taxpayers. In 1978, the city budgeted $6.8 million for the homeless; by 1983, the figure had risen to $38 million. (While the numbers of people using the shelters rose from about 600 in 1978 to 4,235 in 1983, whether the rise was due to an increase in homelessness or whether people left temporary housing for free beds and food is a question intensely debated by sociologists.). . .

While Hayes was fencing with New York City lawyers, Mitch Snyder was beginning to acquire his notoriety. Snyder was an ad-man who, in the early 1970s, founded the Community for Creative Non-Violence (CCNV), a Washington, D.C., commune dedicated to opposing the Vietnam war. Snyder widened his range in the late '70s, engaging in a series of hunger strikes and demonstrations (usually "tent cities") in Lafayette Park, across the street from the White House. While some of these strikes were antiwar, an increasing number were devoted to the homeless.

A Manageable Problem

America's homeless problem is manageable. Recent studies of a number of cities reinforce the 1984 estimate of the U.S. Department of Housing and Urban Development that, on any given night, approximately 300,000 Americans are homeless. Currently there are shelters and emergency beds available to house about half this number. Already, however, private agencies, states, and localities have been providing extra resources at a rapid rate to meet specific, local needs. It is likely that the remaining problem of homelessness can be met with a modest expansion of existing efforts, combined with specialized assistance to the mentally ill, who account for up to half the homeless population.

Kenneth J. Beirne, The Heritage Foundation *Backgrounder*, April 4, 1987.

Snyder began to acquire a local reputation as an expert on homelessness. If he had lived in Los Angeles or Philadelphia, the state legislature would have asked to hear him; but because he lived in Washington, Snyder was asked to testify before the D.C. equivalent of a statehouse—the House District Committee. The congressional committee asked Snyder and his associates at CCNV to compile an estimate of the number of homeless people in the United States.

In December 1980, Snyder delivered his report. There were, he declared, 2.2 million homeless Americans—or one percent of the population. Snyder then attacked the congressmen who asked for the report. "We have tried to satisfy your gnawing curiosity for a number," he said, carping about "Americans with little Western minds that have to quantify everything in sight."

Two years later, with homelessness increasingly in the news, the Community for Creative Non-Violence published *Homelessness in America*, a revised version of Snyder's 1980 testimony. "We have learned nothing that would cause us to lower our original estimate," wrote Snyder and coauthor Mary Ellen Hombs. "In fact, we would increase it, since we are convinced that the number of homeless people in the United States could reach 3 million or more during 1983."

107

These two sentences are the strongest "evidence" ever provided by the Community for Creative Non-Violence on the size of the homeless population. Snyder and Hombs chose to prove their claim, not by providing evidence but by listing dozens of horror stories about individual homeless people. . . .

Newspaper Stories

Most of the major newspapers in America had a story about national homelessness in 1982 or 1983, and most of these stories had one point in common—they all reported Mitch Snyder's estimate of two million homeless (which Robert Hayes also adopted) as a hard fact:

• "1982's Homeless: Americans Adrift in Tents, Autos," *Washington Post*, front page, August 14, 1982: "'From coast to coast, signs of the 1930s reverberate,' says Robert M. Hayes, . . . attorney for the National Coalition for the Homeless, which estimates at least two million people are without shelter in the United States. He notes, 'The soup lines grow. The flophouses fill to overflowing. . . . The newest token of a failed American dream is a cardboard box.'"

• "Millions Hit Bottom in the Streets," *Los Angeles Times*, front page, December 26, 1982: "According to testimony two weeks ago at a congressional subcommittee hearing on the subject, there may be as many as 2.5 million citizens without a place to stay for the holidays." The unnamed provider of testimony was Mitch Snyder. . . .

It was up to *Newsweek* reporter Jonathan Alter to provide the most florid statement of what by now was everywhere dubbed a crisis. "The tattered ranks of America's homeless are swelling," Alter wrote in a January 2, 1984, cover story, "and the economic recovery that made this Christmas merrier than last for most Americans has not brought them even a lump of coal." . . .

The HUD Report

Needless to say, the government was not sitting around letting social activists monopolize the limelight. In 1983, Secretary of Housing and Urban Development Samuel Pierce ordered his Office of Policy Development and Research to produce an estimate of the size and nature of the homeless population. *A Report to the Secretary on the Homeless and Emergency Shelters* was released in May 1984—to howls of outrage from Snyder, Hayes, and the homeless lobby. It was, scoffed Snyder, "a political document."

The HUD report presented four estimates of the homeless population, ranging from 192,000 to 586,000. The authors concluded that "as best as can be determined from all available data, the most reliable range is 250,000 to 350,000 homeless persons. This represents the total number of people, nationally, who were homeless on an average night in December 1983 or January 1984."

It was a meager 10 percent of the 2-3 million figure popularized by Snyder and Hayes.

HUD had tried four ways to come up with some homeless estimates. The highest figure of 586,000 was determined by collecting local newspaper stories, magazine articles, and a few reports by state and local welfare agencies, dividing the total into the population of those areas, and so deriving a national estimate that .25 percent of the population was homeless. HUD's analysts did not question their source material and relied on news reports written as much as two years before the December 1983 "snapshot" date. For example, estimates for Minneapolis and Philadelphia were derived from 1981 newspaper articles, while Tucson and Pittsburgh figures were taken from 1982 newspaper stories.

Snyder's Numbers

Few people outside the homeless lobby, however, now support [homeless advocate Mitch] Snyder's number claims. In an interview, Snyder said that he still believes there are between two and three million homeless in the United States but noted that his numbers are not "scientifically precise."

But "they're not just my numbers," he said in defense. "Check with the American Psychological Association, the U.S. Conference of Mayors, and the National Coalition for the Homeless. They'll back me." Spokesmen for the U.S. Conference of Mayors and the American Psychological Association denied that they had either supported Snyder's statistics or issued comparable estimates. And of course, the National Coalition gets its numbers . . . from Snyder.

Martin Morse Wooster, *Reason*, July 1987.

HUD's other estimates deserve closer attention. Consider the number derived from the opinions of operators of shelters for the homeless.

Shelter operators are not as knowledgeable about the numbers of homeless in their area as one might expect. As Eugene Ericksen, a professor of sociology at Temple University, told a congressional committee in December 1985, "the shelter operators and other providers are so busy running their facilities and taking care of the local clientele that they have little time or motivation to learn about the problem as a whole. Knowing how many homeless people there are in the New York area will not help you run your shelter in the Bowery when your beds are full every night and you have to turn people away.". . .

The estimates HUD did receive varied widely. In New York, for example, estimates ranged from 12,000 to 50,000 homeless people;

in Los Angeles, from 19,500 to 39,000.

"Some of these responses may have been wild guesses," Erickson testified. "In other cases, respondents may have given the number of public shelter beds; estimates may also have been given of the number of persons staying in shelters, missions, or hotels and apartments vouchered for the homeless.". . .

In short, what HUD did was not to count the number of homeless people or to rely on counts compiled by others. It simply collected opinions. Some of the opinions may be better than others, but as Richard Applebaum, a professor of sociology at the University of California at Santa Barbara, points out, most of HUD's research was "subjective opinion. . . . I don't think it matters if it is a shelter operator or a member of the Coalition on the Homeless, it is just a guess. It may be a somewhat more informed guess than my guess, but it is still a guess because of the monumental problem [in counting the homeless]."

Numbers Too High

The homeless lobby obviously didn't care for HUD's huge deflation of their own numbers. But two recent studies suggest that HUD's estimates were *too high*. Peter Rossi, director of the Social and Demographic Research Institute at the University of Massachusetts at Amherst, conducted a study for the National Opinion Research Center to determine the number of homeless people in Chicago. Rossi and his reseachers counted homeless people on 245 blocks in downtown Chicago (including "super blocks" such as train, bus, and subway stations that have a large number of homeless people). They concluded that there were between 2,000 and 3,000 homeless on the nights surveyed (in September/October 1985 and February/March 1986). Rossi estimated that 5,000 people were without homes at some point during the year. HUD, by contrast, estimates Chicago's homeless at 12,000-25,000—three times Rossi's figures.

In a subsequent article in *Science*, Rossi and his researchers reveal that they have "never been able to locate any data from which [HUD's] numbers were derived." They note that "empirically credible attempts to estimate the size of the homeless population have produced numbers well below the expectations of the advocacy community." . . .

Martha Hicks, president of the Skid Row Development Corp., a nonprofit community agency, discounts HUD's estimate that there are up to 50,000 homeless people in Los Angeles. "They'd be falling all over each other if we had that many people here," Hicks told the *Washington Post* recently. "I think there are some people who think there is some money to be made from homelessness.". . .

Politicians and homeless advocates, in trying to "solve" the problem of homelessness by the well-worn method of throwing money at it, underestimate the amount of federal aid already flowing to the homeless. For example, a "fact sheet" put out by the House Select Committee on Hunger claims that only five federal programs serve the homeless.

In fact, as a modest amount of poking around Washington reveals, there are at least *20* federal programs for the homeless, ranging from conversion of surplus buildings to Urban Mass Transit Administration research grants (yes, UMTA is in on the action to figure out how homeless people can use public transportation).

The total amount targeted for homelessness in fiscal year 1986 was between $170 and $200 million. At least $60 million—and as much as $560 million—will be added to this total in fiscal year 1987. And that's just for programs within agencies designated specifically for homeless people; this doesn't count welfare benefits such as food stamps or veterans' benefits for the 25 percent of the homeless population who have served in the armed forces. . . . Calculating *all* federal benefits for homeless people is impossible, since most social welfare programs do not earmark money specifically for the homeless even when that's how it's spent. . . .

Questions

Could the current cornucopia of federal aid—free food, free housing, free electricity—"solve" the homeless problem? Some experts argue that, as the amount of aid increases, the number of people eager to use it increases.

When Thomas Main analyzed New York homeless statistics, he found that 19 percent of the people staying in shelters over a long-term period were "economic-only" clients—men who entered shelters not because of drugs, mental illness, or disability but because life in a shelter is more attractive than either a life on welfare or a life in a minimum-wage job. Main believes that minority youth with "tenuous family ties" may find a shelter more attractive than living with unfriendly relatives.

In an interview, Main said he would like to have lawmakers think about several questions before contributing to the budget crisis by responding to the "homeless crisis" with more and more tax dollars. "Is the best way to approach this problem by building more shelters? Is a national right to shelter the approach that makes the best sense?"

And here's an additional question. Given the vast number of programs already serving the homeless, and given the at-best sketchy evidence offered by the homeless lobby, why should taxpayers believe there *is* a "homeless crisis"?

"Many of the homeless are . . . 'domestic refugees,' people who have turned not against life itself, but against us, our life, American life."

Society Should Be Sympathetic Toward the Homeless

Peter Marin

Peter Marin is a contributing editor for *Harper's Magazine*. In the following viewpoint, he classifies the homeless into two groups: those who have had homelessness forced upon them, and those who have chosen to be homeless. Marin argues that the former group has a right to regain a place in society, and that the latter group has a right to be left alone.

As you read, consider the following question:

1. How does the author define homelessness?
2. According to Marin, how has the homeless world changed in recent years?
3. What does the author mean by "social contract," and how does he apply it to the homelessness problem?

Peter Marin, "Helping and Hating the Homeless." Copyright © 1986 by Harper's Magazine. Reprinted from the January 1987 issue by special permission.

The trouble begins with the word "homeless." It has become such an abstraction, and is applied to so many different kinds of people, with so many different histories and problems, that it is almost meaningless.

Homelessness, in itself, is nothing more than a condition visited upon men and women (and, increasingly, children) as the final stage of a variety of problems about which the word "homelessness" tells us almost nothing. Or, to put it another way, it is a catch basin into which pour all of the people disenfranchised or marginalized or scared off by processes beyond their control, those which lie close to the heart of American life. Here are the groups packed into the single category of "the homeless":

- Veterans, mainly from the war in Vietnam. In many American cities, vets make up close to 50 percent of all homeless males.
- The mentally ill. In some parts of the country, roughly a quarter of the homeless would, a couple of decades ago, have been institutionalized.
- The physically disabled or chronically ill, who do not receive any benefits or whose benefits do not enable them to afford permanent shelter.
- The elderly on fixed incomes whose funds are no longer sufficient for their needs.
- Men, women, and whole families pauperized by the loss of a job.
- Single parents, usually women, without the resources or skills to establish new lives.
- Runaway children, many of whom have been abused.
- Alcoholics and those in trouble with drugs (whose troubles often begin with one of the other conditions listed here).
- Immigrants, both legal and illegal, who often are not counted among the homeless because they constitute a "problem" in their own right.
- Traditional tramps, hobos, and transients, who have taken to the road or the streets for a variety of reasons and who prefer to be there.

You can quickly learn two things about the homeless from this list. First, you can learn that many of the homeless, before they were homeless, were people more or less like ourselves: members of the working or middle class. And you can learn that the world of the homeless has its roots in various policies, events, and ways of life for which some of us are responsible and from which some of us actually prosper. . . .

Choosing To Be Homeless

You can also learn from this list one of the most important things there is to know about the homeless—that they can be roughly divided into two groups: those who have had homelessness forced upon them and want nothing more than to escape it; and those who have at least in part *chosen* it for themselves, and now accept, or in some cases, embrace it.

I understand how dangerous it is to introduce the idea of choice into a discussion of homelessness. It can all to easily be used to justify indifference or brutality toward the homeless, or to argue that they are only getting what they "deserve." And yet it seems to me that it is only by taking choice into account, in all of the intricacies of its various forms and expressions, that one can really understand certain kinds of homelessness.

Punished for Appearance

Most homeless people do nothing objectionable—they only look objectionable.

It used to be that the sight of immigrants or groups of black people was threatening to most people. Yet no one ever did anything about it. Now, however, homeless people are being penalized not for what they do, but for how they look. It is difficult for people not to feel discomfort at seeing homeless people; but it is the homeless who pay for the way people feel about them.

Robert Rosenthal, *The Center Magazine*, September/October 1986.

The fact is, many of the homeless are not only hapless victims but voluntary exiles, "domestic refugees," people who have turned not against life itself but against *us*, our life, American life. Look for a moment at the vets. The price of returning to America was to forget what they had seen or learned in Vietnam, to "put it behind them." But some could not do that, and the stress of trying showed up as alcoholism, broken marriages, drug addiction, crime. And it showed up too as life on the street, which was for some vets a desperate choice made in the name of life—the best they could manage. It was a way of avoiding what might have occurred had they stayed where they were: suicide, or violence done to others.

The Story of Alice

We must learn to accept that there may indeed be people, and not only vets, who have seen so much of our world, or seen it so clearly, that to live in it becomes impossible. Here, for example, is the story of Alice, a homeless middle-aged woman in Los Angeles, where there are, perhaps, 50,000 homeless people. It was set down a few months ago by one of my students at the University of California, Santa Barbara, where I taught for a semester. I had encouraged them to go find the homeless and listen to their stories. And so, one day, when this student saw Alice foraging in a dumpster outside a McDonald's, he stopped and talked to her:

She told me she had led a pretty normal life as she grew up and eventually went to college. From there she went on to Chicago to teach school. She was single and lived in a small apartment.

One night, after she got off the train after school, a man began to follow her to her apartment building. When she got to her door she saw a knife and the man hovering behind her. She had no choice but to let him in. The man raped her.

After that, things got steadily worse. She had a nervous breakdown. She went to a mental institution for three months, and when she went back to her apartment she found her belongings gone. The landlord had sold them to cover the rent she hadn't paid.

She had no place to go and no job because the school had terminated her employment. She slipped into depression. She lived with friends until she could muster enough money for a ticket to Los Angeles. She said she no longer wanted to burden her friends, and that if she had to live outside, at least Los Angeles was warmer than Chicago.

It is as if she began back then to take on the mentality of a street person. She resolved herself to homelessness. She's been out West since 1980, without a home or job. She seems happy, with her best friend being her cat. But the scars of memories still haunt her, and she is running from them, or should I say *him*.

This is, in essence, the same story one hears over and over again on the street. You begin with an ordinary life; then an event occurs—traumatic, catastrophic; smaller events follow, each one deepening the original wound; finally, homelessness becomes inevitable, or begins to *seem* inevitable to the person involved—the only way out of an intolerable situation. You are struck continually, hearing these stories, by something seemingly unique in American life, the absolute isolation involved. In what other culture would there be such an absence or failure of support from familial, social, or institutional sources? Even more disturbing is the fact that it is often our supposed sources of support—family, friends, government organizations—that have caused the problem in the first place.

Fixing the Homeless

Everything that happened to Alice—the rape, the loss of job and apartment, the breakdown—was part and parcel of a world gone radically wrong, a world, for Alice, no longer to be counted on, no longer worth living in. Her homelessness can be seen as flight, as failure of will or nerve, even, perhaps, as *disease*. But it can also been seen as a mute, furious refusal, a self-imposed exile far less appealing to the rest of us than ordinary life, but *better*, in Alice's terms.

We like to think, in America, that everything is redeemable, that everything broken can be magically made whole again, and that what has been "dirtied" can be cleansed. Recently I saw on television that one of the soaps had introduced the character of a homeless old woman. A woman in her thirties discovers that her long-lost mother has appeared in town, on the streets. After much searching the mother is located and identified and embraced; and then she is scrubbed and dressed in style, restored in a matter of days to her former upper-class habits and role.

A triumph—but one more likely to occur on television than in real life. Yes, many of those on the streets could be transformed, rehabilitated. But there are others whose lives have been irrevocably changed, damaged beyond repair, and who no longer want help, who no longer recognize the *need* for help, and whose experience in our world has made them want only to be left alone. How, for instance, would one restore Alice's life, or reshape it in a way that would satisfy *our* notion of what a life should be? What would it take to return her to the fold? How to erase the four years of homelessness, which have become as familiar to her, and as much a home, as her "normal" life once was? Whatever we think of the way in which she had resolved her difficulties, it constitutes a sad peace made with the world. Intruding ourselves upon it in the name of redemption is by no means as simple a task—or as justifiable a task—as one might think. . . .

The Resourcefulness of the Homeless

There is . . . a great deal of supportiveness within homeless groups: the sharing of survival tips, of job possibilities, where to go to keep warm, as well as cigarettes, reading material, food, and clothing. It would be well to identify these strengths and build on them in the process of dealing with homelessness. There is cleverness and street-wisdom in the woman who found a place to shampoo her hair and clean herself or the man in Grand Central Terminal who converted an old wardrobe trunk into a portable earth station, neatly filled with an array of life-sustaining possessions—clothing, cleaning materials, and dishes. These are capable survivors, whose coping strategies and the competence that supports them need to be documented, rather than their weaknesses and needs alone.

Leanne G. Rivlin, *Social Policy*, Spring 1986.

Years ago, when I first came to California, bumming my way west, the marginal world, and the lives of those in it, were very different from what they are now. In those days I spent much of my time in hobo jungles or on the skid rows of various cities, and just as it was easier back then to "get by" in the easygoing beach towns on the California coast, or in the bohemian and artistic worlds in San Francisco or Los Angeles or New York, it was also far easier than it is now to survive in the marginal world.

It is important to remember this—important to recognize the immensity of the changes that have occurred in the marginal world in the past twenty years. Whole sections of many cities—the Bowery in New York, the Tenderloin in San Francisco—were once ceded to the transient. In every skid-row area in America you could find what you needed to survive: hash houses, saloons offering free lunches, pawnshops, surplus-clothing stores, and, most important of all, cheap hotels and flophouses and two-bit employment agencies specializing in the kinds of labor (seasonal, shape-up) transients have always done. . . .

Changes in the Marginal World

But things have changed. There began to pour into the marginal world—slowly in the sixties, a bit faster in the seventies, and then faster still in the eighties—more and more people who neither belonged nor knew how to survive there. The sixties brought the counterculture and drugs; the streets filled with young dropouts. Changes in the law loosed upon the streets mentally ill men and women. Inflation took its toll, then recession. Working-class and even middle-class men and women—entire families—began to fall into a world they did not understand.

At the same time the transient world was being inundated by new inhabitants, its landscape, its economy, was shrinking radically. Jobs became harder to find. Modernization has something to do with it; machines took the place of men and women. And the influx of workers from Mexico and points farther south created a class of semipermanent workers who took the place of casual transient labor. More important, perhaps, was the fact that the forgotten parts of many cities began to attract attention. Downtown areas were redeveloped, reclaimed. The skid-row sections of smaller cities were turned into "old townes." The old hotels that once catered to transients were upgraded or torn down or became warehouses for welfare families—an arrangement far more profitable to the owners. The price of housing increased; evictions increased. The mentally ill, who once could afford to house themselves in cheap rooms, the alcoholics, who once would drink themselves to sleep at night in their cheap hotels, were out on the street—exposed to the weather and to danger, and also in plain and public view: "problems" to be dealt with.

Nor was it only cheap shelter that disappeared. It was also those "open" spaces that had once been available to those without other shelter. As property rose in value, the nooks and crannies in which the homeless had been able to hide became more visible. Doorways, alleys, abandoned buildings, vacant lots—these "holes" in the cityscape, these gaps in public consciousness, became *real estate*. The homeless, who had been there all the time, were overtaken by economic progress, and they became intruders. . . .

The homeless, simply because they are homeless, are strangers, alien—and therefore a threat. Their presence, in itself, comes to constitute a kind of violence; it deprives us of our sense of safety. Let me use myself as an example. I know, and respect, many of those now homeless on the streets of Santa Barbara. Twenty years ago, some of them would have been my companions and friends. And yet, these days, if I walk through the park near my home and see strangers bedding down for the night, my first reaction, if not fear, is a sense of annoyance and intrusion, of worry and alarm. I think of my teenage daughter, who often walks through the park, and then of my house, a hundred yards away, and I am tempted—only tempted, but tempted, still—to call the "proper" authorities to have the strangers moved on. Out of sight, out of mind. . . .

Just Don't Know

Anyone attempting to classify the varieties of misfortune and failure that lead people to homelessness must pause to confess how inadequate the enterprise can be when faced with the living reality. Often you just can't know. For instance, how did this worn, pretty-faced woman of 38 or 40 come to be sitting with a tin can labeled "Donations for the homeless lady" on the pavement beside the Los Angeles City Hall, close by the bushes where she spent the night? She turns a tired face up from her book and mentions a divorce, children she hasn't seen in years, help not given when needed. But what exactly happened? "It's a long story," she says in a voice of despondency just this side of tears. "A long story." And turns back to her book.

Myron Magnet, *Fortune,* November 23, 1987.

The person who has written most revealingly about such things is George Orwell, who tried to analyze his own middle-class attitudes toward the poor. In 1933, in *Down and Out in Paris and London,* he wrote about tramps:

In childhood we are taught that tramps are blackguards . . . a repulsive, rather dangerous creature, who would rather die than work or wash, and wants nothing but to beg, drink or rob henhouses. The tramp monster is no truer to life than the sinister Chinaman of the magazines, but he is very hard to get rid of. The very word "tramp" evokes his image.

Repulsion

All of this is still true in America, though now it is not the word "tramp" but the word "homeless" that evokes the images we fear. It is the homeless who smell. Here, for instance, is part of a paper a student of mine wrote about her first visit to a Rescue Mission on skid row.

The sermon began. The room was stuffy and smelly. The mixture of body odors and cooking was nauseating. I remember thinking: how can these people share this facility? They must be repulsed by each other. They had strange habits and dispositions. They were a group of dirty, dishonored, weird people to me.

When it was over I ran to my car, went home, and took a shower. I felt extremely dirty. Through the day I would get flashes of that disgusting smell.

To put it as bluntly as I can, for many of us the homeless are *shit*. And our policies toward them, our spontaneous sense of disgust and horror, our wish to be rid of them—all of this has hidden in it, close to its heart, our feelings about excrement. . . .

What I am getting at here is the *nature* of the desire to help the homeless—what is hidden behind it and why it so often does harm. Every government program, almost every private project, is geared as much to the needs of those giving help as it is to the needs of the homeless. Go to any government agency, or, for that matter, to most private charities, and you will find yourself enmeshed, at once, in a bureaucracy so tangled and oppressive, or confronted with so much moral arrogance and contempt, that you will be driven back out into the streets for relief. . . .

What Should We Do?

The central question emerging from all this is, What does a society owe to its members in trouble, and *how* is that debt to be paid? It is a question which must be answered in two parts: first, in relation to the men and women who have been marginalized against their will, and then, in a slightly different way, in relation to those who have chosen (or accept or even prize) their marginality.

As for those who have been marginalized against their wills, I think the general answer is obvious: A society owes its members whatever it takes for them to regain their places in the social order. And when it comes to specific remedies, one need only read backward the various processes which have created homelessness and then figure out where help is likely to do the most good. But the real point here is not the specific remedies required—affordable housing, say—but the basis upon which they must be offered, the necessary underlying ethical notion we seem in this nation unable to grasp: that those who are the inevitable casualties of modern industrial capitalism and the free-market system are entitled, *by right*, and by the simple virtue of their participation in that system, to whatever help they need. They are entitled to help to find and hold their places in the society whose social contract they have, in effect, signed and observed.

Look at that for just a moment: the notion of a contract. The majority of homeless Americans have kept, insofar as they could, to the terms of that contract. In any shelter these days you can find men and women who have worked ten, twenty, forty years, and whose lives have nonetheless come to nothing. These are people who cannot afford a place in the world they helped create. And in return? Is it life on the street they have earned? Or the cruel charity we so grudgingly grant them?

But those marginalized against their will are only half the problem. There remains, still, the question of whether we owe anything to those who are voluntarily marginal. What about them: the street people, the rebels, and the recalcitrants, those who have torn up their social contracts or returned them unsigned? . . .

What Do We Owe?

Do we owe anything to these men and women, who reject our company and what we offer and yet nonetheless seem to demand *something* from us?

We owe them, I think, at least a place to exist, a way to exist. That may not be a *moral* obligation, in the sense that our obligation to the involuntarily marginal is clearly a moral one, but it is an obligation nevertheless, one you might call an existential obligation.

Of course, it may be that I think we owe these men something because I have liked men like them, and because I want their world to be there always, as a place to hide or rest. But there is more to it than that. I think we as a society need men like these. A society needs its margins as much as it needs art and literature. It needs holes and gaps, *breathing spaces*, let us say, into which men and women can escape and live, when necessary, in ways otherwise denied them. Margins guarantee to society a flexibility, an elasticity, and allow it to accommodate itself to the natures and needs of its members. When margins vanish, society becomes too rigid, too oppressive by far, and therefore inimical to life.

It is for such reasons that, in cultures like our own, marginal men and women take on a special significance. They are all we have left to remind us of the narrowness of the received truths we take for granted. "Beyond the pale," they somehow redefine the pale, or remind us, at least, that *something* is still out there, beyond the pale. They preserve, perhaps unconsciously, a dream that would otherwise cease to exist, the dream of having a place in the world, and of being *left alone*.

"Neither poverty nor unemployment entitles a person, or a band of persons, to set up camp wherever they choose to light."

Society Should Protect Its Own Interests

Burton M. Leiser

Several cities in America have dealt with homelessness by making it illegal to steal food from trash containers or to sleep in parks or streets. In the following viewpoint, Burton Leiser, a professor of philosophy at Pace University in New York City, defends such laws. He argues the community has a right to defend its property against vagrants and that the "rights" of people to food and shelter are a matter of charity, not entitlement.

As you read, consider the following questions:

1. How does the author justify banning the use of public property to homeless people?
2. According to Leiser, what problems arise when talking about the "rights" of the poor to food and shelter?
3. Do vagrancy laws discriminate against the poor, according to the author? How does he defend them?

Burton M. Leiser, "Vagrancy, Loitering, and Economic Justice," from Kenneth Kipnes and Diana Meyers, (eds.) ECONOMIC JUSTICE (Totowa, New Jersey: Rowman & Allanheld, 1985).

As late as 1953, forty of the forty-eight states defined vagrancy as a crime, which could be "committed" by living in idleness or without employment and having no visible means of support; being a common prostitute; being a common drunkard, a common gambler, a keeper of a house of prostitution, or a keeper of a gambling house or gaming equipment; being a wanton, dissolute, or lascivious person; and being an associate of known thieves. In addition, roaming, wandering, or loitering, especially when one had no visible or lawful purpose in so acting, could give no satisfactory account of his presence, or was wandering at "late or unusual hours," was defined in some states as vagrancy. Many states included begging or being a beggar, at least when one was able to work, as vagrancy. Lodging or sleeping outdoors or in buildings other than residences without the permission of the owner or without being able to give a good account of oneself was punishable in a number of states, and failing to support one's family was vagrancy in about ten states.

The crime or offense of vagrancy was not an act, but a state of being. As a California court put it:

> That which has been done is not to declare that it is unlawful to get drunk, or to prostitute oneself, or to peep in another's building, nor have these acts been declared to be misdemeanors. The punishment provided by section 647 is not for doing, but for being; for being a vagrant. . . .

Justice Douglas Objects

In an important article published in 1960, Justice William O. Douglas denounced vagrancy statutes and the manner in which they were enforced. "I am sure," he wrote, "that my old friend Carl Sandburg, whom America loves, feels warm inside when I address him as Fellow Hobo. The term implies independence, a restless spirit, the quest for a better life, rebellion against submission to orthodoxy." Justice Douglas went on to quote at length Robert Louis Stevenson's paean to the vagabond, contrasting it with the Tucson police department's "war" on "winter vags." He had known judges and lawyers, he said, who had wandered the streets at night during a bout with insomnia, and recalled the days of his own youth when he had ridden the rods with the casual laborers of the Pacific West, sharing their meals under railroad bridges, sleeping with them in the open air. "I came to know that the 'consumers of injustice' are not the sleepless judges and lawyers," he wrote, "but the wanderers who have no prestige of class or family." . . .

Justice Douglas was concerned about what he perceived to be the complete ineffectiveness of penal statutes to cure the problem—which after all is nothing more than poverty.

In 1972 the Supreme Court, in *Papachristou* v. *City of Jacksonville*, struck down the Jacksonville vagrancy ordinance and impelled state governments and municipalities to repeal or revise their vagrancy statutes and ordinances. In his opinion for the Court, Justice Douglas argued that loafing and loitering, like walking and strolling and wandering, are "part of the amenities of life as we have known them, amenities that have been in part responsible for giving our people the feeling of independence and self-confidence, the feeling of creativity, . . . [that] have dignified the right of dissent and have honored the right to be nonconformists and the right to defy submissiveness. They have encouraged lives of high spirits rather than hushed, suffocating silence." The presumption that people who walk, loaf, loiter, or stroll, or who frequent liquor stores or taverns, or who are supported by their wives or look suspicious to the police are about to become involved in criminal behavior is "too precarious for a rule of law," he said, an assumption "too extravagant to deserve extended treatment." With that, he dismissed the subject and brought his *Papachristou* opinion to an end.

The Question of Public Safety

This decision has considerable appeal. But there is reason to believe that the Supreme Court is modifying the stand that it took in *Papachristou*. A number of statutes and ordinances forbidding loitering or disorderly conduct have been upheld on various grounds, principally the fear that peace, order, or public safety are threatened. . . .

What Can Be Done

People sleeping on the streets depress property values, decrease tourism, tarnish a city's reputation and inhibit customers from entering shops. In subtle ways, we already are paying the price for the homeless. I would rather pay higher taxes and get these people off the streets. . . .

Every community has factories and warehouses that have closed down. Nearly every community has abandoned houses. These can be converted at minimal cost into a shelter that provides light, heat and plumbing. Call them tax-supported flophouses, call them almshouses, I don't care.

People can't be *forced* to live there, of course. They have their rights. But so do we. Once we have made shelter available, we have the right to say this: the streets are not for sleeping anymore.

Stuart D. Bykofsky, *Newsweek*, December 1, 1986.

The recent cases lead one to wonder whether, for example, the known pickpocket should be permitted to loiter in a bus terminal when he has nowhere to go and is not waiting to meet anyone in particular. Or is it necessary to wait until after he has stolen someone's wallet and been caught and convicted before his thievery can be brought to an end?

Similarly, must the lone wanderer be permitted to hide behind the bushes late at night in a residential area where he has no business and cannot provide a reasonable explanation of his presence? In light of common experience, it is not unreasonable to presume that his motives may not be pure and to insist that he either explain what he is doing there or suffer arrest on some charge designed to protect homeowners and residents against the depredations of burglars, thieves, and muggers. The mere claim that they are innocent nightwalkers who just happen to be fifteen miles from home ought not to be construed to be sufficient to overcome the presumption.

Social Costs of Homelessness

Neither poverty nor unemployment entitles a person, or a band of persons, to set up camp wherever they choose to light, intruding upon the peace and harmony of any community that happens to be in their path. When parks, streets, and sidewalks are converted into temporary residences, there can be no doubt of the deleterious impact upon the local community. The stench of human excrement fills the air. Benches intended for the enjoyment of local residents are occupied by sleeping vagabonds. Grounds become littered with the refuse left by persons who use them for purposes for which they were neither intended nor designed. Passersby and householders are intercepted and importuned by beggars and panhandlers, and the peace of the community is disrupted by the influx of strangers, not all of whom are determined to find an honorable way of satisfying their needs.

The fact that a place is not privately owned does not entail its being open to any and all persons for occupation and use for any purpose. Many places are publicly owned, but it is neither unlawful nor immoral to place restrictions upon the persons who may use them and the activities in which they may engage while in those places. A public-school building, for example, is owned by the community; but the school board and its agents are fully justified in demanding that people who are not authorized to be in such buildings because they are not there on business having to do with the public schools must leave the premises or be charged with trespass. The same is true of public hospitals, libraries, courthouses, post offices, and even jails and prisons. If this elementary principle of public ownership were not recognized, it would soon become impossible to carry on the public business for which such structures are erected. . . .

A public park, designed as a place of recreation, may properly be restricted to members of the local community that supports it, and to particular uses. There is no *a priori* reason why residents

124

should feel morally obliged to open their facility to any stranger who happens to pass through town. It could scarcely be argued that they would not be justified in ejecting anyone who attempted to build a campfire in the middle of a tennis court, since it would destroy the surface of the court and render it useless—or at least less useful—for the purposes for which it was intended. By the same reasoning, they might properly eject anyone who erected a squatter's tent on the grounds of the park and attempted to establish a residence there for himself and his family.

Community Rights

We constantly in this country talk about every problem in terms of a clash of individual rights. The community has some rights here. If it is illegal, and it is, and ought to be illegal, to litter the streets, frankly it ought to be illegal for people who must survive in panhandling among other things to sleep on the streets. Therefore there is a simple matter of public order and hygiene in getting these people somewhere else. Not arrest them, but move them off to someplace where they are simply out of sight and no longer a visible, in some cases intrusive, in some cases even an aggressive, public nuisance.

George Will, *The New Republic*, March 18, 1985.

Like many so-called human rights, those fundamental "rights" claimed by the poor (including those to food, drink, clothing, and shelter) are of imperfect obligation. They are pleas or requests directed to the good nature, the kindness, the compassion, the charity of those who find themselves in more fortunate circumstances. Thus it does not follow that *this* community, where these poor persons happen to be located, has the obligation to provide them their needs. Nor does it follow that the poor have a special claim upon the members of that community, or that they have a special moral obligation to fill those needs, just because the poor happen to be among *them*. Any community that recognized such a claim would undoubtedly be inundated by poverty-stricken persons. The end would be the impoverishment of the generous citizens of that community and the termination, for lack of resources, of the benefits they might otherwise have extended to the poor among them.

In any event, although one might want to argue that the members of a community in which poor persons happen to be located (whether those impoverished individuals are long-term residents or newly arrived migrants) are morally obliged to assist their less fortunate neighbors by providing them the necessities of life, there is no moral imperative that lays upon anyone in that community or upon the collective whole the duty to make such provisions, when making them would entail sacrificing goods or amenities for which they have worked. Why should *these* individuals or *this* community be saddled with the burden of providing for these impoverished individuals? If such an obligation exists at all, it surely cannot be acquired by mere physical proximity. If a poor person comes uninvited to my door asking for (or demanding) shelter, what moral principle lays the duty of fulfilling his demand upon me rather than upon my neighbor or someone who lives a thousand miles away—or, for that matter, upon the government of China? And if, instead of visiting my home, he visits my city's park, a bus station, or a boxcar and claims the right to camp there on the ground that he will otherwise be denied his fundamental human right to shelter and a place to lay his head, what moral principle obliges the city, the bus company, or the railroad company to allow him to do so? It is evident that they are under no greater obligation to permit him to camp on their grounds than I am to permit him to pitch his tent in my front yard. . . .

The mere invocation of the expression, "human right," is not sufficient to establish that any particular person is being denied anything to which he had a legitimate claim, or that any particular person or community has failed to meet his or its moral obligations. Even supererogatory duties and duties of imperfect obligation have some meaning. One might ask, then, what moral duties persons and communities have with respect to the poor. I chose *not* to address myself to that question here, where the issue is not what is owed to the poor, but what is *not* owed to them. There are ways of dealing with the problems of poverty, many of them reasonably well known and well tested. People *ought* to be kind and generous, within reasonable limits, both in their private charities and through their governmental institutions. Private institutions exist for dispensing various forms of aid to the needy. Public institutions have fulfilled many of the same functions—in some cases well, and in others not as efficiently as might be desired. Shelters have been erected for the homeless. Clothes have been provided for those who did not have clothes of their own. Food has been dispensed to the hungry. Education and other benefits have been provided for those who could not acquire them with their own resources. All of this and more are highly desirable, and those individuals and communities who have provided them are to be commended for their generosity and their sense of public service.

Rights of Society

But none of this has anything to do with the question presently at issue: Does a community have the right to pass ordinances designed to protect communal property and institutions against uses for which they were not intended—in particular, against persons who happen to be poor and destitute? Harsh as it may sound to put it so bluntly, the answer appears to be affirmative. Those who own private property have the right to deny admission to anyone they choose to exclude from their buildings or lands, and to eject them if they trespass. Without such a right, the very notion of real property ceases to have much meaning. Property rights are valuable for a number of excellent utilitarian reasons, not the least of which is the incentive they give individuals to improve the lands they own, both for their own benefit and for the benefit of the wider community. Similarly, states and municipalities provide public facilities for their residents to enhance the quality of life within their borders. In order to guarantee the preservation and improvement of the conditions under which their citizens live, they are entitled to bar nonresidents from the enjoyment of certain amenities, and to restrict the kinds of activities in which residents and nonresidents may engage—despite the claim that some might make that they are entitled to special privileges beause they are poor.

Enforcement of such regulations is best accomplished by the enactment of laws and ordinances directed against those who do not qualify as residents and who are not able to establish that they are using the facilities—including such public facilities as streets, sidewalks, and parks—in a lawful way for lawful purposes. This is precisely what the vagrancy statutes were designed to do. . . .

The persons most likely to be affected by vagrancy laws are those who are unfortunate enough to be poor. The laws themselves, however, need not make poverty itself a crime. They may facilitate a legitimate governmental objective. The fact that that objective can be met only by depriving some poor persons of privileges they might like to exercise does not render those objectives or the means employed to meet them illegitimate. Poverty is not in itself an entitlement. Don't poor, destitute persons have a right to a place to lay their heads? Surely one cannot argue that they have no moral right to such an elementary requirement of survival! In the same way, they have the right to air to breathe and water to drink and food to eat.

Even if we grant this proposition, it does not follow that *this* community, where these poor persons happen to be located, has the obligation to provide them their needs, or that the poor have a special claim upon the people of that community, who have a special moral obligation to fill those needs, just because the poor happen to be among *them*. Any community that recognized such a claim would undoubtedly be inundated by poverty-stricken persons. The end would be the impoverishment of the generous citizens of that community and the termination of the benefits they would extend to the poor among them for the lack of resources.

127

"The laws need to be changed so that obviously disabled individuals can be hospitalized and treated."

The Homeless Mentally Ill Should Be Forced To Receive Treatment

E. Fuller Torrey

A substantial percentage of the homeless population in America is composed of mentally ill patients who have been released from hospitals. E. Fuller Torrey, a Washington psychiatrist who runs a shelter for homeless women, argues in the following viewpoint that this increase in the homeless mentally ill is due to laws that make it impossible for hospitals to keep patients against their will. He contends that the laws should allow hospitals to force treatment on those individuals that appear too sick to care for themselves.

As you read, consider the following questions:

1. What does the author find frustrating about the problem of homelessness among the mentally ill?
2. Why does the author believe some people should be treated against their will?
3. What changes in the law does Torrey suggest?

E. Fuller Torrey, "Finally, a Cure for the Homeless," *The Washington Monthly*, September 1986. Reprinted with permission from *The Washington Monthly*. Copyright by THE WASHINGTON MONTHLY CO., 1711 Connecticut Avenue, NW, Washington, DC 20009. (202) 462-0128.

Cynthia joined the legions of homeless on Washington's streets on March 26, 1985, when she was precipitously discharged from St. Elizabeth's Hospital. She walked down Martin Luther King Avenue holding a list of the city's public shelters and one week's worth of medication, wearing a light sweater and bedroom slippers because, as her hospital chart phrased it, "she refused to wear her sneakers." The weatherman had said the temperature would drop into the thirties. Passersby glanced at Cynthia and her odd footwear, and walked past this latest graduate of St. Elizabeth's.

Hospital regulations do not sanction such hasty discharges, of course. A patient is supposed to have housing arranged and a follow-up appointment at a community mental health center. But Cynthia was, everyone agreed, a difficult patient—"very demanding" and "not cooperative at all," as the nursing staff wrote on her hospital chart. She had had difficulty getting along with other people even as a small girl. Then, in her early twenties, when she developed schizophrenia, she went from irascible to unlikable.

Released and Alone

The nursing staff had been subtly pressuring the ward psychiatrist for weeks to discharge her. She refused to meet with her occupational therapy group, and was then told she had to attend or she would be released. Cynthia told the nursing staff what she thought of their threat. And she was out the door after one hour's notice.

Packing was easy, for she had come with nothing. Four years and six hospitals earlier she still owned some things—pictures, clothes, bagatelles of a private past—but now they are all gone, forgotten on some park bench or locked away in the unclaimed luggage room of another state hospital. It is difficult for her to keep things; the voices in her disordered brain distract her. Schizophrenia is a disease which affects the brain's chemistry so that its sufferers can no longer think clearly or logically. Cynthia often believes people are trying to kill her.

Cynthia joined the homeless who live on the streets and park benches of downtown Washington. They sleep, importune strangers, gesture to imaginary accomplices, shout angrily at the wind, forage through cans, and sit quietly with glazed eyes. They are daily reminders of the massive failure of one of the Great Society's premier programs: the deinstitutionalization of mental patients out of state asylums and into local Community Mental Health Centers (CMHCs).

Not News

The crisis of the mentally ill among the homeless is certainly not news. In fact, there has been a broad consensus for several years that deinstitutionalization is a major cause of homelessness. . . . A 1983 Senate hearing showed that 30 to 50 per-

Tony Auth, Universal Press Syndicate. Reprinted by permission.

cent of the homeless have severe mental illnesses, and congressional hearings in 1985 drew a *Washington Post* headline: "Experts Decry Dumping of Mental Patients: Streets Called Asylums of the 1980s." Just six days later Cynthia was released from St. Elizabeth's.

The news, then, is not that there is a clear relationship between failed mental health programs and the number of homeless mentally ill. Rather, it is that everybody acknowledges the fact, but does nothing about it. Hospitals like St. Elizabeth's continue to dump disturbed patients into the community, while the CMHCs show more interest in patients with mid-life crises than in those with serious mental illness.

More frustrating still, Cynthia and others like her could lead normal, productive lives if they would take certain medications. While this solution is medically simple, it is politically and legally difficult. Lawyers and politicians have objected on civil liberties grounds. But since homelessness among the mentally ill persists—despite the agreement on its causes—it is time for society to take a seemingly distasteful step: *force* many of these schizophrenics to take their medicine.

The Institution Reform

Deinstitutionalization was conceived in idealism and implemented with the best of intentions. President John F. Kennedy spoke of "the abandonment of the mentally ill and the mentally retarded to the grim mercies of custodial institutions" in his 1963 State of the Union message. One month later, in a historic special message to Congress, Kennedy proposed a network of CMHCs as "a bold new approach." When carried out, "reliance on the cold mercy of custodial isolation will be supplanted by the open warmth of community concern and capability. . . . It has been demonstrated that two out of three schizophrenics—our largest category of mentally ill—can be treated and released within six months. . . . If we launch a broad new mental health program now, it will be possible within a decade or two to reduce the number of patients now under custodial care by 50 percent or more." . . .

The CMHC program was passed by Congress and turned over to the National Institute of Mental Health (NIMH) to administer. It was clear from the beginning, however, that neither NIMH nor the CMHCs had any interest in the severely mentally ill. NIMH wrote its regulations so loosely that the local centers soon geared themselves to people with "problems of living" who could not afford the fees of private psychiatrists. The program that had originally been set up for patients with schizophrenia, manic-depressive psychosis, and other severe mental disorders, became instead a program for married couples having difficulty communicating, young adults concerned about their relations with the opposite sex, and middle-aged individuals undergoing existential crises. In states such as Mississippi, where mental health officials have tried to gear the centers more toward the seriously ill, the staffs that run the clinics have rebelled, claiming they are not equipped to treat such patients. Set up for the suffering sick, Kennedy's program was instead coopted by the worried well. . . .

Dumping the Mentally Ill

Meanwhile, seriously ill patients continued to be dumped from state hospitals into the community despite clear indications that CMHCs were not following up with treatment. Where state and federal officials thought these disabled people were going to get care is a mystery. On the day Cynthia was released from St. Elizabeth's, she may have wondered too; President Kennedy's "open warmth of community concern and capability" was not readily apparent. Most of the women's shelters were full, but she was finally accepted at a small church shelter where the women sleep on mats on the floor. Like most shelters in Washington, the church sends the women out at 7:30 in the morning and doesn't allow them to store anything. If they have any possessions, they must taken them wherever they go during the day. If they are fortunate enough to have an extra 50 cents, they may rent a public locker at the bus station, but that is a luxury few can afford.

Nancy has lived at this shelter for more than two years. She likes clothes and hangs onto them by wearing several layers. She is a familiar site around Lafayette Park, which is across from the White

131

House, and the Smithsonian museums, happily talking to herself and carrying her bags. She was hospitalized years ago but hated it; she refuses all entreaties to take medicine. There is nothing wrong with her, she says, although it is sometimes difficult to get her to focus on your questions, which compete with the several other inaudible voices with which she is carrying on conversations. . . .

Mary says she has been looking for affordable housing for more than a year. She is eligible to receive $359 each month as Supplemental Security Income because of her schizophrenia, though she denies there is anything wrong with her. She can tell you what is available for that income level and she doesn't like any of it. So for several months she has slept on the mezzanine of National Airport; the guards leave her alone as long as she is quiet. She feels safe there from the Israeli agents who she believes inject her with special medicine while she's sleeping. You barely notice her sitting in the airport during the day, apparently waiting for a plane to arrive. Pleasant and intelligent, she is a college graduate with three children. Her family lost track of her for several months until one of her daughters, when catching a flight back to college, ran into her. . . .

The Younger Mentally Ill

The homeless mentally ill are more often not the deinstitutionalized but the younger never-institutionalized—those who got sick after the deinstitutionalization movement had eviscerated the mental health care system. Never diagnosed or medicated, many become sicker by dosing themselves with the street dope or alcohol that temporarily quiets the voices. To imagine it a triumph of civil liberty that people unable to make rational choices are now free to choose is humbug. Says poverty expert Anna Kondratas, head of the Agriculture Department's Food and Nutrition Service: "It's irresponsible to allow people who can't help themselves to be on the streets."

Myron Magnet, *Fortune*, November 23, 1987.

The biggest tragedy is that many of these lives are salvageable. . . . The lithium and antipsychotic medication do not cure mental illness, they control the symptoms. They work the same way that insulin does in diabetics. I would estimate that one-fourth of the women I have known who live in public shelters could be returned to at least part-time employment if they took medication regularly. But most of the homeless who could benefit from medication will not accept it. Their brains tell them there is nothing wrong with them. Their voices whisper that medication is poison. Mary's family tried several times to have her involuntarily hospitalized and treated. She had been on medicine in the past and was much better, even able to hold a job. But she lived alone, with no one to force her to keep taking her medication. Because she didn't believe she was sick, she stopped.

Although the law once said that people could be hospitalized against their will if they were "in need of treatment" or "gravely disabled," well-meaning lawyers, concerned about the patients' civil liberties, have changed that. Now, in most states, no one can be involuntarily hospitalized and treated unless he is a danger to himself or to others. So Mary now has the right to sit at National Airport, safely evading the Israeli agents. And we now have a wonderfully free collection of individuals congregating in the nation's parks and streets. The defenders of civil liberties may be proud of that, but they don't have to live on the streets. Homeless people frequently freeze to death in the winter. Homeless women are frequently raped. . . .

Laws Must Be Changed

Liberty and cruelty have become confused. The laws need to be changed so that obviously disabled individuals can be hospitalized and treated before they become a danger to themselves or others. If they are gravely disabled and refuse help because they can't understand their illness, then psychiatric staff or the police should be allowed to take them—involuntarily—to a hospital for evaluation. Release from a hospital should be made contingent upon the patients' agreeing to continue to take medication. If the patients stop taking their medication (as determined by blood tests) then they can also be returned to the hospital.

Partial conservatorship or guardianship, and similar legal mechanisms for ensuring treatment have all been shown to work. These solutions, however, have been opposed by the American Civil Liberties Union, and others who say that involuntary treatment infringes on an individual's autonomy and right to make his own decisions. Assuming, however, that someone with schizophrenia is capable of making intelligent decisions regarding his or her own needs is like assuming that a person with heart disease has normal cardiac function and can run a marathon. When diabetes causes a person to go into a coma we do not defend the person's right to remain in a coma. Yet when schizophrenia jumbles the brain's chemistry, we insist that the person has the right to remain sick even when he has a history of getting well on medication.

There must be checks and balances available in the system, of course, such as court hearings and specified review periods. Nobody would advocate returning to the 1930s when someone could be hospitalized involuntarily for an indefinite period on the strength of a single psychiatrist's signature. But the present state of affairs is unacceptable.

133

"The expanded use of involuntary hospitalization will not help non-dangerous disordered persons, because we will not spend the money necessary for adequate care."

Forced Treatment of the Homeless Mentally Ill Will Not Help

Stephen J. Morse and Kim Hopper

Stephen J. Morse is the Orrin B. Evans professor of law, psychiatry, and behavioral sciences at the University of Southern California. In Part I of the following viewpoint, he contends that forcing mentally ill patients back into hospitals will not help them or solve the homelessness problem. In Part II, Kim Hopper cites a recent law passed in New York City making it legal to forcibly hospitalize the homeless mentally ill. She argues that besides undermining civil liberties, such laws will help little. Hopper is an anthropologist and advocate for the homeless.

As you read, consider the following questions:

1. What are the limits of drug treatment, according to Morse?
2. According to Morse, what is the only justification for the forced hospitalization of the mentally ill?

Stephen J. Morse, "From Mean Streets to Mental Hospital Is No Cure for Homelessness," *The Los Angeles Times*, August 25, 1987. Reprinted with permission. Kim Hopper, "Homeless Choose Streets Over Inhuman 'Shelters,'" *The Guardian*, November 11, 1987. *The Guardian* is available for $27.50 per year from 33 West 17th Street, New York, NY 10011.

I

The appalling spectacle of mentally disordered homeless people aimlessly wandering the streets and sleeping in doorways has justifiably alarmed the public and the lawmakers. But consigning greater numbers of the non-dangerous disordered to state hospitals by broadening the commitment laws will not solve the problem. A hospital is not a home or, in most cases, the best setting for treatment.

Insufficient Resources

We must simply accept that there are insufficient resources and technology to care for, treat and rehabilitate more than a small fraction of chronic and severely mentally disordered people. Substantial misery and degradation is unavoidable, no matter what policy we adopt. The real question is how to do the best that we can for the mentally disordered and for society as a whole.

The expanded use of involuntary hospitalization will not help non-dangerous disordered persons, because we will not spend the money necessary for adequate care and treatment of increased numbers of inmates. Deinstitutionalization over the past three decades was motivated largely by the recognition that state hospitals are often human warehouses with limited therapeutic potential and that community care is preferable to involuntary hospitalization. Deinstitutionalization wasn't really tried, however. The in-patient population dropped about 80% nationwide in state and county mental hospitals, but the resources and community institutions necessary for successful deinstitutionalization weren't provided.

The Limits of Treatment

Even today, with reduced numbers of patients, the state hospitals have insufficient resources to provide adequate drug therapy, the most efficient form of treatment for the severely disordered. Moreover, the present hospital system cannot provide rehabilitation for the large numbers of people who need these services. Drugs may reduce crazy thinking, agitation and other symptoms, but they do not cure underlying pathology and they cannot teach persons to hold jobs, manage a budget or achieve the myriad other skills necessary for independent living.

If our society was and is unwilling to provide resources for decent treatment, it is naive or cynical to assert that we will spend enough in the future for expanded and ever more expensive hospitalization. We can only justify the infringement of liberty that involuntary hospitalization represents for non-dangerous disordered people if their condition improves—the discomfort that they may cause *us* is insufficient moral or legal justification. And no convincing evidence suggests that "reinstitutionalization" will provide the severely disordered with humane care and a reasonable chance for an autonomous life.

Broadened commitment criteria, even if they appear sensible and require treatment, will be abused. Studies of states with narrow commitment criteria demonstrate that one-third to one-half of persons committed did not really satisfy the statutory criteria for commitment. If the commitment criteria are broad, pressure to remove the disordered from the community will inexorably produce even more overcommitment.

Fundamental Freedoms

Whenever government proposes to remove citizens from the streets and confine them involuntarily in a mental hospital, fundamental civil liberties are at stake. Individuals are deprived of their freedom of movement and association, they are separated from friends and community and they are frequently subjected to intrusive and in some cases potentially harmful treatment procedures without their consent.

Because commitment is, in the words of the Supreme Court, a "massive deprivation of liberty," government's exercise of this power must be limited by statute and constitutional principles. Before a person can be involuntarily confined in a mental hospital . . . , the individual must be shown to have a mental illness and to present a real and present danger of substantial physical harm to himself or others. . . .

Government does not have the power to hospitalize harmless people who are capable of meeting their basic survival needs, even if they appear to be disheveled or their standard of living is considered low.

Norman Siegel and Robert Levy, *The New York Times*, September 17, 1987.

We will simply trade visible misery and degradation in the community for invisible degradation and misery in overcrowded and understaffed institutions. The only major published study of the effects of reinstitutionalization found that in the state of Washington, which broadened its hospitalization criteria, the state hospitals are once again overcrowded, adequate treatment is unavailable, many persons who were able to live in the community without hospitalization are now committed for long periods, and, most ironically, there is insufficient room for patients who voluntarily seek help. We probably will not allow state hospitals to become snake pits again, but who will pay the massive costs if the patient population increases?

The proper response to non-dangerous mentally disordered persons is to allocate sufficient resources to provide community-based treatment and rehabilitation. Many comparative studies demonstrate that community care is less expensive and as effective as in-patient hospitalization; in fact, a recent Vermont study demonstated that it is feasible to dismantle the state hospital system entirely and replace it with a network of community services. Self-help and advocacy groups run by former patients are another promising approach that should be supported. Finally, we should change the provision of care incentives to ensure that far greater numbers of the most talented mental-health professionals work with the severely disabled, rather than with the "worried well."

Homelessness is basically a social-welfare problem. It is not produced primarily by mental disorder. Few rich disordered people are sleeping in doorways, and many homeless people are not disordered. Involuntary hospitalization is not a sensible means of providing shelter to the needy. Excluding the mentally disordered from our communities will only permit us to avoid confronting the misery.

II

For the past decade or so, the number of mentally disabled street-dwellers in New York City and other U.S. cities has dramatically increased. These homeless people live in darkened shop doorways, on the median strips of avenues, in the parks, in the subterranean warren of the subways—anywhere refuge, however tentative, can be had. At night, some roam the streets foraging for food; others howl and scream; most simply do their best to pass the hours unnoticed and undisturbed.

But it can be tough to be inconspicuous when you haven't bathed for months and your clothes are in tatters; when you take on invisible adversaries in animated argument; when your possessions are strewn in large bundles around you.

Now, in the increasingly divided city that is New York, the problem is becoming too severe to ignore. A mayor whose favorite term of opprobrium is "wacko" has decided that the streets need psychiatric policing: The streets are to be swept of those who are "designatable" as so "gravely disabled" as to be incapable of caring for themselves.

Two things distinguish this measure. First, the groundwork was laid by the city's legal, hospital and mental health bureaucracies. And second, the terms of the debate during the initial days of press coverage were neatly biased to the mayor's advantage: It was mayor Edward Koch, the "number one social worker" in the city, against the "crazies," civil liberty lawyers and other advocates who questioned the legality and rational of the program.

Lack Long-Term Plans

Noted but little appreciated was the minuscule scale of the resources lined up—a 28-bed unit in Bellevue Hospital—and the apparent absence of any long-term plans for disposition or placement. It is this fact, rather than the troublesome civil liberty issues, that may prove most consequential in the long run. For in seeking to correct what he sees as the excesses of deinstitutionization, the mayor may succeed in doing what many of us thought was impossible: reopening the state hospitals. The irony, of course, will be that community-based treatment will be judged a failure, when the truth is that, except for isolated demonstration programs, it never had a chance of succeeding.

The mayor's initiative plays to a popular misconception about the forces behind contemporary homelessness, a misconception abetted by some journalists and scholars. As a *Baltimore Sun* reporter told an audience of librarians, homelessness is "just a code word for mental illness." There are clearly people with severe psychiatric disorders among the homeless poor. But that doesn't explain contemporary homelessness.

A Wrong Explanation

It is wrong to explain homelessness by invoking de-institutionalization. The major waves of depopulation of state hospitals occurred in the early and late 1960s. Yet the growing presence of the psychiatrically disabled homeless wasn't noticeable until the mid-1970s. Over half the total decline in in-patients from 1965-1985 took place by 1971; city shelters figures did not begin to rise until five years later.

The Case of Nella King

Nella King, a 59-year-old black woman . . . spent two winters warmly dressed sleeping in the doorway of a Manhattan bank. Presumed mentally ill when she refused the city's offer of shelter, she was handcuffed, strapped to a stretcher and removed to a city hospital. NYCLU's [New York Civil Liberties Union] Levy represented King and secured her release from the hospital. But even though the professionals there determined that she was sane, Nella King and others like her can be picked up repeatedly.

Susan Blank, *Civil Liberties*, Winter 1986.

Clearly other factors were at work. It isn't difficult to identify the critical one: between 1970 and 1982, the city lost 87% of its low-rent residential hotel rooms. For many ex-patients, such quarters, miserable though they were, spelled the difference between a life of hardship and neglect and one on the streets or in the shelters.

The allegation that many street people are impaired mentally easily leads to the inference that their disorder accounts for their refusal to use available shelters. On the contrary, most people living on the streets today, according to the outreach teams that undertake the difficult work of engaging them, have tried the shelters and found them too forbidding. Many are simply registering what a majority of homeless folks would tell you: the shelters offer a rough haven at best, and you had better be ready to protect self and possessions if you take the city up on its offer of refuge.

Will Not Help Most Homeless

Most important, sweeping the streets will not solve homelessness. In all probability, it won't even make much of a dent. Outreach workers generally agree that only a small minority of their clients are "designatable," even under the expanded criteria currently in force. Thus the program will directly affect only a tiny fraction of the homeless poor today—and will not find homes, even for these. . . .

Homeless men and women have gotten the word out among their numbers: it's time to hunker down, cover one's tracks, change location. Dozens of people, according to Diane Sonde, director of Project Reachout, have vanished from long-frequented spots. Sadly, the trust that outreach workers had arduously won now falls prey to new suspicions. And those who had been coaxed to try the hand of humanity one more time have retreated, again suspicious of purported offers of assistance.

The Ability
To Empathize

This exercise is designed to improve your problem-solving skills through empathizing: the ability to understand situations from another's point of view.

In this activity you and your group are asked to imagine yourselves as participants at a meeting to decide what to do about the homeless people in your community. Each group member will play the role of one of the key figures in the decision-making process.

Part I

The situation:

In recent months, homeless people have migrated to the community of Bakersville and have been setting up residence in the town's park. Many residents have complained about their appearance and behavior. The town, working with local church groups, has constructed a makeshift shelter in the basement of the old city hall, but some of the homeless refuse to stay there, saying they would rather live in the park.

Two proposals have been made. One would make it a crime to sleep overnight on public property, punishable by a thirty-day jail sentence or a one-way bus ticket out of town (depending on whether the jail was full). The other proposal, at considerably greater expense, would improve the shelter to include private rooms, a mental health treatment center, and job counseling. When the remodeling is completed, all homeless people would be required to live in the improved shelter.

The roles:

a town council member who is worried about costs and taxes, and whether an improved shelter would attract more homeless to the area

an activist from the National Coalition for the Homeless, who is not a resident of the community

a parent whose children are afraid to play in the park

a psychologist who works with the homeless in his/her spare time

a homeless person who lives with his/her children in the town's shelter

a homeless person who lives in the park, refuses offers of help, and may or may not be mentally ill

The group should discuss which proposal to recommend, if any. Each person should take one of the roles listed and argue that person's point of view. Try to imagine and explain that person's feelings about the issues involved.

Part II

After your group makes a decision, prepare a written rationale to present to the rest of the class in which you explain how you came to your decision.

Periodical Bibliography

The following articles have been selected to supplement the diverse views presented in this chapter.

Paul S. Appelbaum	"Crazy in the Streets," *Commentary*, May 1987.
The Center Magazine	"Caring for the Homeless in Santa Barbara," November/December 1986.
Holly Hall	"The Homeless: A Mental-Health Debate," *Psychology Today*, February 1987.
Jon D. Hull	"Slow Descent into Hell," *Time*, February 2, 1987.
Barry Jacobs	"Under the Boardwalk," *The Progressive*, October 1987.
Mickey Leland	"Toward a National Policy To End Homelessness," *America*, January 31, 1987.
Myron Magnet	"The Homeless," *Fortune*, November 23, 1987.
Thomas J. Main	"Hope for New York City's Homeless?" *The New York Times*, November 27, 1986.
Peter Marcuse	"Why Are They Homeless?" *The Nation*, April 4, 1987.
Scott R. Sanders	"Death of a Homeless Man," *The Progressive*, March 1987.
Society	"Homeless Families: How They Got That Way," November/December 1987.
Richard Stengel	"At Issue: Freedom for the Irrational," *Time*, September 14, 1987.
Marianne Szegedy-Maszak	"How the Homeless Bought a Rolls for Cornelius Pitts," *The Washington Monthly*, July/August 1987.
E. Fuller Torrey	"Fiscal Shell Game Cheats Mentally Ill," *The Wall Street Journal*, November 3, 1987.
William Tucker	"Homeless People, Peopleless Homes," *The American Spectator*, February 1987.
William Tucker	"Where Do the Homeless Come From?" *National Review*, September 25, 1987.
Peter Weber	"Scenes from the Squatting Life," *National Review*, February 27, 1987.

Why Does Poverty Disproportionately Affect Minorities?

Chapter Preface

Blacks are three times more likely to be poor than whites. The 1986 poverty rate was 13.6 percent of the total population, but 27.3 percent of Hispanics. Two out of three poor adults are women. What do these facts mean?

Some people argue that these statistics prove that poverty is strongly affected by racism and sexism. They assert that minorities and women face insurmountable barriers such as discrimination, low wages, and lack of federally subsidized daycare. Many people call for strong government involvement to counter the disadvantages these groups face in the marketplace.

Others argue that America is the land of opportunity where anyone with enough drive and ambition can succeed. They cite the economic success of recently-arrived Asian immigrants as proof that discrimination is not a major factor in poverty. They point out that two-thirds of the American poor are white, and believe this proves racism is not the prevailing factor.

The viewpoints in this chapter debate some of the issues involving minorities, women, and poverty.

"Blacks and other minorities have far more than their share of poverty."

Racial Discrimination Affects Poverty

Milton Meltzer

Milton Meltzer is a historian who has written many books on social issues for young people, including *The Black Americans: A History in Their Own Words*. In the following viewpoint, an excerpt from his book *Poverty in America*, Meltzer blames past and present racism for the persistent poverty of American minorities.

As you read, consider the following questions:

1. Why does the author believe there is more black poverty now than when John Kennedy was president?
2. What ethnic minorities does Meltzer write about? What different obstacles do they face in overcoming poverty?
3. How does racism continue to affect society, according to the author?

Contrary to what most people think, two-thirds of the poor are white.

But blacks and other minorities have far more than their share of poverty. The rates of poverty are highest for those groups that have long suffered the most from racial prejudice and discrimination.

Blacks are about three times more likely to be poor than whites. While one out of every eight whites is poor, one out of every three blacks and more than one out of every four Hispanics and Native Americans is poor. The average black family income is only 58 percent of white family income. And that gap has been widening for many years.

Advances and Setbacks

If you look at black Americans today, you see both the advances and the setbacks in their conditions. Advances include the victory of blacks in mayoral races—from Chicago, Los Angeles, Atlanta, Detroit, and other big cities to hundreds of smaller ones. The soaring into space of the first black astronaut. The adoption of Martin Luther King, Jr.'s birthday as a national holiday. The moving up of better-prepared black workers from low- to higher-paying positions. The great gains in the fight for black dignity, self-respect, and identity.

A short time ago, none of this would have been possible. Older Americans cannot forget how hard it has been for blacks to achieve progress. But their gains have not been enough to bring full equality with whites. Millions of blacks—and their numbers are growing—are still living in poverty, still feel hopeless about their future.

The truth is that there is more black poverty than at any time since Kennedy's New Frontier and Johnson's War on Poverty and Great Society programs. How come, when black sociologists say that "significant positive changes have taken place in white attitudes towards blacks"? The reason: long decades of racism have kept an extremely high percentage of blacks poor and unskilled. Even when times get better, many blacks are not prepared to take advantage of the opportunities.

Economic Changes

It is ironic that between 1960 and 1980 the proportion of blacks in professional, technical, and craft positions went up from 11 to 21 percent. But the percentage of blacks below the poverty line rose from 31.4 in 1973 to 35.7 in 1983. Black Americans keep sliding back in almost every part of life that counts. The reason for some of this is because of changes in the American economy. . . . Some of those forces are international. For example, Japan has 18 percent of the American car market, almost all the videotape-recorder market, most of the television-set market, and large slices of the markets for steel, machine tools, microchips, and office equipment. When have you bought a suit or a dress or a shirt that wasn't made in some Asian or Latin American country? The United States buys more goods abroad than it sells abroad. Imports are killing many American jobs. Traditional American industries are fading away, and so are the jobs these industries provided.

These forces have combined not only to keep poor people poor, but to frighten large numbers of people not yet poor but in real danger of soon being poor. The loss of manufacturing jobs is painful for anyone, but blacks are disproportionately hurt by the decay of our industrial centers.

Older blacks suffer a double danger. Not only is their poverty rate considerably higher than that of aged whites, but they have endured racial hardships all their lives, and now old age makes it even worse. A team of sociologists points out this is because blacks bring

> to their older years a whole lifetime of economic and social indignities, a lifetime of struggle to get and keep a job, more often than not at unskilled labor, a lifetime of overcrowded, substan-

dard housing in slum neighborhoods, of inadequate medical care, of unequal opportunities for education, and the cultural and social activities that nourish the spirit, a lifetime of second-class citizenship, a lifetime of watching their children learn the high cost of being a Negro in America.

Other Minorities

What about the other ethnic minorities? What risk do they run of being poor?

Immigrants continue to enter the country at a high rate. The Population Reference Bureau forecasts that 800,000 to 1,000,000 people will come in annually all through the 1980s. About half of them enter illegally, primarily from lands to the south. The urge to migrate remains high in the Latin American and Caribbean countries because their young-adult population grows rapidly and there are nowhere near enough jobs for them at home.

Hispanics

The Hispanics come with hope, but many find work only in the underground cheap-labor market. They live in fear—victims of hunger, disease, extortion, and an exploitation often close to slavery. Nearly 3 million of the American poor are Hispanics. The largest group are the Mexican Americans. They live mostly in the West and Southwest. One in four of them is poor. A large number are migrant workers. They tend to have large families, earn much less than the median income, and are less well educated than the average person.

In the Texas port city of Brownsville, for example, a school principal reported in 1984 that 90 percent of his students came to school hungry each day. Hunger cripples the attempt to learn. "In my ten years in the Brownsville system," he said, "I find the problem worse now. Most of it is due to poor nutrition. Our children are seeds for the future. The problem is that we're not watering them."

A doctor in the Rio Grande Valley of Texas who directs a health center has grown bitter about the national indifference to the Mexican Americans he serves:

> The majority of my patients wander all over America working the crops. They have no education and poor conditions. They are hungry. Our people have become human garbage. They are damned. I am told that elephants don't die of disease; they die of starvation when their teeth fall out. That is the same thing that happens to my patients.

Mainland Puerto Ricans are the next largest group of Hispanics. One out of three is poor. Only about a fourth are high school graduates. The majority live in the ghettos of New York City. They are generally unskilled or semiskilled workers who are quickly fired when times get bad. Like the blacks, they have seen their jobs vanishing from the cities. They don't have a car or the money for public transportation to follow the factories into the suburbs for low-paying jobs. Nearly 60 percent of all Puerto Rican families are headed by single women. When they work, they earn even less than men.

Cuban Americans are the next largest group. Many from the middle class have adapted readily because of superior education at home in Cuba and have done well. Still, about 14 percent of them are poor.

Race and Jobs

Since the beginnings of our society, race and sex have been major determinants of the division of labor and of the distribution of the fruits of labor. Numerous studies have documented the allocation of the worst jobs—lowest-paying jobs—by race and sex: Blacks, Hispanics and women have consistently found themselves in the lowest-paying jobs. Moreover, race and sex have been fairly constant criteria in allocating the burden of the periodic recessions and crises that characterize the economy. Minority unemployment, especially, runs consistently higher than white unemployment. It seems logical that the combination of excessive unemployment and excessive concentration in the worst jobs would generate excessive poverty.

Howard Stanbuck, *Beyond Reagan*, 1984.

In recent years large communities of Asians have taken root in many sections of the country. They, too, gather in their own neighborhoods, often in crowded tenements. Many work steadily but at very low wages. Their barriers are job discrimination and language.

As for the Native Americans, who number under one million, the poverty rate is estimated to be 45 to 50 percent. Something like half of all Native Americans live on government reservations. And 90 percent of those living on reservations are said to be poor.

Racism

Common to the fate of blacks and other colored Americans is the curse of racism. For the poverty of blacks, Hispanics, and Native Americans society blames heredity, IQ, shiftlessness, immorality. The true trouble lies with racism and the prejudice and discrimination that flow from it.

Racism is the false belief that some "races" are superior and others are inferior. Modern science has proved that no group of people is superior to another. There are simply no innate differences in ability or character from one racial or national group to another.

But racism goes back centuries in America and existed

149

worldwide before the first whites brought it to this continent. The white colonists believed that the colored peoples—the red people and the black people—were inferior, were less than human. It gave them an excuse for enslaving Africans and killing off large numbers of Native Americans. It was convenient and profitable to assert that colored people were good only for doing the hard and dirty work the whites did not want to do.

Past and Present

Over the centuries those racist beliefs were woven into custom, law, education, and religion. Racism was no longer only an act by an individual white against an individual member of a minority. It took the form of the whole white community discriminating against an entire minority. Members of racial minorities became systematically excluded from an activity or function that the larger society believed to be important. Or they were permitted only a subordinate part in it.

It became "natural" and "necessary" to segregate minority peoples and discriminate against them. Jobs, schools, churches, housing, transportation, politics—almost every area of human life was infected with racism. Even the most respected newspapers and journals—from the *New York Times* to *Harper's*—were once guilty of the crudest racism. Articles, stories, poems, editorials, cartoons, jokes by the thousands depicted blacks as stupid, ignorant, dull, lazy, vicious. And similar stereotypes, often with fresh negative variations, circulated about other minorities.

Racism may be less open and less harsh today than in the past. The civil rights struggle and changes in the law of the land have helped make a vital difference. But racism still exists, and its victims are always within its reach. It has much to do with the creation of some of the poverty detailed in these pages and in its perpetuation.

"Not only history but also economics argues against the widespread assumption that group income differences are largely a function of discrimination."

Poverty Is Not Caused by Racism Alone

Thomas Sowell

Thomas Sowell is an economist and a senior fellow at the Hoover Institution at Stanford University. His many books include *Race and Economics* and *Black Education: Myths and Tragedies*. In the following viewpoint, an excerpt from his book *Ethnic History*, Sowell argues that racial discrimination alone does not explain minority poverty. He points to Japanese-Americans, Jews, and other groups who have succeeded economically despite severe racial prejudice and discrimination.

As you read, consider the following questions:

1. How does the author compare American racism and discrimination to other countries?
2. What economic and historical reasons does the author give for questioning the link between racism and poverty?
3. How does Sowell draw the distinction between individual and group discrimination? What significance does he attach to this distinction?

Discrimination has obviously influenced the incomes of American ethnic groups. All have been discriminated against to one degree or another. Yet some of the most successful—such as the Orientals—have experienced worse discrimination than most, and the extraordinary success of the Jews has been achieved in the face of centuries of anti-Semitism. The *moral* offensiveness of discrimination has attracted much attention, but whether its *cause-and-effect* role is equally important is another question. . . .

Every ethnic group has encountered obstacles to its progress in the United States. But the obstacles and suffering they experienced before arriving here usually exceeded anything experienced on American soil. Anti-Semitism in the United States meant encountering snobbery and occupational restrictions, but not living under the threat of mass expulsions and massacres. Even the historic bitterness of slavery was worse for Africans enslaved to the Arabs or in the rest of the Western Hemisphere, where slaves died off faster than they could reproduce. In short, America has never been exempt from the ages-old sins that have plagued the human species. What has been distinctively American is the extent to which other factors have also been at work, usually for the better. . . .

Many discussions of group differences in income or occupation freely invoke such terms as "discrimination" or the even more emotionally charged (and empirically elusive) term "exploitation." While clear instances of discrimination have been encountered by many ethnic groups at various periods in their history, determining how much of the group differences in income, occupations, or housing represent discrimination is a complex and uncertain process. The very meaning of discrimination varies across a spectrum, from underpaying individuals for their current capabilities to the existence of historic barriers that inhibited the development of capabilities. Employer discrimination as an explanation of current income differences usually means that a given group is underpaid relative to its current capabilities. Historical and current empirical evidence on this point is far from conclusive, despite the axiomatic certainty of many assertions.

Differences Within Groups

Employer discrimination cannot, for example, explain large income differences among various segments *within* a given ethnic group, if employers are generally unaware of these internal differences. The poverty that is as common among Hong Kong Chinese as affluence is among native-born Chinese Americans cannot be explained by the existence of racist employers, to whom Chinese "all look alike." The substantial differences in income between first- and third-generation Mexican Americans are likewise difficult to explain by employer attitudes, when generational information is unlikely to be sought from job applicants in the blue-collar occupations in which most Mexican Americans work. Employers are even less likely to seek genealogical information that would enable them to distinguish descendants of "free persons of color" from other blacks, and it is doubtful if most employers can tell a second-generation West Indian from other blacks, or would even be interested in trying.

The purely internal differences in income have implications for differences between the whole group and the larger society. In some cases, one social segment (the Hong Kong Chinese) earns lower incomes than the national average while another segment (native-born Chinese Americans) earns more than the national average. In the nineteenth century, eastern European Jews lived in poverty, while German Jews were affluent. Today, second-generation West Indians earn more than the national average, while native black Americans earn substantially less. When whole social segments of a group—not just some fortunate individuals—have above-average earnings, it is difficult to explain lower than average earning for the group as a whole by employer discrimination, if employers do not make such distinctions within the group.

White vs. Black Talk

About 35 percent of black Americans are poor. But they're not poor mostly due to racism, age or slavery. They're poor because too many well-meaning white and black people won't deal honestly with poverty.

The polite and white talk goes like this:

"Racism causes poverty."

"We must expand opportunity to include all Americans."

"Don't blame the victims." . . .

Black talk is quite different. . . . Among themselves—when no whites are present—working blacks bad-mouth the "sorry" poor.

Some call this talk self-hatred. But that label doesn't fit. What the hard-working black American simply is saying to the black welfare recipient is, "Look, *I* have to struggle. But I'm making it. And I'm as black as you."

Lawrence Wade, *The Washington Times*, April 22, 1987.

The existence and effectiveness of economic discrimination depend on far more than the existence or degree of prejudice against a particular group. The historic prejudice and legal discriminations encountered by the Japanese were at least as severe as those encountered by Puerto Ricans, and yet Japanese incomes are more than double the incomes of Puerto Ricans and are significantly above those of Anglo-Saxons. Not only history but also economics argues against the widespread assumption that group income differences are largely a function of discrimination, rather than human capital differences or differences in age, geographic distribution, and other factors. Translating subjective prejudice into overt economic discrimination is costly for profit-seeking competitive firms, although less so for government, public utilities, regulated industries like banking, or nonprofit organizations such as universities or hospitals. Just how costly was shown by the repeated failures of white employer cartels to control the wages of newly freed blacks after the Civil War—despite having almost every imaginable economic, legal, political, and social advantage. Statistics that today compare the incomes of ethnic individuals with the "same" education, for example, as members of the general population usually ignore large *qualitative* differences in educational substance and performance. Where these qualitative differences are even approximately taken into account, intergroup differences among comparable individuals shrink dramatically or even disappear.

Other Causes

Assertions of consumer discrimination—claims that "the poor pay more"—likewise turn on group differences that are often ignored. Differences in crime rates, for example, affect the cost of running a store in many ways, leading to different prices for the same item in different ethnic neighborhoods. The honest consumer pays costs created by vandals, hoodlums, and criminals in his neighborhood, but that is different from saying that his neighborhood as a whole is being "exploited" by the store located there or by other ethnic groups. The steady exit of stores from high-crime neighborhoods suggests that there is no great profit being made there.

Ethnic groups also differ in credit repayment, and not always solely by income. Even low-income Italian Americans, for example, are considered good credit risks. The revolving credit devices, used by the Chinese, Japanese, and West Indians to finance their businesses, work only where prompt and full repayment can be relied on. Groups without the level of dependability that would enable them to use this device to raise capital among themselves are usually unable to raise capital from commerical sources for the same reason. Their failure to develop businesses cannot be arbitrarily attributed to lack of access to banks, for most small businesses (including those of Chinese, Japanese, and West Indians) are not launched with bank loans anyway.

In housing markets as well, the high cost of slum dwellings has been denounced for years, going back to the nineteenth-century immigrant ghettos on the lower east side of New York. But despite bitter denunciations of slum landlords there, the actual records show no particularly large profits being made on slums in general. High rents were indeed *charged* for a given amount of space, but profits are made only on the rents actually *paid*—and thousands of evictions per year on the lower east side indicate that the two are not only conceptually but also empirically very different. Again, the honest renter paid for the others, and the average profit rates indicate that the lower east side tenants *as a whole* were not "exploited."

The Persecution Complex

One of the problems in dealing with the expanding array of claims of discrimination—reaching far beyond the obvious and paramount victims in American history, the blacks—is that anyone looking for bias can always find it. The persecution complex is a standard psychological ill and its sufferers of every race, creed, and condition have little trouble confirming, to their own satisfaction, their visions of a hostile world.

The last thirty years in America, however, have seen a relentless and thoroughly successful advance against the old prejudices, to the point that it is now virtually impossible to find in a position of power a serious racist. Gaps in income between truly comparable blacks and whites have nearly closed. Problems remain, but it would seem genuinely difficult to sustain the idea that America is still oppressive and discriminatory.

George Gilder, *Wealth and Poverty*, 1981.

Individuals may be devastated by discrimination, even if it does not explain the economic conditions of a group as a whole. W.E.B. Du Bois pointed out, at the turn of the century, that "the individual black workman is rated not by his own efficiency, but by the efficiency of a whole group of black fellow workmen which may often be low." Race is one of many sorting devices used because of the costliness of individual knowledge. The question of group discrimination is a question about whether the group as a whole is misjudged or underpaid—a question about average performance, not individual variation. The "representative Negroes" were, according to Du Bois, "probably best fitted for the work they are doing," and if the racial prejudices of whites were to disappear overnight it "would not make very much difference in the positions occupied by Negroes" as a whole, although "some few would be promoted, some few would get new places" but "the mass would remain as they are. . . . " What Du Bois expected the lowering of racial barriers to accomplish was to provide incentives for successive generations of blacks to improve their skills and efforts. Whatever the empirical validity of Du Bois' assessment, the important point here is that he distinguished discrimination against the individual from discrimination against the group.

Even where the current capability of the group is accurately assessed in the market, particular individuals in the group may still be grossly undervalued. Du Bois himself was perhaps the classic example. But no recitation of such examples provides evidence that discrimination against the group as whole explains the group's poverty. The galling tragedy of a Du Bois or a Paul Robeson—men with superb educations and individual brilliance—was that they were held back solely by racial prejudice and eventually ended up embittered Communists.

A Complex Question

In other groups as well, it has been precisely some of the most acculturated and talented members who have been the most bitter, militant, or extreme. The inference made by them and by others was that no amount of *group* acculturation, skills, or efforts would be any more successful than their individual development had been. Some of the Japanese interned during World War II reached the same despairing conclusion. But however understandable their anger and despair, later events showed that the inference was neither logically conclusive nor historically correct. Within a generation after the internment, Japanese Americans were among the most affluent, socially accepted, and generally respected groups in the United States. This took about half a century from the beginning of Japanese immigration, and many of the virulent racists they encountered along the way could not have been changed by any conceivable thing the Japanese could have done. But the mortality of human beings, and therefore the turnover of individuals in the population, enabled the quiet persistence of the Japanese to ultimately win out on every economic, social, and political front. . . .

The point here is not to definitively solve the question as to how much of intergroup differences in income, social acceptance, etc., have been due to the behavior and attitudes of particular ethnic groups and how much to the behavior and attitudes of the larger society. The point is that this is a complex question, not a simple axiom.

"Our society's economic deck is stacked against women . . . more than any other group in our society."

Sexism Keeps Women Poor

Vicki Kemper

Vicki Kemper is a writer and editor for *Sojourners*, a magazine published by the Christian organization of the same name. In the following viewpoint, Kemper notes that two out of three poor adults in America are women and that poverty among women is rising. She cites two reasons for this discrepancy. One is that women looking for work are traditionally segregated into jobs with low pay. The other is that despite changes in American society, women are still primarily responsible for raising children, and this task has been supported less and less by government programs and absent fathers. Kemper concludes that these poverty trends, if continued, could have serious effects on society.

As you read, consider the following questions:

1. What lessons does the author draw from the story of Nona? Do you agree with her conclusions?
2. According to the author, why are jobs not the "ticket out of poverty" for women? What evidence does she provide tò support her opinion?
3. What has caused the increase of one-parent families, according to the author? What significance does she attach to them?

Vicki Kemper, "Poor and Getting Poorer," *Sojourners*, March 1986. Reprinted with permission from *Sojourners*, Box 29272, Washington, DC, 20017.

That women are poor is nothing new; that women are poor is nothing unusual. Women have been exploited as property to be bought and sold, as goods to be bargained and bartered, since biblical times. Women have been forced to depend upon men for their economic survival in primitive, feudal, industrial, capitalist, socialist, communist, and even our most "advanced" societies. . . . Economic, political, professional, and sexual discrimination have been experienced by women of every race, class, and culture.

Women have always been disproportionately poor, and many women have been poor their entire lives. But many of the social movements of the past 20 years, particularly the women's movement, have attempted to redress the social and economic inequalities suffered by women throughout history. Yet for all our "progress," for all the gains made in women's rights, . . . there are more poor women than ever, and they are getting poorer.

Two out of every three poor adults in this country are women. And a 1981 study by the National Advisory Council on Economic Opportunity, to stress its point about the rapidly growing impoverishment of women, concluded that if the current trend were to continue "to increase at the same rate as it did from 1967 to 1978, the poverty population would be composed solely of women and their children before the year 2000." It is the frightening picture painted by these sobering statistics that social scientists and feminists have labeled the "feminization of poverty."

Lowering Expectations

Forty-six-year-old Nona, like many black women from the South, wears poverty like a birthright:

> I've been poor all my life. I've never owned anything. I have always had to get out and work. . . . I never had anything where I could go to the bank and get money. Most things I own are secondhand.

So effective was Nona's society in lowering her expectations that she doesn't think of her poverty as related to the fact that she is a black woman. Her life has been "sorta tough," she says, quickly and proudly adding that she's managed all right and humbly mentioning that she can't complain because, after all, she's made some mistakes.

"Mistakes" and Causes

However, many problems and "mistakes" that might appear to be causes of poverty actually are the effects of manifestations of long-term poverty. Nona talks openly about her lack of education, her now-reformed alcoholism, the fact that she wasn't married to any of the three men who fathered her five children, and that, although she is unemployed and receives welfare payments, she recently turned down a job offer. But she discusses the many difficult circumstances of her life—many of them completely beyond her control—only after more direct questioning.

Nona was born in South Carolina to a poor, unmarried woman. She describes her mother as an alcoholic who never married but lived with a man who sold whiskey and ran an in-house gambling operation. "Life was sorta tough. . . . I didn't have too much of a childhood before I was a mother [at age 15]. . . . I wasn't married to the father of any of my children. . . . I was married for a few years. We lived together for two years before we married, and that time was better than after we married. He beat me."

Fourteen years later Nona still remembers the biggest paycheck she ever got: $189.17 for two weeks' work, plus overtime, running the electric knife and saw at a turkey factory. But the work was sporadic and offered little pay and no benefits, so in 1971 Nona moved to Washington, D.C., hoping to find better work. She often worked two jobs at a time—housekeeping and commercial laundry most often—but due to alcoholism and unrelated health problems, she hasn't been employed for several years now.

She "barely makes it" supporting her two youngest children—one slightly mentally retarded—and one of her seven grandchildren on her welfare and Medicaid benefits, food stamps, and some support from the children's father. But she recently decided

THE MAJORITY OF THE FUTURE POOR WILL BE WOMEN AND CHILDREN. (NEWS ITEM)

© Huck/Rothco

not to take a job cleaning dormitories at Washington's Howard University because she would have earned less on her minimum-wage salary than she now receives in welfare benefits. . . .

Nona is fed by her modest hopes and dreams for her children. "Even though she is a girl," she says of her 7-year-old daughter, "I want her to make a decent living for herself. Even though they say girls just get married . . . even if she does, I want her not to have to depend on someone else."

But throughout history most social and economic systems have been based, in part, on women's economic dependence and their subjugation to men and the male-ordained values of profit, power, and patriarchy. And while American women have made many social, economic, educational, and political advances in the last 20 years, their contributions to the labor market continue to be valued far below those of their male counterparts—an inequity that further perpetuates their dependence. Yet the very male-dominated system that fosters such dependence has become less and less dependable. . . .

Two Unique Factors

Our society's economic deck is stacked against women—particularly black and Hispanic women—more than any other group in our society. In addition to our society's structural factors that affect all people, certain gender factors also are at work to increase the likelihood that a certain woman, and women as a class, will be poor. There are two major factors unique to women's economic status: women's unequal position in the labor market and women's child care responsibilities.

Until very recently the structures and demands of the American economic system—legitimized, supported, and reinforced by religion, patriarchal families, education, and popular culture—dictated that family and career were mutually exclusive for most women. At the end of the 19th century, more than 95 percent of all married women in the United States stayed at home to do unpaid household work. As late as 1940, only 15 percent of married women were being paid for work outside the home.

But as birth rates declined, mass schooling for children increased, and labor-saving devices in the home became more widely available, more women, including wives and mothers, moved into the labor force. The percentage of women who were wage workers increased from 18.2 percent in 1890 to 45 percent in 1974, and their representation in the labor force increased from 17 percent to 39 percent over the same period.

"Women's Work"

Yet women did not enter the labor market at the same level as their male counterparts. As a result, jobs—usually considered the best way to get out of poverty—offer no such ticket for women.

160

In 1870, when very few women were in the labor market, 97.5 percent of all clerical workers were men, and they earned twice as much as blue-collar workers. As women began taking jobs outside the home, several types of occupations became "women's work," and the pay was correspondingly lowered. Today 80 percent of all clerical workers are women, and their median income is $10,435 a year—considerably less than that of most blue-collar workers.

Poverty Is a Disease

Poverty is a disease whose symptoms are depression, frustration, and exhaustion. The desperation of poverty spreads like a cancer on our society. Once afflicted, a woman no longer has the luxury to choose her destiny. She cannot afford to take a job and pay for day care, and thus lose Medicaid and Food Stamp benefits. She is exhausted by the trauma of living in substandard housing, from the harassment of landlords, the power company, the welfare system; from standing in line for commodities; from rummaging through Salvation Army clothing bins, and keeping her home clean when there's no money left for cleaning supplies, from caring for her children with little or no relief. And society calls her lazy.

Dorothy Campbell, *Daughters of Sarah*, November/December 1986.

In 1984 almost 50 million women were employed, representing a record 43 percent of the U.S. labor force. More than 53 percent of all women over age 16, and 55 percent of all mothers, work outside the home. But about half of all working women work in occupations that are at least 80 percent female and that usually have lower pay and benefits than predominately male categories. Women earn, on the average, about 60 cents for every dollar a man earns; for minority women the figure falls as low as 54 cents per dollar.

Employers have used varying rationales to justify lower salaries for women. For years employers argued that women worked outside the home only for "pin money" rather than to support their families and, therefore, should not be paid as much as male laborers. Yet studies conducted by the Women's Bureau of the Department of Labor as early as the 1920s and 1930s—when women earned only 43 percent of what men did—found that about 90 percent of all working women were working out of economic necessity.

The male-female pay differential has been most commonly explained as a function of differences in skill, education, training, and experience. But a recent study concluded that "about 35-40 percent of the disparity in average earnings is due to sex segregation," which results in lower-paying "women's work." Occupa-

161

tional sex segregation was not created and has not been maintained by women's own career choices; it is due largely to discriminatory barriers such as "social stereotyping," hiring and training practices, and the education system's record of steering women into lower-paying jobs, the study found. . . .

Some other statistics about women and work:

• It takes a woman nine days of full-time labor, on the average, to earn what a man makes in five days.

• Sixty percent of all female full-time, year-round workers earn less than $15,000 a year.

• Black mothers who work full time, year-round, have a poverty rate of 13 percent, the same rate as white men who do not work at all.

• Minority women are most likely to work in the lowest paid of all women's jobs and to experience the most extreme poverty of all.

• If wives and female heads of households were paid the same as similarly qualified men, half the families now living in poverty would not be poor. . . .

Raising Children Alone

The low-paying jobs and occupational discrimination women face in the labor market mean greater poverty in the home, especially in homes where no adult male is present. Women have always had the primary responsibility for raising children, but as more and more women are forced to raise their children alone, the impoverishment of women and children increases proportionately.

The number of one-parent families has doubled since 1970, increasing from 13 percent to 26 percent—more than one-quarter of all families with children under 18. Here again the problem is even more acute for minority families. Among white families the proportion of one-parent families has increased from 10 percent to 20 percent since 1970; for black families the increase was from 36 percent to 56 percent. But, even though nine-tenths of those families are headed by women, the statistics that focus strictly on female-headed families are even more staggering. The percentage of families headed by women has increased 84 percent since 1970.

There is no widely accepted explanation for the dramatic increase in single-parent families. But changing societal attitudes about sexuality and marriage certainly account for some of the shift. As premarital sex has become more and more widely accepted and as many couples have chosen to delay or reject marriage, the number of children born to unwed mothers has skyrocketed. In 1982 more than 55 percent of all black children were born to single mothers. And while ideas about sexual morality have changed, the perception of gender roles has not.

162

As a result, men now have new opportunities to avoid responsibility for supporting their children—leaving women to bear the
load alone. Divorce and the high unemployment rate for young
black men also play a role in the increase of single-parent families.

The welfare system also has been a factor. Until the 1960s
families headed by men were automatically ineligible to receive
Aid to Families with Dependent Children (AFDC) payments. Even
now 29 states still refuse to make welfare or Medicaid payments
available to two-parent families, no matter how poor. The inevitable result of such policies is to break up such families or
discourage marriage between parents caught in poverty. . . .

Whatever the reasons for the astounding increase in female-
headed families, the impact on women and their children has been
devastating. While the poverty rate for the general population is
14.4 percent, 40 percent of all families headed by white women
are poor, and the poverty rate for families headed by black women
is 60 percent. . . .

Government Policies

Even in the very brightest moments of the history of the U.S.
government, its welfare policies have been designed to treat only
the symptoms of poverty rather than to address the systemic
causes of widespread poverty. Rather than compensating for the
racist and sexist injustices of the nation's economic system, government policy reinforces, maintains, strengthens, and, in many cases,
encourages the injustices. But current U.S. government policy fails
even to adequately compensate the victims of such systemic inequities, much less to attack the root causes of poverty. . . .

Federal spending programs to aid poor Americans—62 percent
of whom are women—has decreased 16 percent. Military spending, meanwhile, has increased by 38.5 percent. This shift of
public resources represents a net transfer of roughly $30 billion
a year from the poor to the Pentagon. . . .

In their traditional roles as wives and mothers, women have provided the emotional, logistical, and physical sustenance, support,
and stability that have often proved to be the very foundation of
our society. Though they have often been relegated to menial positions or excluded from participation altogether, women have provided the labor and support most essential and intrinsic to the
survival of the workplace, places of worship, and other social
institutions.

Because women have offered our society so much, their poverty affects all of us. As increasing numbers of women become
poor, society as a whole will suffer. Cracks already can be seen
in our societal foundation; there are small rips in the social fabric.
The increasing impoverishment of women must be arrested and
reversed for women themselves, for their children, and for all of
us.

"If every vestige of discrimination were to vanish instantly, their [poor women's] situations would remain essentially unchanged."

Sexism Does Not Explain Female Poverty

Mary Mainland

Mary Mainland is a mother of three and a lawyer. In the following viewpoint she challenges feminist "myths" about poverty and sexism. She questions statistics showing women are paid less than men and concludes that discrimination has little effect on women in the work force. Mainland believes many feminist proposals such as comparable worth will do more harm than good to poor women.

As you read, consider the following questions:

1. According to Mainland, what has the greatest impact on female wages? Does she believe this signifies sexism? Do you agree?
2. Why does the author believe that comparable worth proposals would harm poor women?
3. What does the author think about feminist proposals for a "just" society? What do you think?

Mary Mainland, "Feminist Myths Reconsidered," *America*, December 15, 1984.
Reprinted with permission of America Press, Inc., 106 West 56th Street, New York, NY 10019. © 1984 All Rights Reserved.

In [an] issue of *America*, Rhode Island state senator David R. Carlin Jr. characterized the contemporary women's movement as part of the quest for human rights, an assessment reflecting the consensus, particularly among the educated, that discrimination by a male-dominated society has made women, in important respects, second-class citizens.

Although the feminist movement has gained women some of the rights historically denied them, the battle is not yet won. Enactment of the remainder of the feminist political agenda is necessary if women are to realize their full human potential. In synopsized form, this is the conventional wisdom subscribed to, not only by feminists, but by virtually every politician and mainstream journalist. Rare dissenters like George Gilder and Phyllis Schlafly are routinely dismissed as reactionaries determined to perpetuate sexism. . . .

Oppressed?

Yet, to paraphrase that politically effective query, "Where's the evidence?"

A dispassionate observer of women in the developed West, the locus of feminism, will find few, if any, of the usual indices of an oppressed or seriously disadvantaged group. Women live longer than men, on the average, and are at least as healthy. Their lower suicide rates and the lack of any cogent evidence that they are more likely than men to be unhappy or embittered, or to be afflicted with mental illness, belie the bleak psychological portrait painted by feminist writers. . . .

Lies and Statistics

Much ideological ammunition has been generated from the statistic that women's earnings average only 62 percent (recently up from 59 percent) of those earned by men. Closer analysis of the figure gives credence to the old quip that there are "lies, damn lies and statistics"; the real disparity is between married women, who share their husband's income, and all other wage-earning adults, including single women. Married women average about 25 percent as much income as married men, the group with the highest earnings. However, single women earn about 91 percent as much as single men, even though substantially fewer women are in such highly paid occupations as the construction skilled trades and medicine, and many more must cope with the conflicting demands of single parenthood and paid employment.

Marriage and motherhood, not gender per se, clearly have the greatest impact on female earnings. Married women are more likely to work part time and to drop out of the labor force for extended periods of time, both factors associated with lower incomes. In addition, women's career choices have tended to reflect their role as the primary caretakers of children. Teaching has been attractive because it permits women to be home after school and during summer vacations; nursing shifts may be timed to coincide with the husband's return from work. Moreover, such fields as teaching, nursing, editing and clerical work involve knowledge and skills that do not readily become obsolete. The editor or nurse who leaves the profession for a few years typically suffers less damage to her career than, say, a physicist, who is likely to return to a field revolutionized by discoveries made in the intervening period.

Feminism and Poverty

Feminists are becoming increasingly aware of the role of divorce and out-of-wedlock births in generating poverty for women in the United States. Previously it was thought that poverty was simply a function of omnipresent sexual discrimination. But the feminization of poverty in this country has come about precisely as sexual discrimination has decreased—thanks to social and legal prohibition. Divorced and unmarried women with children frequently do not marry; as a result, their children are raised in single-parent households. There are now 10 million female-headed households in the U.S.; 35 percent of them live below the poverty line.

Dinesh D'Souza, *Policy Review*, Winter 1986.

So long as large families, delayed weaning and shorter life spans were the norms, marriage effectively ended women's career aspirations. Biology is no longer so determinative, although maternity leaves, however brief, are still essential, while paternity leaves are not. Nevertheless, even among couples where the woman's career choice reflects an aversion to sexual stereotypes, the traditional male-female division of labor seems to be continuing.

Work and Family

In the public law office where I now work, seven of the 15 lawyers are women, three of whom have small children and are married to lawyers. Two of the three work part time and the third has expressed the desire to do so, once a slot becomes available. Each of their husbands works full time, as do all of the male lawyers in the office, married or single. Apparently, my office is not unusual. A recent article in the Los Angeles Daily Journal, a legal publication, reported trends among married women lawyers of childbearing age to work less than full time and to choose specialties, such as estate and tax work, that adapt more easily to part-time careers than, for example, litigation.

Nothing suggests that these women feel pressured to subordinate their careers to those of their husbands, or that they are unhappy with the arrangement. Why should they be? An intellectually and financially rewarding career coupled with more time for children and personal pursuits makes an enviable combination.

Like most men, most women work because they need the income. Black women have traditionally worked more consistently than white women, even after marriage, because the higher unemployment rate among black men has forced them to do so. Some years ago, a middle-aged black woman with whom I was working expressed her gratitude to her husband, despite his fairly obvious faults. His steady employment had allowed her to remain home with their children, a luxury unavailable to many of her friends. . . .

Discrimination?

In her recent book *Sexism and Godtalk*, feminist theologian Rosemary Ruether notes, without examining the implications, that the previous peak of female employment in high-status, traditionally male professions occurred between 1900 and 1920. The 19th Amendment, however, was not ratified until 1920, and it seems improbable that discrimination against women increased after they obtained the vote. A more persuasive explanation is that educated women in the earlier period were marrying later, if at all, and having fewer children, demographic factors also associated with the more recent influx of women into predominantly male professions. Those who would credit the women's movement with the recent increase ignore the fact that the upward trend had begun before the affirmative-action policies and signal court victories of the early 1970s.

The class with which I entered Stanford Law School in 1968 had the then highest percentage of women in the school's history, slightly more than 10 percent, as I recall. In succeeding years, women have risen to become about 37 percent of the nation's law students, and at some schools are at least 50 percent. Women have apparently not needed the recruitment and preadmission measures widely instituted to draw more blacks and other ethnic minorities into the law. For some time, for example, one of the Stanford deans has been assigned to recruit qualified blacks, Hispanics and Native Americans; to my knowledge, no comparable efforts have been directed to women. Medical schools have seen similar increases in the number of women students. Again, there has been no apparent dearth of women with the requisite educational background and admissions test scores. The speed and relative ease with which they have penetrated male strongholds do not, of course, prove that women have not been subjected to overt discrimination or subtly sexist pressures. It strongly suggests, however, that discrimination against women has been of a vastly different order of magnitude from that against blacks and has been far less damaging.

However, during the same period that the percentage of women in law and medicine nearly doubled, female-headed households came to account for almost half of all those living below the poverty line. Mr. Carlin acknowledges that poorer women have gained little from "their" movement. Nevertheless, he is confident that its benefits will eventually "trickle down" because of his belief that it is essentially a human rights movement. Such optimism seems warranted only if the so-called "feminization of poverty" is attributable to some form of sex-based discrimination. Even the most superficial analysis discloses the lack of foundation for such a view.

The largest category of poor women consists of unmarried mothers of dependent children. Some are widowed, but most are the victims, if you will, of divorce, desertion and unwed pregnancy, not discrimination. No one has come up with policy proposals that offer promise of reducing the divorce rate, and the usual feminist prescriptions for curbing unwed pregnancies are, to say the least, unconvincing: If more freely available abortions, contraception and sex education are the answers, why is the unwed birth rate higher now than before abortion was legalized and contraception and sex education became widespread? California is not immune to the trend, even though its state supreme court has ruled that abortions for poor women must be publicly funded. As the columnist William Raspberry pointed out, Washington, D.C., with one of the highest unwed birth rates in the nation, is also one of the three jurisdictions where sex education is mandatory.

Ignoring the Facts

While the pay of men and women is significantly different in many cases, there is very little evidence that this is due to widespread discrimination on the part of American business.

To charge that the situation is the outcome of some vast plot—as do many activist feminists—is to ignore the facts and rely on emotionalism and unsubstantiated conjecture.

Martin Lefkowitz, *Human Events*, January 10, 1987.

The salient characteristic of female-headed households is that only one adult is available both to care for children and to work. Any single parent, no matter how affluent, knows the problems entailed. However, the women at the bottom of the economic ladder tend to have limited educations, few job skills and, if they are among the increasing number of unwed teen-age mothers, neither the maturity nor the discipline necessary for both parenthood and employment. If every vestige of discrimination were to vanish instantly, their situations would remain essentially unchanged.

None of the current feminist demands is likely to be of much utility to the women whose plight evokes serious public policy concern, and one, comparable worth pay, can only further handicap the woman with minimal job skills and experience. An employer forced to upgrade the pay for a given job will naturally seek to hire qualified and, hence, more productive workers. The woman formerly employable at the lower wage will now be competing, not only with better qualified women, but with men attracted by the higher pay the job now affords. In some cases, it will be possible for employers to substitute capital for labor, just as automatic elevators supplanted human operators when it became cost-effective to do so. The net effect will be the foreclosure of some of the limited number of options now open to poorer, but striving women.

Wholly ignored are some foreseeable, if unintended, consequences of various feminist proposals. If pensions become more easily obtainable, and therefore more costly for employers, fewer will offer them and/or the benefits will be reduced. If all jobs, irrespective of the nature of the work involved, must be restructured to accommodate women's employment patterns, productivity will inevitably be impaired. Some jobs adapt fairly easily to job-sharing, flex-time and similar modifications; others do not. No lawyer, for example, would have the temerity to demand that judges schedule proceedings so as to accommodate child-care arrangements and maternity leaves, nor would clients, other lawyers, witnesses and jurors be appreciative. With the exception of criminal defendants, participants in judicial proceedings invariably want them concluded as soon as possible.

However equitably intended, public policy cannot obviate the necessity for choice, or its consequences. Women and men seeking to reach the peaks of demanding professions will have little time to devote to children. Teen-age girls who are sexually active are likely to become pregnant. If both spouses in a two-lawyer household work part time, neither will be eligible for lucrative partnership status.

"Having It All"

To the more extreme feminists, trade-offs are merely manifestations of pervasive injustice. In a truly just society, "having it all" would be a viable and societally guaranteed option. The nebulously democratic socialist society envisioned by Rosemary Ruether in *Sexism and Godtalk* is illustrative: "[It will be one] that dismantles sexist and class hierarchies, that restores ownership and management of work to the base communities of workers themselves who then create networks of economic and political relationships. Still more, we seek a society built on organic community, in which the processes of child-raising, of education, of work, of culture have been integrated to allow both men and women to share child-nurturing and homemaking and also creative activity and decision-making in the larger society."

During several of my years as a lawyer I was also the single mother of three; I can only marvel at Professor Ruether's faith in the capacity of the political process to transform human nature and eliminate life's more trying exigencies. The amorphous beings who will populate this equally amorphous society will evidently need little sleep, yet have vast reservoirs of energy. Husbands and wives will have careers and schedules that mesh perfectly; clients and customers will be unfailingly patient; appliances will be totally dependable, or, alternatively, service people will arrive when scheduled; activities ranging from the ridiculous to the sublime will be juggled easily and without frustration; conflicts, if they arise at all, will be settled reasonably and without rancor. Most awe-inspiring of all, children will have been programmed to time illnesses, school problems and demands for attention so as never to interrupt or inconvenience their creative and decision-making parents.

As Jake Barnes in Hemingway's *The Sun Also Rises* said in response to Lady Brett's view that life could have been beautiful despite her nymphomania and his impotence, "Isn't it pretty to think so?"

"Our work today is not to change the minds of white people, but to involve ourselves in the lives of black people."

Lack of Initiative Keeps Blacks Poor

Glenn C. Loury

Glenn C. Loury is a professor of political economy at the John F. Kennedy School of Government at Harvard University. His writings have appeared in *The New York Times* and *The Wall Street Journal*. In the following viewpoint, Loury says American blacks must take responsibility for their own problems, rather than blaming racism and looking to the federal government for solutions.

As you read, consider the following questions:

1. Why does the author feel that black economic development ultimately depends on "black action"?
2. What problems does Loury see with government "solutions" to poverty?
3. What lessons does the author draw from black history?

Glenn C. Loury, "A Prescription for Black Progress." Copyright 1986 Christian Century Foundation. Reprinted by permission from the April 30, 1986 issue of The Christian Century.

Black Americans confront a great challenge, and an enormous opportunity. The black struggle for equality, born in the dark days of slavery and nurtured with the courage and sacrifices of generations who would not silently accept second-class citizenship, now threatens to falter and come to a stop—short of its historic goal. Throughout America, in the rural counties of the Black Belt, in the slums of Harlem, in North Philadelphia, on the west side of Chicago, on the east side of Detroit, in south-central Los Angeles, in East St. Louis, Illinois, in the ghettos of Houston, Oakland, Newark and scores of smaller cities and towns, literally millions of blacks live in poverty, and, all too often, despair.

Of course, it is not only blacks who experience poverty or who deserve our concern. I focus on this group for two reasons. First, the problems associated with civic exclusion are especially severe for blacks and originate from a unique history of central importance to our nation. Second, I am convinced that group cohesion, identity and mutual concern are key assets in the struggle for equality. So I address the situation of this particular group—my group. Undoubtedly much of what I say can be applied to other groups as well.

Must Accept Responsibility

The great challenge facing black America today is the task of taking control of its own future by exerting the necessary leadership, making the required sacrifices, and building the needed institutions so that black social and economic development becomes a reality. No matter how windy the debate becomes among white liberals and conservatives as to what should be done, meeting this self-creating challenge ultimately depends on black action.

It is unwise (and dangerous) to suppose that any state or federal government would, over the long haul, remain sufficiently committed to such a program of black revitalization. It is to make a mockery of the ideal of freedom to hold that, as free men and women, blacks must sit back and wait for white Americans, of whatever political persuasion, to come to the rescue. A people who languish in dependency, while the means through which they might work for their advancement exist, have surrendered their claim to dignity. A genuinely free people must accept responsibility for their fate. Black America's political leaders have too often failed to face up to this fact.

One way of framing the choice now confronting blacks is to ask, "What does it mean today to be an advocate for the poor?" I propose a different answer to this question than one could infer from the historic practices of those now most widely recognized as "black leaders." My central theme is that poor black people have the wherewithal to begin to make fundamental improvements in their lives, given the opportunity. An advocate for the poor, from this perspective, is one who provides the means for poor people to help themselves develop to their full potential. An advocate for the poor is not someone who perpetuates the dependency of poor people, teaching them by example that their only option is to hold out their hands to accept gifts from others.

Obstacles

In order for the black self-help movement to flourish and prosper, several forces which work to impede or distract this effort must be recognized. As a case in point, some elected officials at the state and federal level are unwilling to consider efforts that would spur self-help activities because of their attachment to past, misguided programs. These legislators retard progress when, for example, they oppose even trying urban enterprise zones in areas of high urban unemployment, but instead urge a return to massive Great Society schemes which have no chance of passage in this era of $200 billion deficits. . . .

Racial Discrimination Has Declined

Racial discrimination has declined as a fact of American life. Poor, non-white immigrants have come to the country in large numbers in the past two decades. Many blacks have themselves moved out of the ghettos and into the middle class. It's simply no longer plausible to hold that limits on opportunity alone account for the pathological conditions of social life in ghetto communities.

Glenn C. Loury, *New Perspectives Quarterly,* Winter 1987.

Yet another major obstacle to the goal of black empowerment is the quality of leadership supplied by many black elected officials. In local, state and federal elections around the country, the black masses are constantly told that sending a black elected official to the mayor's office, the state capital or Congress will lead to the solution of their plight, simply because the candidate is black. Yet, in many big cities around the country where blacks are in positions of power, the same lack of economic development can be observed in the black ghettos (which constitute the politicians' key political base) that can be seen in white-controlled cities. It is not suggested that all black politicians are unworthy of their people's support; but there should be mechanisms to evaluate and discipline indifferent political leaders so that they would be forced to adopt positions and pursue programs that contribute to the economic and social advancement of their constituents. The sad fact is that these disciplining forces are few in number.

Unfortunately, poor blacks seldom seem willing to exercise this kind of critical judgment of the performance of their leaders. Black elected officials who have done little, other than parrot the lines of white liberals, seem to be re-elected regularly. Because of the long history of racism, many blacks mistakenly place group solidarity and considerations of loyalty above a common-sense evaluation of a politician's on-the-job performance. Many black incumbents seem immune to challenge by another black, since it is easy to cast the challenger as somehow being "a white man's nigger."

Some of these rascal incumbents should be voted out of office. But even before that, poor blacks should structure an ongoing system of monitoring a politician's day-to-day performance. Regularly scheduled public political forums and community-based newsletters are but two examples of how to match deed with need.

"Experts" and Communities

John L. McKnight, associate director of the Center for Urban Affairs and Policy Research at Northwestern University, has made an accurate assessment of how our society views its poor: "What we have done for many poor people is to say to them you are sentenced to be a consumer and a client, you are denied the privileges to create, to solve problems, and to produce; you have the most degraded status our society will provide."

McKnight, recounting an experience he had in a low-income community during the 1960s, tells of "poverty experts" who came into a town of 20,000 residents to conduct "needs surveys." All too predictably, they discovered there were severe problems in the areas of housing, education, jobs, crime and health.

In his role as a community organizer, McKnight took note of the "public-policy experts" from both the public and private sectors who were sent in to "solve" the community's problems. They included public housing officials, land clearance experts, housing development counselors, daily-living skills advisers, rodent removal experts, weatherization counselors, teacher's aides, audiovisual specialists, urban curriculum developers, teacher trainers, school security advisers, civil rights consultants, job developers, job counselors, job classifiers, job location specialists, relocation program specialists, job trainees, small business advisers, police aides, correctional system designers, rehabilitation specialists, a juvenile counselor, diversion specialists, social workers, psychologists, psychiatrists, health outreach workers, health educators, sex educators, environmental reform workers, caseworkers, home-budget management trainers, lead inspectors, skills trainers, and administrators and managers to coordinate all of these activities. In short, overkill. McKnight termed this situation an example of an economic development plan for people who *don't* live in the neighborhood.

McKnight concluded his observation by remarking with bull's-eye accuracy:

> I know from years in the neighborhoods that we can rely on community creativity. You have heard about it today over and

over again. It is the most exciting thing that's happening in America. America is being reinvented little by little in the little places, but there is much more wealth that could be freed up, made available,, if we understood that we have a big investment in the poor but their income is radically misdirected into the hands of service professionals.

McKnight's example is all too familiar to those who are aware of the profusion of misdirected and misinformed approaches to "solving" the problems of the country's low-income citizens. This miscalculation of black capabilities is not by any means restricted to white America. . . .

Past Achievements

Blacks must examine their past objectively, taking what is valuable from it and rejecting those notions that have proven unworkable. Over many decades and under much more adverse circumstances than exist today, blacks have made impressive progress—without the benefit of the civil rights laws and welfare transfers that now exist. I do not suggest repeal of those laws. I merely urge that we not permit ourselves to become wholly dependent on them.

There are many examples of the impressive accomplishments which our ancestors managed under difficult conditions. The literacy rate among blacks rose steadily after emancipation, though free public schools were virtually unknown in the South. Independent black businesses and entire black towns flourished in the late 19th century. Modern research has shown that despite the terrible economic and social oppression to which the slaves were subjected, they created a vibrant familial, religious and cultural tradition which continues to enrich black America.

Working the System

There has always been racism, and there's always going to be racism. What you have to do is get around it. You can't use racism as an excuse. Black people can learn how to work their way through the system, and we don't give enough credit to those who do. The energy you spend complaining about racism is energy you could have spent trying to figure out how to work the system.

Frank Mingo, *Harper's Magazine*, February 1987.

Among the black migrant communities in the North in the early years of this century, the kind of social dislocation and family instability that plagues today's black ghettos was virtually unknown. In 1925 in Harlem, 85 per cent of black families were intact, and single, teenage mothers were virtually unknown. In Buffalo, New York, in 1910, blacks exhibited similarly strong family structures, despite the virulent racism which they faced at that time. The point is that without liberal apologists to tell them what little they could do for themselves or how inevitable their misery, poor black folk in years past were able to maintain their communities and establish a firm foundation for their children's progress.

Local Development

This heritage is the underpinning of a collective black strength waiting to be tapped today. To revive a value system that nurtured and enriched the lives of yesterday's black America, a dynamic and continuing process of economic, political and social development must be initiated to furnish the soil in which the seeds of black pride and accomplishment can take root and sprout. Some activists, like Robert Woodson of the National Center for Neighborhood Enterprise in Washington, D.C., have begun to explore the components of an economic rejuvenation process that could launch such a large-scale self-help movement. To be successful, however, these suggested programs must be built upon, expanded, revised and adapted to the varying conditions of local communities. We must, in the words of Chairman Mao, "let a hundred flowers bloom!" The time is now ripe for blacks to spearhead such an effort. With everything to gain and little to lose, a spirit of black adventurism could lift the community beyond dependency to self-sufficiency.

It is important to understand that I am *not* arguing here against the ancient and still valid notion that there is a public responsibility in a decent society to contribute to the alleviation of poverty, black or otherwise. In the areas of education, employment training, and provision of minimal subsistence to the impoverished, the government must be involved. Some of the most innovative and useful private efforts are sustained by public funds. There are publicly supported programs—preschool education, for one—which are expensive, but which research has shown pay an even greater dividend. It is a tragic error that those of us who make the self-help argument in dialogue concerning alternative development strategies for blacks are often construed by the political right as making a case for "benign neglect."

The Self-Help Philosophy

Black America cannot lift itself by its bootstraps into great wealth overnight. But there is a great unexploited potential for change at the level of the black individual and the local black community. In the current environment it is evident that blacks must exploit this dormant opportunity. The self-help approach—more a philosophy of life than a list of specific projects—must be initiated as a matter of necessity, not ideology. . . .

It is crucial that blacks not become so caught up in seeking welfare state handouts that we lose our own souls. The very important, but essentially private, matter of the indignities our ancestors suffered due to their race must not be allowed to become a vehicle for cheap brokering with the welfare state. The generations of blacks who suffered under Jim Crow deserve something more than simply having their travails used as an excuse for current failures. Our work today is not to change the *minds* of white people, but to involve ourselves in the *lives* of black people. Past black sufferings should not be hauled out to gain guilt money. Such a posture is pitiful and unbecoming of black America's proud heritage. Dependency, even when one is dependent on sympathetic and generous souls, is destructive of dignity—and dignity is a necessary precondition of genuine freedom and equality.

"The social and economic devastation of black America is just too vast to be remedied by self-help efforts alone."

Lack of Government Help Keeps Blacks Poor

Roger Wilkins

Roger Wilkins is a senior fellow at the Institute for Policy Studies, and the Robinson Professor of History at George Mason University. He also writes a regular column for *Mother Jones*. In the following viewpoint, he states that racism is still a major problem in America today, and that government has a responsibility to help the poor and combat racism. Wilkins contends that black leaders acknowledge and promote community development and "self-help," but that these efforts are not enough to solve the enormous problem of black poverty.

As you read, consider the following questions:

1. What flaws does the author find in the conservatives' arguments?
2. In what forms does racism exist in America, according to Wilkins? Do you agree or disagree?
3. According to the author, when should a society take collective action instead of individual action? Are the author's examples relevant to race and poverty?

Roger Wilkins, "Not by Bootstraps Alone," *Village Voice*, February 4, 1986. Reprinted with permission of the author and the Village Voice © 1986.

On one of those rare summer nights when the brutal Washington heat had temporarily succumbed to a gentle breeze, I sat around a suburban swimming pool with my wife and some good friends and ate by the light of flickering candles. . . .

The guests were educators, government officials, people from the Hill, successful business people and journalists. The guests were, in the main, all sleek and accomplished, and they were all black.

Despite the laughter and the table of flowers, I couldn't fully enjoy myself that night because the raw wound of Tunica, Mississippi, which I had just seen that morning, made my mind retreat time and again from my friends' conversation to gloomy ruminations about the state of black people in this country, about the capacities of fairly affluent blacks to improve the plight of the black poor, and about the conclusion of the conservatives, black and white alike, that self-help and individual initiative are now virtually the only means to a better future for impoverished black people.

Sugar Ditch

Those ruminations tore my thoughts away from that Maryland poolside to the 100-degree heat in Tunica that morning and to the memory of the roaches I had seen crawling around an open bag of Mueller's macaroni that a black woman named Jearline Simmons, who lives in a part of Tunica called Sugar Ditch Alley, had bought with her food stamps just the day before. Sugar Ditch is a five-foot wide open sewer where the people who live between the ditch and alley dump buckets containing their body wastes, used cooking fluids, dirty bath water, and all life's other leftovers that we at the dinner party would simply flush down our toilets, grind-up in our disposals, or let run down our drains.

Sugar Ditch emits an overwhelming stench, which seeps into the dilapidated wooden dwellings and carries a swarm of germs that, according to the residents, makes all of them—especially the children—sick a good deal of the time. Some of the houses in Sugar Ditch Alley are owned by white Tunica city officials; the rest are owned by other substantial white citizens of the community. . . .

Standing in the alley . . . it seemed almost inconceivable that 38 millionaires could live in that county. . . .

White Wealth and Black Poverty

Inconceivable, that is, until I recalled the lush green fields of soybeans and new cotton that stretched to the horizon along both sides of the road from Memphis. Tunica calls itself the Gateway to the Mississippi Delta, which is one of the most fertile agricultural areas in the country. And then, of course, I knew that it was not at all inconceivable for great white wealth and bitter black poverty to coexist on rich farm land. That is the stuff of

179

"WHEN THE PRESIDENT TAKES HIS ECONOMIC PROGRAM TO THE PEOPLE, DOES THAT MEAN *US*, MA?"

which much of the economic history and much of the lyrical literature of the South is made. The blacks of Sugar Ditch Alley whose human substance was being squeezed for white profit were the lineal descendents of generations of black slaves and the generations of black peasant sharecroppers who succeeded them. . . .

A question kept troubling my thoughts through the evening. It was the charge that those of us at dinner were doing a disservice to our fellow blacks by persisting in pointing to the continuing ravages of racism and by insisting that white America had an obligation to face and fight racism rather than pretend it has gone away. This is the posture adopted by President Reagan in his practice of virtually ignoring black leaders such as members of the Congressional Black Caucus and heads of major civil rights and black service organizations while appointing and heeding a handful of blacks who have greater followings among white conservatives than they do among black people. That basic attack on traditional black leadership is augmented by arguments from such black conservatives as Clarence Pendleton of the United States Commission on Civil Rights, Thomas Sowell of the Hoover Institution at Stanford, and Glenn Loury of Harvard, that go something like this: The civil rights battles have been fought and largely won; social programs have been marginal at best and harmful in the main; black self-help efforts in entrepreneurial ventures and education will provide virtually the only solution to remaining problems.

At the heart of this argument there is an assumption that traditional black leaders willfully ignore the "fact" that conditions are ripe for self-help programs to become the sole engine for black progress because they don't want to dwell on problems that cast blacks in a bad light. The conservatives have in mind here such problems as the high rate of teen pregnancies or a diminished work ethic or limited interest in school found in some segments of poor black communities. Thus, their argument goes, conventional black leaders' continued demands on the larger society are unimaginative extensions of the failed strategies of the sixties. . . .

False Ideas

The accusation that black leaders only know how to ask for bigger government is clearly false; the claim that the possibilities for black self-help are being ignored, and that self-help alone can provide the answer to the problems of black Americans, is both wrong and simplistic. No matter how necessary self-help efforts may be, they are only a part—and, considering the intractability of continuing racism and the massiveness of the need—only a small part of the overall answer. Self-help alone, for example, can not possibly be the entire answer to the racism and the misery of Tunica, Mississippi. . . .

Moreover, conservatives tend to link their calls for self-help with attacks on the Great Society as if the efforts were mutually exclusive. Great Society money and the heightened expectations of the times gave blacks all over the country the wherewithal and the motivation to engage in the most broadscale and most vigorous self-help program in modern history. Many blacks who had never believed they could participate in activities and efforts to improve their own lives became active in everything from early childhood education to such a bewildering array of entrepreneurial efforts that even the coldest heart in the Opportunity Society claque would have been warmed. As the federal funding disappeared, many of these activities melted like the snow before the springtime sun, but a strong residue remains. . . .

A final problem with the conservatives' position is that it asserts that the civil rights victories have all been won, that the legal propositions are now all settled, and that it thus is time to move on to perfecting the black community. To assert this while the Reagan Justice Department and Civil Rights Commission are doing everything they can to tear down the principle and enforcement structure of civil rights makes no sense at all.

The Powers of Government

Only the government can break the hold of structural unemployment which has permanently laid off black men or denied first time jobs to their sons. We have created over 30 million jobs since 1950, but only a million of them are in manufacturing and most of those are far removed from the central city.

Only government—not the black community—can create an economy of mainstream, high paying jobs, the kind that made this a middle-class society for the majority of white Americans. Only government can do something about the fact that in 27 states families are forced to break up because no form of welfare is available for two parent families that are unemployed. Only government can enforce equal employment laws and affirmative action which brought about the amazing progress in the last 15 years that led to the creation of the black middle-class.

Eleanor Holmes Norton, *New Perspectives Quarterly*, Winter 1987.

Racism is an organic part of American culture; it adapts and metastasizes as the society changes. We now know that the *Brown* decision did not automatically desegregate the schools of America or improve the education of black children. We also know that many school boards in this country are shortchanging black children just as many employers are shortchanging current and potential black employees. Moreover, as the syndicated columnist Neal Peirce recently pointed out, America is rapidly resegregating itself by erecting new high-tech, high-priced, and mostly white suburban communities. These unplanned communities—like those along Route I near Princeton, and Route 128 near Boston—rob the nearby older cities of a tax base and their inhabitants of both housing and employment opportunities.

The social and economic devastation of black America is just too vast to be remedied by self-help efforts alone. Forty-five per cent of black men over the age of 16 are jobless; more than half of the black children under six are growing up in poverty, and more than a third of the black population is impoverished. It is not just the magnitude of these problems, but their impact on the broader society, that makes them national rather than black problems. These statistics also give the lie to the notion that the nation's struggle for civil rights is over. . . .

Outside Help Needed

So, it is important to separate carefully those tasks that blacks should be tackling by themselves and those for which massive outside help is still required. It should be remembered, however, that even in those areas where strong initiatives should come from the black community, much outside help will someday be needed. Thus, community-restoring efforts such as changing teenage sexual attitudes and behavior requires school systems to provide effective sex education and postnatal educational opportunities. Programs to drive drugs out of black neighborhoods need to be supplemented by strong and sustained police work. Programs to instill black youngsters with the work ethic and good work habits need to be joined with public and private commitments to provide them with skills and job opportunities. . . .

Values and Jobs

When I was employed by newspapers, editors would sometimes show me pictures of hundreds—sometimes thousands—of blacks lined up for jobs at a new enterprise that, at best, would be hiring 50 people. They would print such pictures with the best will in the world to communicate the message that blacks *did too* want to work. And it was right for them to do so. But another message was communicated to those who stood unsuccessfully waiting out there. The message was that the work ethic can't work when there is no work, and people had to find another way to "get over." Values cannot be changed in a jobless vacuum. So even here, at the heart of black responsibility, it is not a question of either/or, but rather a matter of self-help plus the assistance of others.

Finally, the scale and the complexity of the *entire* problem of black poverty are the issues which ultimately undermine the "self-help is the sole answer" argument. That brings me back to Tunica. The people there are in urgent need of health care, of better housing, of water and sewage services, and of jobs. As Margaret Boyd told us:

"What I need is a job. There's no jobs around here. You can't fight nothing and you can't fix nothing without a job."

In Tunica, the cause and effect are easy. It is clear that the plight of the people in that community stems directly from the racism and the greed of at least a segment of the people who run the town. That plight is perpetuated by other powerful people whose indifference permits them to worship with their shutters and their eyes closed to the suffering of their fellow citizens. Though the connections don't leap up and bash an observer in the head as they do in Tunica, Mississippi, the connections are just the same and just as clear for the Tunica called Central Harlem and the Tunica called South Central Los Angeles.

A Civilized Society

Now all the effective, affluent, and idealistic black people in America could probably band together and deplete their energies and their bank accounts and fix Tunica, Mississippi, but they surely can't do that for all of the Tunicas all over this country. A civilized society takes collective action because it has certain standards and because there are some things that are too large and too complex for even the sturdiest and most resourceful individuals to do for themselves. We have laws against drunk driving because that activity is a known menace to human well-being. And we have laws subsidizing the irrigation of farmland in the West because we don't believe they can do it for themselves and because we believe we're all better-off if those lands don't lie fallow.

Racism is alive and deadly in America today. Anyone who doesn't believe so is as ignorant and willfully ideological on this subject as President Reagan has been on South Africa. The impact of racism is every bit as menacing to human well-being as that of drunk driving. And it is worse to allow human beings to lie fallow than it is to do so to land. It is not civilized for people to suffer helplessly and jobless as too many do both in Tunica and in Central Harlem. As American capital engages in both a ceaseless worldwide search for cheap labor abroad and plays Russian roulette with businesses at home—with virtually no regard for what happens in local labor markets like Detroit, Youngstown, and Pittsburgh, where tens of thousands of blacks and good, lifelong work habits are now unemployed through no fault of their own—it is stupid to suggest that blacks can go it alone. This nation must adjust to new international economic realities, get hold of its own economy, its capital, its bloated military appetite—all with a view toward the well-being of its people, including the most vulnerable of them.

The devastating impact of two and a half centuries of slavery and another century of legal segregation are not in the past. They live with us every day in American places both high and low, but in some places like Tunica, they are absolutely murderous. It is true that we blacks who are closer to the problems have a special responsibility to extend ourselves in these difficult times even more than we have in the past. But so has our national community a special responsibility to expend effort and resources to help us all out of the horrible historical rent in the fabric of our civilization that racism always has been and still continues to be.

Recognizing Stereotypes

A stereotype is an oversimplified or exaggerated description of people or things. Stereotyping can be favorable. However, most stereotyping tends to be highly uncomplimentary, and, at times, degrading.

Stereotyping grows out of our prejudices. When we stereotype someone, we are prejudging him or her. Consider the following example: Mr. Smith believes all poor people are lazy. Whenever he sees a homeless person on the street or on television he asks himself, "Why won't that person look for a job?" He disregards any other possible reason why that person is homeless. Why? He has prejudged all poor people and will keep his stereotype consistent with his prejudice.

The following statements relate to the subject matter in this chapter. Consider each statement carefully. *Mark S for any statement that is an example of stereotyping. Mark N for any statement that is not an example of stereotyping. Mark U if you are undecided about any statement.*

If you are doing this activity as a member of a class or group, compare your answers with those of other class or group members. Be able to defend your answers. You may discover that others will come to different conclusions than you. Listening to the reasons others present for their answers may give you valuable insights in recognizing stereotypes.

S = *stereotype*
N = *not a stereotype*
U = *undecided*

185

1. Many Jews have succeeded economically despite anti-semitism.

2. Jews have a way with money.

3. Two out of three poor adults are women.

4. Most people on welfare are lazy.

5. Many black youths do not have jobs.

6. Many black youths don't want to work.

7. Divorced men are chauvinists who refuse to pay child support.

8. Mothers do not make good workers.

9. Many poor people live in single-parent households.

10. Most Hispanics are illegal immigrants.

11. Women are more likely than men to quit work to raise their children.

12. All white businessmen discriminate against women and minorities.

13. In cities across the country millions of blacks live in poverty.

14. Many women have babies in order to go on welfare.

15. All people who want to cut welfare are racists.

16. The poor are different from the rest of us.

17. Most feminists are social radicals.

18. The median income of Japanese-Americans is higher than that of Anglo-Saxons.

Periodical Bibliography

The following articles have been selected to supplement the diverse views presented in this chapter.

William R. Beer "The Wages of Discrimination: Comparing Salaries," *Current*, November 1987.

Donna Day-Lower "Her Shattered Dream: A Look at Women and Unemployment," *Sojourners*, March 1986.

Dollars & Sense "Women at Work: Gender and Inequality in the 80s." Special issue available from the Economic Affairs Bureau, Inc., 1 Summer St., Somerville, MA 02143.

Troy Duster "Purpose and Bias," *Society*, January/February 1987.

The Economist "The New Poorest," September 13, 1986.

Barbara Ehrenreich and Frances Fox Piven "The Feminization of Poverty," *Dissent*, Spring 1984.

M. Stanton Evans "The Facts Behind 'Vanishing Family,'" *Human Events*, February 8, 1986. Available from 422 First Street, S.E., Washington, DC 20003.

Gertrude S. Goldberg and Eleanor Kremen "The Feminization of Poverty: Only in America?" *Social Policy*, Spring 1987.

Peter Goldman "Inside Trey-nine," *Newsweek*, March 23, 1987.

Harper's Magazine "Forum: Moving Up at Last?" February 1987.

Kristin Helmore and Karen Laing "Exiles Among Us: Poor and Black in America," *The Christian Science Monitor*, November 19, 1986.

David Maraniss "The Third World Here at Home," *The Washington Post National Weekly Edition*, September 7, 1987.

Sylvester Monroe "Brothers," *Newsweek*, March 23, 1987.

Salim Muwakkil "Merging Strategies To Aid Black America," *In These Times*, February 26-March 11, 1986.

M.G. Pat Robertson "The Wealth of Black Families," *Conservative Digest*, June 1987.

Can Government Programs Alleviate Poverty?

Chapter Preface

America does not have a unified system of helping the poor. The welfare system includes a variety of federal, state, and local programs described by former President Jimmy Carter as "a crazy-quilt patchwork system stitched together over decades without direction or design." Reforming the system, however, is complicated by widely differing opinions on the government's proper role in helping the poor.

Some people argue that welfare programs actually increase poverty: By enabling both fathers and mothers to forego supporting their children, welfare fosters a dependency on government that is self-perpetuating. This view asserts that, instead, the primary goal of welfare reform should be to make people self-sufficient. Many advocate workfare programs in which welfare recipients must work or participate in job training programs.

Other people say the primary goal of welfare is to ensure protection from poverty and its effects. They argue that whether a person has enough money to live on is more important than whether that money came from a job or from the government.

The following viewpoints illuminate some of the debates about the role of government in aiding the poor.

"What we are buying with all these programs is a vast reduction in poverty, misery and sickness."

Welfare Has Reduced Poverty

Spencer Rich

The welfare system in the US was developed in order to, among other things, increase the standard of living for the poor and provide them with opportunities that normally may not have been a possibility. In recent years, these programs have been attacked as being costly and extremely inefficient. In the following viewpoint, Spencer Rich, a reporter for *The Washington Post*, takes issue with these arguments. He documents that welfare has indeed improved the lot of the poor.

As you read, consider the following questions:

1. How many Americans would fall below the poverty line if welfare were eliminated, according to the author?
2. According to the author, what would be the direct effects on the poor if welfare were scrapped?
3. If the vast sums spent on welfare were diverted into the public economy, would this advance economic growth, according to Rich?

Spencer Rich, "Look Again: The Anti-Poverty Programs Do Work," *The Washington Post National Weekly Edition*, May 21, 1984. Reprinted with permission of The Washington Post.

Was the federal government's war on poverty in the 1960s and 1970s a failure? Many Americans think so.

In November 1980, a CBS-New York Times national poll found that 62 percent of the public believed that the anti-poverty programs of the '60s either had little impact on the poor or made things worse for them. Another poll taken in 1982 found that 41 percent of all Democrats thought that providing government benefits to poor people encourages them to remain poor.

President Reagan has said, "In the early '60s, we had fewer people living below the poverty line then we had in the later 1960s after the great war on poverty got underway. And there has been from that moment on a steady increase in the level of poverty right up to" the present.

These skeptical views, however, have a serious flaw. The evidence clearly shows that a much smaller percentage of Americans live below the poverty level today than when the effort to attack the problem got underway in earnest. There has not been a "steady increase in the level of poverty," as the president said. Indeed, the opposite is true. . . .

Census Bureau Statistics

Census Bureau data back up this analysis. The official poverty rate stood at 22.4 percent in 1959, three years before publication of Michael Harrington's "The Other America," which described the nation's poverty subculture. The percentage of Americans living below the official poverty level dropped rapidly during the 1960s. In 1965 it had fallen to 17.3 percent. It hovered between 11 and 12 percent in the 1970s and only began rising again in 1980, when a severe recession began. It reached 15 percent in 1982, but was still considerably lower than in 1959.

In 1959, according to the official Census Bureau definition, 39.5 million Americans out of about 180 million were living in poverty. In 1982, 34.4 million were counted as poor, even though the nation's population had risen to 230 million. (The official definition of poverty has been basically unchanged for a generation. It covers anyone whose cash income from all sources is less than three times the cost of an adequate diet as defined by the government. In 1982, a family of four with income below $9,862 was considered poor.)

The total number of poor people is even lower when non-cash benefits such as Medicare, food stamps and rental subsidies are counted.

The strong American economy of the past two decades undoubtedly helped improve the economic status of the nation's disadvantaged. But so did the intricate mesh of programs enacted in that period.

According to a study done for the House Ways and Means Committee by the Congressional Research Service, one American in four would now fall below the poverty level without government support programs, compared with the actual portion of about one in seven in 1982, the latest year for which accurate data are available. Put another way, government cash benefits of one kind or another are keeping some 23 million Americans out of poverty who otherwise would be there.

Even more dramatic, 55 percent of the nation's elderly would be living in poverty today if there were no government programs at all. . . .

The Benefits of Good Intentions

"The costs of good intentions" has become a term of ridicule when used by conservatives of liberal programs. Well, what about the "benefits of good intentions"? Due in large part to federal programs, the percentage of Americans called poor was cut in half in the 1960s. Current government studies indicate that some 40 million more Americans would be below the poverty line if there were no government transfer programs. According to a 1960 Senate report, "at least one-half of the aged cannot afford decent housing, proper nutrition, adequate medical care." Today, the percentage of elderly who are poor approximates the percentage for the non-elderly population, about 13 percent. Recent follow-up studies of children who participated in the Head Start Project—which aims to stimulate pre-school cognitive development of disadvantaged children—found they had significantly higher reading and arithmetic test scores than peers who had not participated in the program. Sar Levitan and Robert Taggart, manpower experts at George Washington University, conclude in their book *The Promise of Greatness* that "the 1960s programs and policies and their continuation had a massive, over-whelming beneficial impact and that the weight of the evidence convincingly supports this view."

Mark Green, *Winning Back America*, 1982.

The [Reagan administration's] casual dismissal of the post-1965 programs as ineffective in reducing poverty is puzzling.

It is indisputable that the initiatives of the Johnson-era war on poverty, and actions taken in the Nixon administration that followed it, substantially enlarged New Deal income-support programs and added a battery of new "safety net" devices.

From the start of the Kennedy administration to the end of the Ford administration, the federal government vastly increased the flow of aid to the poor, the near-poor, the elderly, the disabled and the jobless.

In 1972, Social Security benefits were increased 20 percent and were indexed to inflation, a development that Sheldon Danziger of the University of Wisconsin's Institute for Research on Poverty calls "the single most important factor in reducing poverty in the last 20 years." In 1965, Johnson and Congress pushed through two giant medical aid programs: Medicare for the aged and Medicaid for the poor. A tiny food stamp started on a pilot basis by John F. Kennedy as his first official act in office in 1961 was gradually expanded until, in 1974, Congress made it into a full national program. It now has 21 million beneficiaries a month— nearly one American out of 10 at any one time.

The federal government also united into a single program aid to the aged, blind and disabled who were poor, with a guaranteed minimum benefit. The price tag on this ran to the billions of dollars. And the government undertook to increase the amount of money flowing to the poor to help pay rents.

Alleviating Poverty

All this more than tripled the real amount of federal and state income and medical support laid out between 1965 and 1982 to low-income, elderly and disabled people, many of whom would otherwise be poor. By 1982, the actual dollar figure had risen to more than $300 billion. And this does not even include federal aid to education, job training and various other types of programs.

These programs, costly as they have been, have had a major impact on alleviating the poverty that existed in the early 1960s. The best way to measure the effect of all these income programs, according to [former Reagan administration social welfare expert] Martin Anderson, is to calculate how many people would be poor were it not for these programs. Such calculations have been made by a number of economists and by the government.

Statistics published by the Congressional Research Service and by Danziger estimate that a quarter of the American population would have fallen below the official poverty line in 1982 were it not for government-support programs. That would total about 58 million people, according to CRS. . . .

There are two ways of calculating the impact of the programs. One counts the effect only of cash benefits. That is the official Census Bureau method, unchanged for a generation. According to this method, payment of cash benefits such as Social Security, welfare and unemployment checks cuts the poverty rate to 15 percent—in effect, removing 23 million people from the poverty category.

But if the value of non-cash benefits such as food stamps, housing aid and medical assistance is factored in, the poverty rate goes down even more. There are controversies about how to make these measurements. Liberal politicians do not believe, for example, that medical benefits should be included, arguing that this is tantamount to saying the sicker a person is, the richer he or she is.

Nevertheless, many economists believe these benefits should be included in some form. Timothy M. Smeeding, an economist

193

at the University of Utah and consultant to the Census Bureau on poverty measurement, made his own estimate of what the rate would be if the non-cash benefits were included. According to Smeeding, the 15 percent rate for 1982 would drop to between 8.5 and 9 percent. The Census Bureau, in its own calculations, puts it slightly higher, at 10 percent or so.

As that suggests, non-cash benefits have been among the fastest growing of all social benefits since 1965, climbing from $5.8 billion to $98.5 billion when measured in 1982 dollars. That is why the poverty rate goes down so sharply when these programs are included.

The System Works

The welfare system has worked. It's alleviated a great deal if not all of the deprivation in the US.

Sar Levitan, *The Christian Science Monitor*, April 5, 1985.

These calculations raise some interesting questions about what life would be like for Americans if there were no such benefits.

According to the CRS calculations, if it were not for government programs there would be 14 million to 16 million elderly people in poverty instead of only a few million now. This would mean a vastly greater dependence on their children, including sharing homes to a much larger extent than now.

Suppose all the government programs were wiped out for people of all ages.

"There would be a lot of starvation. A lot of people would be willing to accept extremely menial jobs. A lot of people would be living together," says Henry Aaron, economist at Brookings Institution and a former assistant secretary of what was then the Department of Health, Education and Welfare in the Carter administration.

Dr. Jacob A. Brody, associate director of the government's National Institute on Aging, says experts agree that the health of the aged has improved in recent years, with higher life-expectancies and, beginning shortly after Medicare (which now covers 30 million Americans), "an astonishing decline" in death rates. "I don't think there can be any doubt that Medicare is a factor in improving the health of the aged," he says.

For example, "lowering blood pressure is one of the very potent life-prolongers" and Medicare treats the elderly for that. Since Medicare, blacks, who as a group tend to suffer more than others from high blood pressure, "are going to doctors" for high blood pressure.

194

Cataract operations, cancer surgery, pneumonia treatment—all these life-preserving or life-enhancing treatments—and many more are now available to many older people who couldn't previously obtain them.

Welfare and Economic Growth

The argument has occasionally been made that if the vast sums spent by the government on the income and related programs were somehow stopped and diverted into the general economy, it would produce such an increase in economic growth that everyone would ultimately be better off, even those to whom those benefits now go.

But Alice Rivlin, former director of the Congressional Budget Office and now director of economic studies at Brookings, says, "We don't know what would happen. Certainly a lot of people would be worse off. There is no evidence that I know of that saving would be much larger" or that it would be a great spur to the economy.

John Palmer, former assistant secretary of Health and Human Services, states, "There would be somewhat stronger economic growth. But it wouldn't begin to pay for the income loss to these people."

"I haven't seen any demonstration backed up by any statistics to show that wholesale elimination of income assistance programs would increase economic growth in the U.S.," according to Brookings' Aaron. Even if it did, he adds, it wouldn't help elderly people unable to work or welfare mothers with children who would find it difficult to get and keep jobs.

So the secret is out. What we are buying with all these programs is a vast reduction in poverty, misery and sickness. Whatever the cost of these programs, it must be acknowledged that they have changed the American social landscape for the better. They have moved the country closer to its own lofty ideals of a society that is compassionate to the disadvantaged, as well as rewarding to the fortunate.

"We have to start rethinking what constitutes compassion and appropriate intervention."

Welfare Has Not Reduced Poverty

Charles Murray

Charles Murray is a senior research fellow for the Manhattan Institute for Policy Research. In 1984 he published *Losing Ground,* a controversial and influential study of American poverty and the Great Society welfare programs of the 1960s. Murray concluded that these programs discouraged work and self-sufficiency and helped to create the poverty they were supposed to cure. He concluded that welfare programs should be stopped entirely. In the following viewpoint, an interview with journalist James Bovard, Murray discusses his ideas.

As you read, consider the following questions:

1. What is the "structuralist" view on poverty? Does Murray hold this view?
2. According to Murray, what was the fundamental mistake of the Great Society programs?
3. What does Murray think would happen to the poor if all welfare programs were scrapped?

Charles Murray, "Conservatives, Liberals, Both Wrong on Poverty," *Human Events,* December 8, 1984. Reprinted with permission.

Question: Mr. Murray, in your book you say that American social policy took a grave turn for the worse in the 1960s. Where exactly did the Great Society go wrong? What were Presidents Kennedy's and Johnson's original goals and what happened?

Answer: It's very important to keep separate what Kennedy and Johnson wanted to do, and also to keep separate what Johnson initially wanted to do, from what was being done by the end of his term. Kennedy wanted to use training and economic opportunity to give people a hand, not a handout. That was also the goal of the people who first manned the Office of Economic Opportunity under Johnson.

The first anti-poverty bill was entirely comprised of measures that would give opportunity to people who were looking for a chance to better themselves. Then, at the same time this was going on, the structuralist view of poverty (of which Michael Harrington was the most visible proponent) took over. The structuralist view said that it is not the poor's fault that they are poor, it is not their fault they are on welfare, it is not their fault they are unemployed. . . . The system is to blame.

That intellectual consensus took over with little public debate. By 1965 or 1966, it was assumed intellectually that of course the system is to blame, of course you can't expect people to be getting off welfare. . . .

The Welfare Explosion

Question: What caused the explosion of AFDC rolls in the 1960s and 1970s?

Answer: The explosion in AFDC [Aid to Families with Dependent Children] rolls is most easily explained by the fact that between 1960 and 1970 what became reasonable behavior changed radically both for women and men who were poor.

This whole issue has been hard to talk about because it has gotten so intertwined with the racial issue. I say we can explain what happened without worrying about the racial issue at all. If you take a look at the set of incentives facing a young woman in 1960 if she found herself pregnant, versus those in 1970, you see vast changes.

In 1960, if she went ahead and had the child and tried to keep the child, she would be getting a very small AFDC payment and that would be just about her only source of support. There were no food stamps, no Medicaid, no other kinds of housing support that she could get.

Secondly, she could not supplement that AFDC payment by looking for a job because she would lose her welfare payments. And thirdly, she could not live with the man who was the father of the child without getting married because she would lose benefits.

So all her incentives pushed her toward getting the guy to marry her—and if that didn't work, to put the child up for adoption or make some other arrangement. And there were also a lot of women who tried a lot harder to avoid getting pregnant in the first place.

By 1970, all three of those situations had changed. The money she could put together from a package of AFDC and food stamps

"WHY, HONEY CHILE, IF IT WASN'T FOR MAH GRACE AN' BENEVOLENCE, YOU AN' YO' FAMILY WOULDN'T BE WHERE YOU ARE TODAY."

Steve Benson. Reprinted by permission: Tribune Media Services.

and a variety of other supports was about equal to what she could earn from a minimum wage job.

Furthermore, she could supplement that income with a job, thanks to the 30-and-a-third earnings deduction rule. Finally, not only could she live with the father of her child, or any other man if she chose, it was financially to her advantage to do so. Because the man who was not married to her was not legally responsible for the care of her child.

Women did not necessarily sit down and rationally calculate that "I'm going to have a baby so that I can get on welfare." But, in the way that people make day-to-day decisions about their lives, it was easier to end up on AFDC even if you'd never planned that in the first place. The AFDC rolls exploded because of the same kinds of incentives that you and I respond to all the time.

Question: You mentioned the 30-and-a-third rule, whereby AFDC recipients were allowed to keep the first $30 they earned and a third of everything on top of that. What effect did this have? Wasn't this intended to give welfare mothers an incentive to work?

Answer: The 30-and-a-third rule exemplifies a classic mistake of the Great Society programs. We always focused on the incentives for the people who were already in the condition we wanted to change. We never took a look at the incentives affecting people who were not in that condition.

The 30-and-a-third rule suffered from tunnel vision. What are the effects of the earnings incentive for the women already on AFDC? Well, she will have some incentive to get a job and maybe eventually get off AFDC. What we neglected to note is that it also had an effect on women who were not on AFDC but could potentially become eligible for AFDC.

And what has been determined by economists with their models, and what could also be determined by less elaborate means, is that the downward pull is much greater than the upward push. We have found that again and again. In educational policy, in crime and justice policy, in jobs programs, in all these cases, we ignored the effects of the change on people who were not yet exhibiting the problem that we were trying to cure.

Changing the Rules

Question: You say in your book that the past 15 years have produced much worse social and economic conditions for blacks than could reasonably have been expected in 1966. Why?

Answer: Let me start out by saying what didn't change them. And this is a message that conservatives need to pay attention to. We did not simply add a few dollars on to welfare payments and cause these problems. And it was not simply a few minor changes in the rules that now we can turn back and everything will go right.

We had a complex, interlocking series of changes in the rules that affected every dimension of life for poor people. When we changed the eligibility rules for welfare, and we increased the benefits for welfare, and we decreased the penalties for engaging in criminal behavior, and we decreased the penalties for not attending and behaving in school, and we decreased the rewards for learning in school—all of these interacted with each other.

So that a young person in 1970 was dealing with a world in which the sensible thing for him to do in the short term was something that probably was going to lock him into poverty for the rest of his life.

We too often think in terms of the welfare loafer living off the dole. That's not what really happens. What happens is that young people, age 16 to 24, go through that critical period in their lives

199

moving in and out of the labor market. And a lot of the job leaving is not people getting laid off, but people just walking away from the job. People work in the underground economy for awhile, or they have access to welfare payments through a girlfriend, or parents, or whatever.

Making Things Worse

There are many more people currently living below the poverty line than there were prior to the start of the War on Poverty. The poor today suffer from more crime, poorer education, higher illegitimacy rates, and more unemployment—all traceable to the very programs that were supposed to improve their lot. The quality of life among America's poor is far worse today than before the Great Society programs; the likelihood of the poor escaping from the poverty trap is much less. While our goal was giving the poor more, what we really did was create more poor. We thought we were breaking down barriers that would help the poor escape from poverty, but we only ended up building a poverty trap from which little escape seems likely. Anyone who doubts the truth of these claims needs only to spend a short time in the abject misery of a big-city ghetto.

Ronald Nash, *Christianity Today*, June 14, 1985.

By the time they are 22, 23, 24, they have no skills, they have no record as a worker that will enable them to slowly get more seniority that will get them a better job.

They are locked into the very bottom layer of the job market and they will never get out. This is the tragedy: they have behaved quite sensibly from week to week and month to month and suddenly they find themselves with no way out.

Question: So government encourages the young to sell short the future?

Answer: That's a very good way of putting it.

Latent Poverty

Question: You invented a term called "latent poverty" and called it "the most damning statistic." What is latent poverty and why is it so important?

Answer: When we first started the War on Poverty, virtually everybody wanted to make this the measure of success: Are people able to make a decent living and depend on themselves? That was the commonly understood goal of these programs. The best measure of success is the percentage of people—especially working-age people—able to make a decent living by their own efforts.

The official poverty measure is not meaningless. But it includes all income—including payments from government. Latent poverty refs to all those people who either are poor, or would be poor, in the absence of government aid. It subtracts all the income coming from government and asks whether the remaining income is above or below the poverty line.

What we find is that latent poverty was going down steadily from earliest figures from the end of World War II until about 1969. Then latent poverty began to increase. The number of people who were poor, or would be poor without government help, started to climb, and climbed consistently through the 1970s and into the 1980s.

Explanations

The question we have to ask is, why this should have happened? The first explanation is the increase in the number of elderly. But that does not really explain it. Latent poverty has been climbing more rapidly among the working-aged than among the elderly.

The crucial explanation is that the few years preceding the turnaround in latent poverty saw an unprecedented, extraordinary withdrawal from the labor force by people most likely to be in poverty—young black males.

In 1965-66, at a moment when the national unemployment rate was under 4 per cent, at a time when the economy was red-hot, young black males started dropping out of the labor force at rates much faster than they had before, and at the same time that white male teenagers were increasingly coming into the labor force.

During the same years, the unemployment ratio of young blacks to young whites got worse. If you have people who are not participating in the labor force, you have poor people. And you have the increase in latent poverty as one of the consequences. Of course, the big increase in single mothers also had a lot to do with the increase in latent poverty. . . .

Removing Status

Question: You state in *Losing Ground* that government destroyed status rewards for the poor in the 1960s. What do you mean?

Answer: In poor communities, as in wealthy communities, there are very elaborate structures of status that make a lot of difference in how happy you are from day to day with your life. If you have the respect of your neighbors, if you have a reputation in the community, it makes a great deal of difference in how you fare.

Once we decided that the system was to blame for people being without jobs, or poor, or on welfare, there was an inevitable flip side to that.

Once it became impossible to blame people for being chronically unemployed, it also became impossible to praise people for plugging away—for working at a menial job and taking care of their families.

Once we introduced what we called means-tested programs that had nothing to do with whether you were disabled or out of a job, but with your income level, we in effect put all poor people on welfare—made them all eligible for welfare.

Poor people could no longer brag that they had never taken a penny of charity and always pulled their own weight. Because to do that after a certain time was not a boast, but rather a statement of how naive you were if you continued to behave that way.

To refuse to take food stamps, to refuse to take public assistance when your income was low enough to make you eligible was the behavior of the foolish, not the proud. A very important source of status was removed. . . .

The Limits of Social Programs

Question: You claim in your book that social programs in a democracy almost always do more net harm than good when dealing with the most intractable problems. Are you sure that is not an exaggeration?

Answer: That law is stated specifically to deal with the most intractable problems. I argue that such programs—for example, ones that try to deal with hard-core unemployed as opposed to the youngster looking for his first job—will inherently tend to have enough of an inducement to produce bad behavior and not enough of a solution to stimulate good behavior; and the more difficult the problem, the more likely it is that this relationship will prevail. The lesson is not that we can do no good at all, but that we must pick our shots to focus on those who are *not* the most intractable problem cases. . . .

Welfare Subsidizes Poverty

We are subsidizing divorce, unwed teenage pregnancy, the abandonment of the elderly by their children, and the wholesale dissolution of the family. Unfortunately, people are responding to these incentives. . . .

The U.S. welfare system is reaching crisis proportions. It threatens not only our economy but also our culture. If we are sincere about helping the poor, and serious about reducing poverty, we will put a stop to encouraging welfare dependence.

John C. Goodman, *Conservative Digest,* January 1985.

If you go to work in a social welfare program, you are doing it in part because you are worried about the plight of the people you are trying to help. The problem is keeping separate your desire to help everybody and the ways you must behave if you want to do more good than harm. And it is really tough to make that distinction. . .

Question: Does that mesh with your proposal to abolish all welfare payments except for unemployment compensation?

Answer: In the recommendations about education and welfare, I am trying to get people off the dime in thinking about solutions. We have a dialogue in this country which is abolutely stuck, with a liberal constituency on one side that says we must be more compassionate and generous and a conservative constituency on the other that is worried about welfare cheats and how much money we are spending. Both sides are pretty much bankrupt intellectually in their approaches. We have to start rethinking what constitutes compassion and appropriate intervention.

I ask in the book, what would the world look like if we had no federal social welfare system at all, except unemployment compensation insurance? One of the most foolish and ahistorical reactions to that is that we'd have people starving in the streets. The U.S. has not had people starving in the streets at any point in history.

What Would Happen?

Question: Weren't people starving in New York City around the turn of the century, with the flood of illiterate immigrants?

Answer: I can't cite chapter and verse on that. We had a lot of malnutrition. We surely had a few who starved. I am not going to say there has never been a single case—but I am not sure even then that we had cases in which people starved after they had used every resource. At that time, even with the influx of immigrants and rapid industrialization, there existed a quite well-defined and active welfare system—maintained by cities, by private philanthropies and, in a few cases, by states.

My point is that in the late 20th Century, our extraordinary affluence is so much greater than it was earlier that the most plausible assumption is that even if federal programs were ended, we would have quite extensive systems of public welfare of various levels of funding and sophistication. The new programs would be very different, and it might well be that it would be tougher to be poor in Mississippi than in Iowa.

How To Tackle the Problem

I'm not saying it would solve all our problems. But I am saying that we have got to quit believing that there is no suffering, malnutrition or misery right now. We not only have it right now, but as far as I can tell it's been increasing in recent years, antedating the Reagan Administration.

And we do not have a choice between making everything perfect and not making everything perfect. We have a choice between different ways of tackling the problem.

"The small-scale, voluntary interdependence of families . . . is threatened by the very existence of welfare benefits."

Welfare Victimizes the Poor

Michael S. Christian

Michael S. Christian is a student at Harvard Law School. In the following viewpoint, he uses his childhood experiences to defend his belief that the welfare system dehumanizes people. He argues that welfare leaves the poor with feelings of shame and helplessness.

As you read, consider the following questions:

1. Why does the author conclude that a dollar spent on welfare does not equal a dollar of poverty reduced?
2. What does the government take away from the poor, according to the author? Does he think this is an inevitable process?
3. How does the author define wealth? How might he define poverty?

Michael S. Christian, "I was a Victim of Welfare." Reprinted with permission from the August/September 1986 issue of REASON magazine. Copyright © 1986 by the Reason Foundation, 2716 Ocean Park Blvd, Suite 1062, Santa Monica, CA 90405.

I grew up on welfare and it is a raw deal. For about nine years, middle-class life was my lot. Then my father left without a word, never again to provide sufficiently for my mother or her four children. We became welfare recipients. Years later, when I saw him again, he explained that act of abandonment: "Sorry son, but I had to leave, and I knew that the state would take care of you kids and your mother."

Family and Government

The social engineer might call that an example of the disincentive effects of welfare; the welfare eligibility of abandoned families removes the onus of responsibility from the father. But this is also an example of the demoralizing effects of welfare; the integrity of the family is invaded by the state. The small-scale, voluntary interdependence of families—and the sense of responsibility and security that go with it—is threatened by the very existence of welfare benefits. And what benefits can outweigh the deterioration of poor families?

The state, of course, did provide—just enough money for my mother to carry on under constant fear of eviction or loss of welfare eligibility. She would wait in line at a neighborhood distribution center to receive boxes of overproduced foodstuffs such as flour, oatmeal, sugar, powdered milk, powdered eggs, and corn syrup, everything clearly marked "Department of Health, Education, and Welfare." Later, she bought our meals with food stamps, a handy means of publicizing one's dependence.

The social engineer would call this "the elimination of poverty," the greatest virtue of the welfare system. And although the elimination of poverty seems easy to quantify, it is not. A dollar spent on welfare is not equal to a dollar's worth of poverty eliminated. For it is impossible to know in which cases need would persist in the absence of state aid. I will never know how my family would have fared without welfare. Would my father have left in the first place? Would my uncle have helped? Would private organizations have willingly helped provide for my family?

Give and Take

Assuming that nothing but governmental redistribution could have kept us from even worse poverty, there are still costs to be considered that are usually ignored. The state does not give without taking. Yes, it takes from the rich in the form of taxes, but it takes from the poor as well. It takes for itself the right to inquire repeatedly into one's affairs, financial and personal. It takes away privacy and dignity. And remember, the state justifies all this taking and giving in the name of humanity. Gratitude is in order.

Yet every day of the many years that my family was on welfare, I was angry. The indignities of bureaucratic inquisitiveness and my mother's shame were to me the government's way of punishing us for the checks we got in the mail. These feelings of resentment and humiliation have no place in the analysis of the social engineer, yet they are the greatest costs of the welfare system.

Who Is To Blame?

The resentment of the welfare recipient is especially burdensome because it has no constructive or sensible direction. When I was a child, who was I to blame? My mother, who after 15 years as a dependent housewife could not earn enough to support a large family? My father, who, thanks to the state, felt that he could abandon his family with moral impunity? Or should I have blamed the state, my humanitarian benefactor?

Welfare Is a Narcotic

Continued dependence upon relief induces a spiritual and moral disintegration fundamentally destructive to the national fiber. To dole out relief . . . is to administer a narcotic, a subtle destroyer of the human spirit.

Franklin D. Roosevelt, State of the Union Address, 1935.

If anyone is to blame for this mess, it is you—or those of you who are members of the educated, liberal, humanitarian middle or upper-middle class. You have never been poor. You don't want anyone else to be poor. You think something should be done for those who live below some government-determined poverty line. But you never wonder whether the state can take responsibility *for* individuals without taking responsibility *from* them.

Money and Power

Real wealth is seldom money; it is power. That power is exactly what the liberal social engineers and their followers have reserved to themselves by advocating welfare. As a boy, I wondered at the altruism of those who, with no special relationship to me, would give some of their income to my family through taxes. But we all know that welfare beneficiaries almost never take what you really cherish. No need to fear that people of different backgrounds, ideas, or colors might supplant you or even join you at the top of the hierarchy—not under a welfare system.

Redistribution is in your interest. It starches the social fabric. It keeps people in their places. It steals the sense of righteous ambition from the poor. The welfare beneficiary cannot point his finger at you or hold out his hand to his neighbor, because he has been provided for and he does not know that the hidden social benefits of that provision are yours. As long as he looks to you for the next check or the next box of surplus food, you are safe; your real wealth is enhanced.

What should be done? Or, better yet, what can you do? You can keep your money and let go of your sanctum. Eliminate the redistribution of wealth. What will the poor do without your aid? We will struggle, challenge, and win as individuals. Because, as you have always claimed to believe, we are your equals. Otherwise, the best egalitarian ends you can expect from your programs are the rare exceptions—welfare beneficiaries who succeed in your system in spite of it and who want to bite the hand that fed them.

"The worst problem with it is not that it causes demoralization . . . or craven dependency. The worst problem is that welfare doesn't pay enough."

Welfare Does Not Victimize the Poor

Barbara Ehrenreich

Barbara Ehrenreich is an author and a contributing editor to *Ms.* In the following viewpoint, she describes a friend who is on welfare. She concludes that the main problem with the welfare system is not that it fosters a lack of responsibility, but rather that it does not pay enough.

As you read, consider the following questions:

1. What picture of Lori is Ehrenreich trying to paint? What point is she trying to make?
2. How does Lori's situation compare with the one described in the opposing viewpoint? What significance does Ehrenreich attach to marriage and family support?
3. How does the author compute what welfare benefits should be?

The latest academic thinking on welfare is that it is positively unkind to shower the poor with largesse, even in the low four-figure range. Give an unemployed and bankrupt person a little help, according to the welfare critics George Gilder and Charles Murray, and he or she will lapse into the psychic slough known as demoralization—from which few ever venture forth again to seek honest employment at an hourly wage. The implication for public policy is that it would be much kinder to spare the poor the misery of demoralization, which is after all only a product of big government and other human errors, and let them experience the hunger that is natural to their condition.

One Welfare Recipient

There is someone I would like to introduce to the aforementioned gentlemen. She is a friend and former neighbor of mine, who will have to remain anonymous until public opinion takes a more generous turn. "Lori," let us call her, makes an excellent first impression. She is vivacious, smart and, although it shouldn't matter, disconcertingly pretty. She is also on welfare—and those who imagine the average welfare recipient as a slatternly mother of six or a young man apprenticing in street crime should know that Lori is a far more representative case: She is a single mother, as are close to 90 percent of recipients; she has only one child, which puts her among the 70 percent that have two or fewer; and, although this shouldn't matter either, she is white, as are a majority of welfare recipients.

Lori is no more demoralized by welfare than I am by an unexpected royalty check. True, she resents the days spent in the welfare office, the long waits, the interrogations about her limited inventory of household possessions. But she feels that she and her daughter have rights in the matter, like the right to a standard of living on some level exceeding vagrancy. She was not always, she will tell you, so assertive—certainly not in the two years when she was married to a man who routinely beat her and had once chased her around the house with a gun. Only welfare had made it possible to leave him, a move she says was like being born again, "as a human being this time."

Cheating

In one way, though, Lori fits the worst stereotypes: She is a "cheat." That is to say, she has sources of income that she does not report to the welfare office. When she can find a friend to watch her daughter (welfare doesn't provide funds for child care), she rushes out to whatever job she can find: babysitting, waitressing, cleaning other people's houses, anything so long as it's off the books. I wouldn't want to swear to it in court, but she sometimes brings in close to $100 a week in this manner—not enough to enable her to get off welfare, but a useful supplement, along with the occasional house plant or pizza pie she accepts from an admirer.

If I were made of sterner stuff, if, for example, I were tough enough to disport myself in thousand-dollar-plus outfits while, only blocks away, my fellow citizens were warming themselves over bonfires in vacant lots, then I suppose I would turn Lori in. And if I were a welfare critic of the stature of Gilder or Murray, I suppose I would tell her I was doing it for her own good. Instead, I merely sit back and reflect on what Lori's case reveals about welfare. The worst problem with it is not that it causes demoralization, atrophy of the work ethic, or craven dependency. The worst problem is that welfare doesn't pay enough.

Welfare Creates Independence, Not Dependence

Given the realities of the labor market . . . it is the availability of welfare benefits that introduces a measure of independence into the circumstances of workers. Knowing they can turn to unemployment benefits or welfare benefits if they are fired probably makes workers a little more secure in their dealings with employers and therefore a little more "independent.". . . Contrary to the stereotype of a large permanent underclass created by welfare usage, many people move on and off the welfare rolls, and a majority stay on rolls for relatively short periods of less than two years. . . . These facts suggest that, rather than miring them in dependency, welfare benefits help people cope with unsettled and difficult life circumstances, including unsettled and difficult employment circumstances. It is not farfetched to say that income-protection programs make many people a little more self-reliant.

Frances Fox Piven and Richard A. Cloward, *The Mean Season*, 1987.

This, I have realized, is the true cause of the demoralization critics are so concerned about: It is one thing to spend a day queueing up in a crowded stuffy room if the setting is OTB and you end up winning $50,000 in cash. But it is dispiriting to do the same thing for no greater reward than a $17 allowance for a child's winter jacket. And, as should be obvious, it is inadequate benefits, rather than depravity, that are the cause of cheating. Lori, for example, does not use her illicit income to build up a fleet of Cadillacs, but to buy little things that some pebble-hearted bureaucrat has determined are inessential to a welfare recipient's well-being: deodorant, hand lotion, an occasional commercial haircut.

The only question, then, is how much welfare benefits should be increased. Bearing in mind that the primary purpose of welfare is to support mothers and young children, we might use an estimate offered in a *Newsweek* cover story on Yuppies, in which a young woman said she ordinarily required $200,000 to live on, but would of course need more if she were to have a baby. If $300,000 or so a year seems high, we might just go with the market value of the average mother's work: approximately $7 an hour, for both child care and housekeeping, for what is minimally a 10-hour day, or about $26,000 a year.

Degrades Middle Class

Now, I can imagine the objections of the welfare critics, who will speak out manfully against this latest proposal to drive the poor beyond demoralization to outright despondency. Well, if they cannot understand that it feels better to have some money rather than none and more rather than less, I will base my argument on middle-class self-interest: Welfare, as it is now, is degrading to the middle class. It makes us mean and petty, bad neighbors and worse citizens. In fact, the more misery welfare is, the more anxious we feel, deep inside, about our own economic security. And the more anxious we feel, the more we are inclined to bluster about "not taking any handouts," and the nastier we get toward those who most need our understanding and support. It is a terrible cycle that we, the taxpayers and breadwinners have entered into, and perhaps for more debilitating in the long run than any "cycle of dependency" experienced by the poor. Never mind the welfare recipients, we can't afford to go on like this.

"The central ambiguity of our welfare system—whether single mothers should work— . . . [should] be resolved cleanly and clearly in favor of work."

The Government Should Make Welfare Recipients Work

Mickey Kaus

Mickey Kaus is a senior writer for *Newsweek*. In the following viewpoint, he proposes his own plan for welfare reform. He believes the fundamental goal should be to enforce the work ethic, which he believes has been lost in the "welfare culture" of the ghettos. Under his plan, every able-bodied person, including young mothers, would be provided a job and *not* be provided cash benefits. He raises and refutes possible objections to his plan, and differentiates his proposals from others by saying it would need large government involvement, including a federal day-care program for children.

As you read, consider the following questions:

1. According to Kaus, what is the central dilemma of our present welfare state? How does he resolve this dilemma?
2. What is the difference between the Bribe Theory and the Umbilical Cord Theory on welfare, according to Kaus?
3. What objections does the author make to his own proposal? Does he adequately answer them?

Mickey Kaus, "The Work-Ethic State," *The New Republic*, July 7, 1986. Reprinted by permission of THE NEW REPUBLIC, © 1986, The New Republic, Inc.

What's wrong with the current welfare state, anyway? The basic features of our current system for the poor are these: Fairly generous benefits are available to those who are deemed totally and permanently disabled. Very little in the way of benefits (mainly Food Stamps and stingy state "general relief" money) is available to able-bodied men and women, single or married. But if you are a single parent (almost always a mother) responsible for taking care of a child, you qualify for Aid to Families with Dependent Children (AFDC), which is what most people mean by welfare. In California and New York the AFDC benefit, combined with other benefits, is high enough to bring a welfare mother close to the poverty line. In most Southern states the AFDC benefit is much lower.

The central dilemma of our welfare state, then, is not the age-old general tension between "compassion" and "dependency." For most of the able-bodied, Americans have decided against much cash compassion. Ours is a more specific and modern dilemma: what about a single able-bodied woman who must also care for a child? If we give her no more aid than we give able-bodied men, we may be punishing the child. But to aid the child, we must aid the mother, as AFDC does—and then we risk the "social hazard" of encouraging women to put themselves in that disastrous position. To women, the AFDC system seems to say, "Have a kid and the state will take care of you—as long as you don't live with the father." To men, it says, "Father children and the state will take care of them."

Two Theories

This can't *help.* But the current attack on welfare by conservatives mixes up two quite distinct theories as to how it might hurt. In theory #1, prospective mothers and fathers are influenced directly by the economic blandishments of AFDC, much as if by bribes. A mother might have a baby "to go on welfare." A father might leave his wife or girlfriend so she qualifies for the program. Believers in this theory are apt to say that welfare *caused* the growth of the underclass. . . .

But there is a second, and far more plausible, theory that implicates welfare in this cultural catastrophe. It holds that although welfare might not *cause* the underclass, it *sustains* it. With AFDC in place, young girls look around them and recognize, perhaps unconsciously, that girls in their neighborhood who have had babies on their own are surviving, however uncomfortably (but who lives comfortably in the ghetto?). Welfare, as the umbilical cord through which the mainstream society sustains the isolated ghetto society, permits the expansion of this single-parent culture. . . .

The implications of this second view of welfare are far nastier than those of the Bribe version. If the Umbilical Cord Theory is

213

correct, it isn't enough to *extend* welfare benefits so that intact families are well off in comparison to single-parent families. You have to deny benefits to the single-parent families, to unplug the underclass culture's life support system.

Those of us who don't have the stomach to go through with Murray's "experiment" (and Murray himself waffles) are compelled to come up with a more humane way of changing the welfare culture. And there remains the possibility that something less than Murray's "let-them-starve" solution might work—something that doesn't cause pain exactly, but that does impose upon individuals the consequences of their choices, at the same time that it offers them a way out. Something like work. . . .

Set Clear Standards

The only practical way to improve behavior at the bottom of society is to set clearer standards for able-bodied welfare recipients. No one should be denied assistance, but no aid should be given without conditions. We should require that adult recipients work, that they avoid crime and drugs and that their children stay in school in return for support. People on welfare must begin to live by the same rules of reciprocity—giving something in order to get something—that other, nondependent Americans live by. Welfare must begin to mean obligations as well as rights. Only then will recipients be accepted as equals by other Americans.

Lawrence M. Mead, *The New York Times,* November 12, 1985.

What would a program that had a real chance of undermining the underclass look like? The deficiencies in the efforts currently underway give us some idea. First, it would be a program that expects women to work even if they have young children. Second, it would offer work to ghetto men and single women as well as to the welfare mothers. Third, it will have to deal with the related Take Away and Low Wage dilemmas: how can you require welfare recipients to accept private jobs if they pay less than welfare? How can you avoid making workfare or training more lucrative than private sector work?

Solving these problems will take something more radical than any existing workfare plan. It must be far bigger, in order to offer jobs to men, and far tougher in its dealings with young mothers. Above all, the program must unambiguously announce the cultural norm it seeks to promote in place of the culture of welfare.

What is required, I think, is something like this: replacing all cash-like welfare programs that assist the able-bodied poor (AFDC, general relief, Food Stamps, and housing subsidies, but not Medicaid) with a single, simple offer from the government—an offer of employment for every American citizen over 18 who wants it, in a useful public job at a wage slightly below the minimum wage. If you could work, and needed money, you would not be given a check (welfare). You would not be given a check and then cajoled, instructed, and threatened into working it off or "training it off" (workfare). You would be given the location of several government job sites. If you showed up, and worked, you would be paid for your work. If you don't show up, you don't get paid. Simple.

Unlike "workfare" jobs, these jobs would be available to everybody, men as well as women, single or married, mothers and fathers alike. No perverse "anti-family" incentives. No "means test" either. If David Rockefeller showed up, he could work too. But he wouldn't. Most Americans wouldn't. The low wage itself would "ration" the jobs to those who needed them most, and preserve the incentive to look for better work in the private sector. Instead of paying what in effect are high workfare "wages" and then relying on the stigma of welfare to encourage people to leave, this program would pay low wages but remove the stigma. Those who worked in the jobs would be earning their money. They could hold their heads up. They would also have something most unemployed underclass members desperately need: a supervisor they could give as a job reference to other employers. Although the best workers could be promoted to higher paying public service positions, for most workers movement into the private sector would take care of itself. If you have to work anyway, why do it for $3 an hour?

Those who didn't take advantage of these jobs, however, would be on their own. No cash doles. Mothers included. (Remember, we're only talking here about those able to work.) People who show up drunk for their jobs, who show up high, or who pick a fight with their supervisor could be fired (though they could show up again after a decent interval). There would be no need to "require" work. Work would be all that was offered. . . .

Objections

Will the wage be enough to support a family? No. This is the Low Wage dilemma. The poverty line for a family of three is $8,750. A full-time, minimum-wage job brings in only $7,000, and the government jobs proposed here would pay less than that. But there are ways to supplement the incomes of low-wage workers outside the welfare system (while preserving an incentive to seek better pay). The current Earned Income Tax Credit is one, the innovative Wage Rate Subsidy system of Brandeis professor Robert Lerman (which would pay half the difference between the family breadwinner's wage and $6 an hour) is another. . . .

A subsidized wage would, in effect, be a guaranteed income *for those who work* (a far more affordable proposition than an income guarantee that doesn't have a base of wages to start from).

There is no objection, in the Work Ethic State, to the government sending out checks as long as able-bodied people only get them if they work. Supplementing wages is a much better solution to the Low Wage problem than pretending the underclass can get "good jobs" that pay enough in themselves to support a family.

People Who Refuse Work

Will people be allowed to starve? The state's basic obligation, in this scheme, is to provide dignified work for all who can work, and a decent income for the disabled. There will be those who refuse work. Many ghetto men, at least initially, will prefer the world of crime, hustle, and odd jobs to working for "chump change." One advantage of the Work Ethic State is that criminals can be treated as criminals, without residual guilt about the availability of jobs. Others—the addled and addicted—will simply fail at working, or not even try. Even a fraction of welfare mothers, the most employable underclass group, will have trouble. "The workplace is so foreign to so many people who are second- and third-generation dependents," says Tom Nees, a Washington, D.C., minister whose Community of Hope works with welfare families poor enough to be homeless.

The Permissive Welfare State

Washington does give too much to the poor—in the sense of benefits given as entitlements. It also gives too little—in the sense of meaningful obligations to go along with the benefits. What undermines the economy is not so much the burden on the private sector as the message government programs have given that hard work in available jobs is no longer required of Americans. The main problem with the welfare state is not its size but its permissiveness, a characteristic that *both* liberals and conservatives seem to take for granted. The challenge to welfare statesmanship is not so much to change the extent of benefits as to couple them with serious work and other obligations that would encourage functioning and thus promote the integration of recipients. The goal must be to create for recipients *inside* the welfare state the same balance of support and expectation that other Americans face *outside* it, as they work to support themselves and meet the other demands of society.

Lawrence M. Mead, *Beyond Entitlement*, 1986.

The first underclass generation *off* welfare will be the roughest. Those people who fail at work will be thrown into the world of austere public in-kind guarantees—homeless shelters, soup kitchens, and the like—and the world of private charitable organizations like Nees's. This aid would be stigmatizing (as it must be if work is to be honored), but it could be compassionate. Nobody

216

would starve. Counseling, therapy, training, could be offered, even subsidized by the government, in order to help these people back on their feet. The one thing the government would not offer them is cash.

Mothers

What about mothers with young children? The government would announce that, after a certain date, single mothers would no longer qualify for cash welfare payments. The central ambiguity of our welfare system—whether single mothers should work—would be resolved cleanly and clearly in favor of work. This hard choice is a key way the Work Ethic State would hope to break the self-perpetuating culture of poor, single-parent families. Teenage mothers who had babies could no longer count on welfare to sustain them. They would have to work like everyone else, and the prospect of juggling motherhood and a not-very-lucrative job would make them think twice, although it would also offer a way out of poverty that Charles Murray's starvation solution would deny.

What would the children do when their mothers were working? If the government is going to expect poor mothers to work, then it will have to provide day care for all those who need it. This will be expensive (Massachusetts pays $2,800 a year for each day-care slot). But it won't be as prohibitively expensive as many who raise the day-care issue seem to believe. In every state in which free day care has been offered to AFDC mothers, demand has fallen below predictions. "It is never utilized to the extent people thought it would be," says Barbara Goldman of MDRC. Most mothers, it seems, prefer to make their own arrangements. Whether those arrangements are any good is another question. The government might actually have to take steps to encourage day care, as part of the general trend toward getting kids out of underclass families and into school at an early age.

The Child Dilemma

What about mothers with very young children, two years and under? A destitute mother with a newborn infant presents the basic AFDC dilemma in its starkest form. It *is* a dilemma, meaning there are arguments on both sides. One alternative is to allow temporary cash welfare for the first two years of a child's life, with a three-year limit to avoid the have-another-kid loophole. A two-year-free ride is better than a six-year free ride. Teenagers are likely to be friends with someone in their community who has a two-year-old kid and is "up against it," as Murray puts it. On the other hand, no free ride at all (except for in-kind nutritional assistance during pregnancy and infancy to avoid disastrous health problems) would clearly have stronger impact. It would also put mothers into the world of work without letting them grow accustomed to dependency. Oklahoma applies its soft workfare requirements to mothers as soon as their kids are born, with no apparent ill effects.

And if a mother refuses? The short, nasty answer is that if a mother turns down the state's offer of a job with which she might support her children, and as a result her children live in squalor and filth, then she has neglected a basic task of parenthood. She is subject to the laws that already provide for removal of a child from an unfit home.

What about teenagers who haven't even finished high school? They could receive free day care while finishing, and in-kind nutritional assistance, but no cash. To obtain any extra cash necessary to support a baby, they would have to work, in one of the guaranteed government jobs if necessary. Again, the government could offer as many free training programs as it wanted, but without cash entitlements. Since training would no longer be an alternative to working, trainees would have every incentive to make the most of it.

Will there be enough jobs these people can do? As noted above, the objection can't be that there aren't enough worthwhile jobs to be done. The crumbling "infrastructure" that preoccupied Washington three years ago hasn't been patched up overnight. All around the country governments have stopped doing, for financial reasons, things they once thought worthwhile, like opening libraries on Saturday and picking up trash twice a week. Why not do them again?

What Workers Can Do

But there are plausible doubts whether the welfare recipients who would need public service employment are suited to doing all these worthwhile jobs. One objection has to do with women and physical labor. Are we really going to have teenage girls repairing potholes and painting bridges? One response is, why not? Women can fill potholes and paint bridges (and water lawns and pick up garbage), just as women can be telephone repairmen and sailors. Feminism has rightly destroyed the sex stereotypes that used to surround much physical work. Anyway, there are many non-arduous "women's" jobs that need doing—nurses' aides, Xerox operators, receptionists, clerks, coat checkers, cooks, and cleaners. Private schools often require parents to keep order on playgrounds twice a month. Public schools might employ one or two parents to do the same full-time. Day-care centers could too. Is there any point of offering women free day care and then putting some of them to work in day-care centers? Yes. First, that would still free up a lot of women for employment. Second, and more important, the day-care jobs would exist within the culture of work—with alarm clocks to set, appointments to keep, and bosses to please—rather than the culture of welfare. . . .

Yes, public works jobs would be relatively inefficient compared with their private sector counterparts. The government would have to learn to work with the dregs of the labor market, and the program (like the most successful War on Poverty program, the Job Corps) would have to be relatively authoritarian. Boondoggles would happen. But at least the public would be getting *something* for its money. . . .

A Cultural Offensive

The point is to enforce the work ethic. This is a long-term cultural offensive, not a budget-control program or an expression of compassion. The sharpness and simplicity of its choices—no cash welfare for the able-bodied, no exceptions for parenthood—are its main virtue, because they embody with unmistakable clarity the social norms that are in danger of disappearing in the underclass culture. . . .

Welfare doesn't work. Work "incentives" don't work. Training doesn't work. Work "requirements" don't work. "Work experience" doesn't work and even workfare doesn't quite work. Only work works.

"For a mother on AFDC, there is often little economic gain . . . to endure poor working conditions in a dead-end job at the expense of time spent with her children."

The Government Should Not Make Welfare Recipients Work

Russell Roberts and *Dollars & Sense*

The following viewpoint consists of two articles. The first is by Russell Roberts, a professor of economics and political science at the University of Rochester in New York. He examines the poorhouse common in England and America in the 1800s, and claims they ultimately failed because people lacked the will to enforce the harsh laws. Part II is taken from an article that appeared in *Dollars & Sense*, a magazine written and edited by a collective of economists who write from a socialist perspective. They conclude that programs forcing welfare recipients to work at low pay only help business, not the poor.

As you read, consider the following questions:

1. What basic dilemma does Roberts see in helping the poor?
2. According to the authors, what are the motivations behind workfare proposals?
3. What solutions are proposed at the end of the viewpoint?

Russell Roberts, "Welfare Doesn't Work," *The New York Times*, October 10, 1985. Copyright © 1985 by The New York Times Company. Reprinted by permission. "The Retreat from Welfare," *Dollars & Sense*, June 1987. Reprinted with permission. *Dollars & Sense*, a progressive popular economics magazine, is located at One Summer Street, Somerville, MA 02143.

I

Maimonides, the 12th-century Jewish scholar, defined eight ascending levels of charity. At the lowest level is charity given grudgingly, where donor and recipient know each other. The levels ascend according to willingness to give and anonymity. At the highest level, a donor gladly helps a stranger until he can break free of the need of assistance. Legislators in California aspire to the highest virtue by helping the poor in that state find jobs so they will not need charity.

The state Legislature passed a bill changing the largest welfare program in the country to "workfare." Under the measure, which had bipartisan support, all welfare recipients without children six years old or younger are required to have a job, to register for job training or to work at an assigned job in the public sector.

Workfare may be a blossoming idea; since 1981, 36 states have adopted workfare laws but perhaps none as stringent or ambitious as California's. The efforts are all noble but probably wasted. The history of relief programs strongly suggests that workfare laws will not work.

A Dilemma

Private charity and public welfare programs face a terrible dilemma. There are two unavoidable effects of being generous to the poor—reducing the incentive for the poor to help themselves and helping people who the programs are not designed for, those who defraud the system or those who prefer relief to work.

The history of aid to the poor is a chronicle of the conflict between compassion and the desire to see the poor help themselves. Reformers clamor for a program that is generous and also preserves the incentive to work. But such a program is a fantasy.

The English used the poorhouse to try to cope with this problem. A royal commission observed in 1834 that the Poor Law, which allowed people to receive aid outside of the poorhouse, was destroying the incentive to work, causing people to become poor in order to receive aid. Britain's solution was the New Poor Law of 1834, which gave aid only to those who lived in the poorhouse.

The British attempt at improving work incentives failed because the new law was not enforced. Local communities found it too difficult and unpleasant to force every unfortunate individual into the poorhouse.

American Laws

The United States tried a similar experiment in the last half of the 19th century. From 1870 until 1910, public assistance in most cities was given only in the poorhouse. By 1910, poorhouses had lost favor and politicians campaigned to help widows with children (a group that today would be on workfare in California).

A report in 1914 from a New York State commission that ad-

Dan Wasserman. © 1987. Boston Globe. Reprinted by permission.

vocated pensions for widows with children sounds familiar: "The work available to such women outside of the home inevitably breaks down the physical, mental and moral strength of the family and disrupts the home life through an inadequate standard of living and parental neglect."

By 1921, 40 states gave pensions for widows rather than forcing them to work, to enter the poorhouse or to give up their children to foster homes. The poorhouse was dying. After the Great Depression, relief programs rarely required recipients to work.

Modern attempts to encourage welfare recipients to work focus on reducing tax rates for income earned by welfare recipients. But what the public and politicians want is unattainable: a welfare program that helps only the truly needy, enables them to live comfortably and encourages them to help themselves.

We Must Choose

So we must choose. Given the choice between compassion and work, Americans prefer compassion. So we stop requiring aid recipients to work, and the handouts then actually discourage work. Workfare programs in California and elsewhere will fail for the same reasons that earlier efforts failed. Administrators of the laws will find them difficult and unpleasant to enforce just as their English counterparts did. Ultimately, altruists who want to help the poor will be disenchanted with the law's cost and consequences.

Discouraging the poor to work is an unavoidable consequence of compassion. Like the poor, it is a consequence that is always with us.

II

After more than a decade of only minor tinkering with the welfare system, policymakers in Washington and across the country have decided it's time for a major overhaul. . . .

Democrats and Republicans in nearly every state—including governors, legislators, and human service bureaucrats—have put forward their ideas for revamping the system. . . .

The National Governors' Association has generated the unifying theme for the various proposals: "Making America Work." As the slogan suggests, the current calls for reform come down to one thing: forcing those on public assistance into the labor market. Nearly all the new programs seek to change the welfare system from an income support program to a jobs program through an administrative mix of carrots and sticks designed to compel welfare recipients to take low-paying jobs.

A Workhouse Without Walls

None of the proposals speaks adequately to the real reasons most adult welfare recipients don't take paying work: they are already working—raising children. But rather than recognize the value of this unpaid work, reformers want those on welfare to "get a job." The reforms now under consideration offer minimal training, poor job placements with inadequate health coverage, and too-small subsidies for childcare.

But what is bad for welfare recipients is good for local employers. In the 19th century, welfare reform meant the establishment of workhouses in which the poor, many of them men, split wood or farmed in exchange for room and board. Welfare reform in 1987 is more subtle: it's a workhouse without walls, and most of the workers are women.

Welfare: An "Enabler"

According to the new breed of reformers, which includes both conservatives and liberals, welfare must be overhauled because it breeds illegitimate children and dependency and erodes the work ethic. In his 1986 State of the Union Address, President Reagan blamed welfare for "the breakdown of the family," and said the "welfare culture" was responsible for "female and child poverty, child abandonment, horrible crimes, and deteriorating schools."

A White House report on welfare reform gave a sense of why conservatives are so bent on changing the welfare system. The report called the main income support program for poor families, Aid to Families with Dependent Children, an "enabler—a program which enables women to live without a husband or a job." In other words, conservatives' recent rush to reform welfare reflects their agenda for the labor market and the family. If a woman can live without of job, that's a problem for employers, particularly employers who depend on women's cheap labor. If a woman can live without a husband, that means major changes in the balance of power between men and women.

Liberals have responded with rhetoric of their own, avoiding some of the right wing's moralism, but arriving at remarkably similar conclusions. For the National Governors' Association, dominated by Democrats, welfare must "create a system where it is always better to work than be on public assistance."

For conservatives, welfare reform means workfare: forcing welfare recipients to work off their benefits or lose them. Liberals add a few carrots like training and childcare subsidies to the work requirement stick. But nearly all the state demonstration projects, liberal and conservative alike, make the job programs mandatory. . . .

Motherhood vs. McDonald's

Where would welfare recipients find work? The only labor shortages in today's economy are in very low-skilled positions in the service sector. But wages at McDonald's and Dairy Queen will not make up for the welfare mother's loss of Medicaid, nor will they pay the costs of child-care. The net result of "reform" that forces single women off welfare and into these low-paying, dead-end jobs will be simply to plunge them deeper into poverty.

The latest "workfare" proposals demonstrate how undervalued child-rearing has become in our society. Welfare mothers *are* working—and they are performing socially more useful work than frying potato sticks or swirling soft ice cream. Why force them out of the home?

The Progressive, August 1987.

If Congress approves a work requirement for those who receive public assistance, it will not be the first time government has tailored welfare to the needs of the labor market. Historically, welfare has played an important role within capitalism. Public assistance has appeased dissent when protest by the poor threatened to disrupt society. It is no accident that the periods of greatest expansion of the welfare system have been those following the unrest of the Great Depression and the urban riots of the late 1960s.

In addition to regulating the poor, the welfare system has been used to regulate the supply of workers to employers paying low wages. When there is a shortage of workers willing to take low-paying work, government historically tightens eligibility requirements to force more recipients into the work force. The Work Incentive Program (WIN), which created workfare and training programs that compelled welfare recipients to find jobs, was established in the full employment years of the late 1960s.

Low Paying Jobs

Over the past 15 years, the number of low-paid jobs in the United States has been rising. This has been especially true in the Reagan years. Despite chronically high unemployment rates, there is a shortage of workers willing to take the low-wage service jobs that are replacing the high-wage union jobs lost in recent years. The labor shortage is particularly acute in urban areas where many welfare recipients reside. Employers have responded with minor incentives, but still have difficulty attracting workers. The current proposals for welfare reform are designed to increase the supply of workers to low-wage employers.

The immigration reform bill passed by Congress also has employers worried. The law is expected to reduce the supply of undocumented workers who do much of the low-wage work in the United States. Many employers fear a shortage of people willing to work for the low wages they pay.

Welfare mothers represent a labor pool to be tapped by these employers. Some proposals, such as New Jersey's REACH, require employment or training for mothers of children as young as two. New Jersey's plan even provides the jobs: new casinos in the Atlantic City area have agreed to employ 1,500 graduates of the state's AFDC work and training program. Just in case there's any doubt as to whose interests welfare reform is serving in New Jersey, REACH will be administered by Private Industry Councils made up of local employers.

One of the reasons economic compulsion is no longer sufficient to generate enough low-wage workers is that the real value of the minimum wage has fallen even faster than the value of welfare benefits. In 1981—the last time the minimum wage was raised—monthly earnings from a full-time minimum wage job were frozen at $558. At that time, average AFDC benefits per family were $277, 50% of earnings from minimum wage work. Since then, benefits have fallen in real terms but risen in relation to the minimum wage. By 1985, AFDC benefits were worth 61% of minimum wage earnings.

So despite the falling value of benefits, the financial advantage to taking a job has been declining for welfare recipients. This is particularly true when the value of other benefits is taken into account. Few low-wage jobs provide company-paid health care to replace lost Medicaid benefits, and childcare costs are high and rising. Increased cash income also reduced food stamp benefits. For a mother on AFDC, there is often little economic gain—if any—in taking a job over welfare. If she does, she is usually forced to endure poor working conditions in a dead-end job at the expense of time spent with her children. . . .

The Purpose of Work Relief

Work relief is designed to spur people to offer themselves to any employer on any terms. And it does this by making pariahs of those who cannot support themselves. This object lesson in the virtues of work is accomplished by the terrible treatment accorded those who do not work. The resulting immiseration and degradation of the pauperized poor then becomes yet another justification in the campaign against social provision.

Frances Fox Piven and Richard A. Cloward, *The Mean Season*, 1987.

The current range of reform proposals doesn't address the basic problems that generate poverty: unemployment, low-paying jobs without benefits, inequitable wages for women, and an inadequate supply of affordable childcare.

In the abstract, there is nothing wrong with some aspects of the welfare reform proposals being considered by Congress. Increasing economic opportunity for welfare recipients through vocational training and job placement is a worthy goal. And it is a step forward for legislators that they are proposing at least some form of childcare subsidy.

But as long as politicians insist on making participation by welfare recipients with no children under three years of age mandatory, the introduction of job training programs is not a positive development. As long as legislators continue their retreat from the commitment to provide a sufficient, basic income to the poorest members of society, their proposals will only oppress welfare recipients.

Alternatives

A more progressive welfare reform would recognize that a job is not an automatic ticket out of poverty for single-parent families. A meaningful system of income supplements for low-income families, such as the European family allowance system, comes closer to what is required. In this system, the government pays a uniform subsidy to all families with children. In Western Europe as a whole, between 1% and 2% of gross national product is devoted to family allowances. Devoting the same share of GNP to alleviating family poverty in the United States would require between $40 and $80 billion, roughly twice what we are currently spending on AFDC and Food Stamps.

If the policy goal is to expand the labor market options available to welfare recipients, the most important consideration should not be welfare reform but rather raising the effective wages of the work that is available to them. Such a change, which workers have as much interest in demanding as those on public assistance, would involve mandating both higher cash wages—by at least raising the minimum wage—and employer-provided benefits like health insurance and childcare. Then those welfare recipients who want to enter the labor market will not have to bear such economic hardship to do so.

Evaluating Sources of Information

A critical thinker must always question sources of information. Historians, for example, distinguish between *primary sources* (a "firsthand" or eyewitness account from personal letters, documents, or speeches, etc.) and *secondary sources* (a "second-hand" account usually based upon a "firsthand" account and possibly appearing in a newspaper or encyclopedia). A published diary of a welfare mother is an example of a primary source. A book review of the mother's diary is an example of a secondary source.

Interpretation and/or point of view also play a role when dealing with primary and secondary sources. For example, the welfare mother might strongly believe that any form of welfare is degrading. Her personal experience affects her view of the welfare system. The secondary source, too, should be questioned as to interpretation or underlying motive. The book reviewer might have strong feelings regarding the necessity of welfare, and criticize the diary because of his personal bias. It is up to the researcher to keep in mind the potential biases of his/her sources.

This activity is designed to test your skill in evaluating sources of information. Imagine you are writing a report to the governor on how to reform the state welfare system. You decide to include an equal number of primary and secondary sources. Listed below are a number of sources which may be useful for your report. Carefully evaluate each of them. Then, *place a P next to those descriptions you believe are primary sources*. Second, *rank the primary sources* assigning the number (1) to what appears to be the most accurate primary source, the number (2) to the next most accurate, and so on until the ranking is finished. *Repeat the entire procedure, this time placing an S next to the descriptions you feel would serve as secondary sources and then ranking them.*

If you are doing this activity as a member of a class or group, compare your answers with those of other class or group members. Be able to defend your answers. You may discover that others will come to different conclusions than you. Listening to the reasons others present for their answers may give you valuable insights in evaluating sources of information.

_____ 1. copies of the forms people fill out to _____
receive welfare

_____ 2. interviews with children growing up on
welfare

_____ 3. a book on poor Americans and welfare _____
programs from 1900 to 1950

_____ 4. an article by a social scientist who com- _____
pares state-by-state welfare benefits and
poverty statistics

_____ 5. a local television news feature about a _____
pastor who works with poor families in
her neighborhood

_____ 6. a statewide poll on how people feel _____
about welfare

_____ 7. viewpoint three in this chapter _____

_____ 8. viewpoint four in this chapter _____

_____ 9. a novel based on the author's childhood _____
growing up under welfare

_____ 10. a magazine article about a company _____
which hires people on welfare

_____ 11. a speech by a US senator on welfare _____
cheats

_____ 12. a pamphlet published by a conservative _____
organization titled "How Welfare Ex-
ploits the Poor"

_____ 13. a pamphlet published by a leftist _____
organization titled "How Welfare Ex-
ploits the Poor"

_____ 14. welfare mothers speaking as guests on _____
the Oprah Winfrey show

Periodical Bibliography

The following articles have been selected to supplement the diverse views presented in this chapter.

The Annals of the American Academy of Political and Social Science — "The Welfare State in America: Trends and Prospects," May 1985.

Ken Auletta and Charles Murray — "Saving the Underclass," *The Washington Monthly*, September 1985.

Lucy Braun — "She Helps Moms Kick Welfare," *Reason*, August/September 1987.

Gregory A. Fossedal — "The Second War on Poverty," *The American Spectator*, February 1986.

Harper's Magazine — "Forum: What Does the Government Owe the Poor?" April 1986.

Robert M. Haveman — "The War on Poverty and the Poor and Nonpoor," *Political Science Quarterly*, Spring 1987.

Robert Kuttner — "The Welfare Strait," *The New Republic*, July 6, 1987.

Jacob V. Lamar Jr. — "From Welfare to Workfare," *Time*, February 3, 1986.

Stephen V. Monsma — "Should the Poor Earn Their Keep?" *Christianity Today*, June 12, 1987.

Tom Morganthau — "Welfare: A New Drive To Clean Up the Mess," *Newsweek*, February 2, 1987.

The New Republic — "Welfare & Work: A Symposium," October 6, 1986.

The New York Times — "Rewriting the Social Contract for America's Have-Nots," April 27, 1987.

Robert D. Reischauer — "Welfare Reform: Will Consensus Be Enough?" *The Brookings Review*, Summer 1987.

Society — "Safety Nets and Welfare Ceilings," January/February 1986.

Carol Twopines — "My Life in Crime," *The Progressive*, August 1985.

Laurie Udesky — "Workfare: It Isn't Fair and It Doesn't Work," *The Progressive*, December 1987.

Organizations To Contact

The editors have compiled the following list of organizations which are concerned with the issues debated in this book. All of them have publications available for interested readers. The descriptions are derived from materials provided by the organizations themselves.

Bread for the World
802 Rhode Island Ave. NE
Washington, DC 20010
(202) 269-0200

Bread for the World is a Christian citizens' movement which is concerned about hunger-related issues. Its members contact U.S. Congressional representatives to lobby for changes in policies which impact these issues. The organization publishes *Background Papers, Contact,* and a newsletter, monthly; *Leaven,* a quarterly, and has published a book, *Bread for the World.*

Cato Institute
224 Second St. SE
Washington, DC 20003
(202) 546-0200

The Institute sponsors programs designed to assist scholars and laypersons in analyzing public policy questions. It is dedicated to extending the social and economic freedoms of the capitalist system. The Institute publishes the monthly *Policy Report* and the *Cato Journal.*

Center for Community Change
1000 Wisconsin Ave. NW
Washington, DC 20007
(202) 342-0519

The Center assists community groups of urban and rural poor in making positive changes in their communities. The organization lends technical assistance to communities and works to make government more responsive to the needs of the poor. It publishes newsletters and citizen action guides.

Center on Social Welfare Policy and Law
95 Madison Ave.
New York, NY 10016
(212) 679-3709

Founded in 1965, the Center provides legal aid and develops materials for welfare rights groups. A publications list is available on request.

Eagle Forum
Box 618
Alton, IL 62002
(618) 462-5415

Eagle Forum is a conservative organization led by Phyllis Schlafly that opposes comparable worth and government programs that it believes undermine the free market and traditional values. Eagle Forum publishes *The Phyllis Schlafly Report,* a monthly newsletter.

Fisher Institute
6350 LBJ Freeway, #183E
Dallas, TX 75240
(214) 233-1041

Fisher Institute is a non-partisan research organization that believes competitive markets can solve America's long-range economic problems. The Institute's conferences and seminars offer information on economic aspects of public policy in easily understandable terms. It publishes the monthly newsletter, *Enterprise*.

Foundation for Economic Education (FEE)
30 S. Broadway
Irvington, NY 10533
(914) 591-7230

This libertarian organization focuses its research efforts on free-market theory and advocates society without government interference. FEE also maintains a speakers bureau, a library with related materials, and publishes *The Freeman* monthly.

The Heritage Foundation
214 Massachusetts Ave. NE
Washington, DC 20002
(202) 546-4400

The Heritage Foundation is a conservative public policy research institute. It produces a tremendous number of research and position papers on current policy issues and *The Backgrounder*, a series of occasional papers on current political, economic, and social issues.

Interfaith Action for Economic Justice
110 Maryland Ave. NE
Washington, DC 20002-5694
(202) 543-2800
(800) 424-7292 (legislative updates)

Members of Interfaith Action for Economic Justice are the mission boards or program units of national religious agencies. They work for just and effective policies regarding food and agriculture, health and human services, and development and economy. The organization publishes *Interfaith Action* newsletter and *Policy Notes*.

National Committee on Pay Equity
1201 16th St. NW, Room 422
Washington, DC 20036
(202) 822-7304

The National Committee on Pay Equity was organized to examine and educate the general public about wage discrimination and the historical, legal, and economic bases of inequities between women and men and between whites and people of color. The Committee's task forces provide education, research, and advocacy. The Committee also publishes briefing papers.

National Organization for Women (NOW)
Box 7813
Washington, DC 20044
(202) 347-2279

NOW is an organization of men and women who support full equality for women in truly equal partnership with men. NOW acts to end prejudice and discrimination against women, supports the ERA, and investigates the feminization of poverty. The group publishes a newspaper, *National NOW Times*, seven times a year. Local chapters also publish monthly newsletters.

Physician Task Force on Hunger in America (PTFHA)
c/o Harvard School of Public Health
Dept. of Health Policy and Management
Kresge, 4th floor
677 Huntington Ave.
Boston, MA 02115
(617) 732-1265

The Task Force's members are physicians and public health experts who study the extent of hunger and its effects in the US. PTFHA conducts surveys, reviews state and national studies, operates a speakers bureau, and maintains a collection of related publications. The organization publishes the report, *Hunger in America: The Growing Epidemic*, report summaries, and articles and essays relating to hunger in the US.

Population Reference Bureau, Inc. (PRB)
777 14th St. NW, Suite 800
Washington, DC 20005
(202) 639-8040

PRB gathers, interprets, and disseminates information on the facts and implications of national and world population trends. The Bureau believes that population density, particularly in Third World areas, is often a major factor in the local poverty level. PRB publishes a variety of population-related literature, wall charts, and *The Population Handbook*.

Presbyterian Hunger Program (PHP)
341 Ponce de Leon Ave. NE
Atlanta, GA 30365
(404) 873-1531

PHP conducts programs in direct food relief, development assistance, and education, both in the US and abroad. It believes more modest lifestyles would reduce energy consumption and provide more equitable allocation of world resources. PHP publishes a brochure, *Seeds of Hope: What Is the PHP?*, and a quarterly newsletter, *HANdles for Action*.

Reason Foundation
PO Box 40105
Santa Barbara, CA 93103
(805) 963-5993

The Reason Foundation's purpose is to provide a better understanding of the intellectual basis of a free society based on capitalism. It promotes individualist philosophy and free-market principles as the most reasonable way to build a strong economy and fight poverty. Its publications include *Fiscal Watchdog* and *Reason* magazine.

Bibliography of Books

Ken Auletta	*The Underclass.* New York: Random House, 1982.
Fred Block, et al.	*The Mean Season: The Attack on the Welfare State.* New York: Pantheon Books, 1987.
Stuart Butler and Anna Kondratas	*Out of the Poverty Trap: A Conservative Strategy for Welfare Reform.* New York: Macmillan, 1987.
Frank and Janet Ferrell	*Trevor's Place.* San Francisco: Harper & Row, 1985.
Roger Freeman	*Does America Neglect Its Poor?* Stanford: Hoover Institution, 1987.
George Gilder	*Wealth and Poverty.* New York: Basic Books, 1981.
George Grant	*The Dispossessed: Homelessness in America.* Westchester, IL: Crossway Books, 1986.
Michael Harrington	*The New American Poverty.* New York: Holt, Rinehart and Winston, 1984.
Robert H. Hartman, ed.	*Poverty and Economic Justice: A Philosophical Approach.* New York: Paulist Press, 1984.
Henry Hazlitt	*The Conquest of Poverty.* Lanham, MD: University Press of America, 1986.
Marshall Kaplan and Peggy Cucity, eds.	*The Great Society and Its Legacy.* Durham, NC: Duke University Press, 1986.
Michael Katz	*In the Shadow of the Poorhouse.* New York: Basic Books, 1986.
Gerald Leinwald	*Hunger and Malnutrition in America.* New York: Franklin Watts, 1985.
Dale Maharidge	*Journey to Nowhere: The Saga of the New Underclass.* Garden City, NY: Doubleday & Company, Inc., 1985.
Lawrence M. Mead	*Beyond Entitlement: The Social Obligations of Citizenship.* New York: The Free Press, 1986.
Milton Meltzer	*Poverty in America.* New York: William Morrow & Co., Inc., 1986.
Charles Murray	*Losing Ground.* New York: Basic Books, 1984.
National Conference of Catholic Bishops	*Economic Justice For All: Catholic Social Teaching and the U.S. Economy.* Washington, DC: United States Catholic Conference, Inc., 1987.
Michael Novak, et al.	*The New Consensus on Family and Welfare: A Community of Self-Reliance.* Washington, DC: American Enterprise Institute, 1987.
James T. Patterson	*America's Struggle Against Poverty, 1900-1980.* Cambridge, MA: Harvard University Press, 1981.
Physician Task Force on Hunger in America	*Hunger Reaches Blue Collar America.* Available from Physician Task Force on Hunger in America, 677 Huntington Avenue, Boston, MA 02115, 1987.
Robert B. Reich	*Tales of a New America.* New York: Times Books, 1987.
Earl Shorris, ed.	*While Someone Else Is Eating.* New York: Anchor Press/Doubleday, 1984.

Index

225
technology, 23, 31, 78
is often voluntary, 73-75, 200
see also employment
US Bureau of the Census, 36, 37, 39

vagrancy laws, *see* homelessness

Wade, Lawrence, 153
Wasserman, Dan, 222
welfare, *see* government poverty
  programs
Wilkins, Roger, 178
Will, George, 125
Williams, Walter E., 29
Wilson, William Julius, 92, 83
women
  and marriage, 209-210
    effect on career, 166-167
  and welfare
    should be required to work,
      214-218
    con, 223-227
  discrimination against
    and pay scales, 160, 169-170
    statistics prove, 150, 161, 162
    con, 165
  homelessness among, 101-102, 113,
    114-115, 130-133
  poverty among, 77, 78, 209
    childcare as a cause of, 162-163,
      165-166, 197, 210-211
    sexism causes, 157-163
    myth of, 164-170
  roles of, 166-167, 169-170
Wooster, Martin Morse, 105, 109
workfare
  cannot work, 220-227
  is essential, 212-219
  is exploitive, 224-227